Rationality and Modernity

Essays in Philosophical Pragmatics

Publications:

Nihilisme? Oslo, 1958, 2nd ed. 1979 (Engl. transl. 1972).

Dei filosofiske vilkår for sanning [The Philosophical Conditions for Truth], Oslo, 1966.

Er ideologiane døde? [Are Ideologies Dead?], Oslo, 1969, ed. and co-author.

Truth and Preconditions, Bergen, 1970.

Nymarxisme og kritisk dialektikk [Neomarxism and Critical Dialectics], Oslo, 1970.

Politisk filosofi [Political Philosophy], Bergen, 1970, 2nd ed. 1976.

Økologi og filosofi [Ecology and Philosophy], Oslo, 1972.

Den argumenterande fornuft [Argumentative Reason], Bergen, 1977.

Wahrheitstheorien, Frankfurt a.M., 1977, ed. and co-author.

Filosofihistorie [History of Philosophy], Bergen/Oslo. 1980, from 2nd ed. 1987 together with Nils Gilje; fifth ed. 1992.

Praxeology. Oslo, 1983, ed. and co-author.

Ord [Words], Oslo, 1984.

Manuscripts on Rationality, Bergen, 1984; revised version Bergen, 1992.

Objektivitetsproblemet i vitskapane [Problem of Objectivity in Science], Bergen, 1984, ed. and co-author.

Die pragmatische Wende, Frankfurt a.M., 1987, co-ed. and co-author.

Til Djevelens forsvar og andre essays [In Defence of the Devil, and other Essays], Bergen, 1988.

Modernitet - rasjonalisering og differensiering [Modernity - Rationalization and Differentiation], Bergen, 1988, ed. and co-author.

Vernunft und Verantwortung, Bergen, 1992.

Kulturell modernitet og vitskapleg rasjonalitet [Cultural Modernity and Scientific Rationality], Bergen, 1992.

Eco-Philosophical Manuscripts, Bergen, 1992.

The Commercial Ark. A Book on Ecology, Evolution and Ethics, co-ed. and co-author, Oslo, 1992.

Rationalité et Modernité, Paris, 1993.

Geschichte der Philosophie, Frankfurt a.M., 1993, together with Nils Gilje.

Gunnar Skirbekk

Rationality and Modernity
Essays in Philosophical Pragmatics

Scandinavian
University Press

Scandinavian University Press (Universitetsforlaget AS)
0608 Oslo, Norway
Distributed world-wide excluding Norway by
Oxford University Press, Walton Street, Oxford OX2 6DP

Oxford New York Toronto Dehli Bombay Calcutta Madras
Karachi Kuala Lumpur Singapore Hong Kong Tokyo Nairobi
Dar es Salaam Cape Town Melbourne Auckland Madrid and
associated companies in Berlin Ibadan

Oxford is a trade mark of Oxford University Press

Published in the United States by
Oxford University Press Inc., New York

© Universitetsforlaget 1993

ISBN 82-00-21718-3

British Library Cataloguing in Publication Data
Data available

Library of Congress Cataloguing in Publication Data
Data available

Printed in Norway by A/S Foto-Trykk, Trøgstad 1993

Preface

The philosophical horizon of this collection of essays is broadly speaking that of present-day Critical Theory. The way of working is largely that of case-oriented praxeology. And the political and cultural background is that of West-European modernity, Scandinavian style. Apel, Habermas and Wittgenstein are thinkers to whom reference is made – though not exclusively, nor uncritically: in my view, Wittgenstein's relation to modernity remains 'unredeemed', Habermas's reconstructions call for additional contextual elaboration, and Apel's transcendental pragmatics still awaits the cautious test of further 'arguments from absurdity'. Nevertheless, these philosophies are in my opinion highly provocative and promising. They should therefore be honored discursively, i.e. with curiosity and critique – and that is the aim of this collection of essays on rationality and modernity.

Gunnar Skirbekk
Bergen, 1992

Acknowledgement

I thank all those friends and colleagues who have given me valuable criticism during numerous dialogues and discussions on the issues presented in these essays. A very special thank-you to Victoria Rosén and Alastair Hannay for 'language laundering' my essays. I also cordially thank Anne Turner and Scandinavian University Press for a most pleasant collaboration. Finally, my gratitude is due to the Norwegian Research Council for giving its support to the publishing of these essays in philosophical pragmatics.

G.S.

Content

Introduction

A philosophy of modernity is a philosophy of crisis. In a post-metaphysical age, characterized worldwide by plurality and tensions, the quest for a universal rationality is a complex but urgent task. And after Auschwitz and Hiroshima the question concerning the possibility of a universal ethics can hardly be ignored. The most promising answers in favor of a universal rationality, including a minimal ethics, are, I believe, to be found in those philosophies which elaborate procedural and self-reflective conceptions of pragmatic reason.

These pragmatic conceptions of universal rationality have to cope with contextualist objections. They have to deal with the situatedness of their own language and of their own socio-historical embeddedness. Hence there is a search not only for possible deep-level competences inherent in all contextually embedded speech acts but also for a normative notion of cultural modernization in terms of institutional and epistemic differentiations. Within this intellectual setting we encounter the current debate of modernity and post-modernity, from literary criticism to social science – the modernists arguing in favor of some notion of universal rationality, the post-modernists arguing in favor of plurality and an unmasking of the notion of rationality as one of power and repression in disguise.

This collection of essays deals with rationality and modernity. It focuses on the philosophical discussion of contextuality and universality in connection with rationality and basic norms. Its perspective is that of the 'pragmatic turn'.[1] Its discursive dimension is that of a mutual criticism between hermeneutic contextualism on the one hand and trans-contextual pragmatics on the other, or more precisely, between contextual praxeology as it is found in the late Wittgenstein and universal pragmatics as we find it in Apel or in Habermas. Its basic concern is to elaborate an improved conception of rationality as situated but still universally valid. All the essays have this philosophical horizon in common, and they all attempt to elaborate, from different angles, another position or another way of thinking within this discursive dimension. Their philosophical contribution can be indicated, tentatively at this point, by the following catchwords. It sets forth a discursive elaboration of a 'fallibilistic meliorism' with a 'pragmatic' core of universal rationality. Attempts are made, on the one hand, to defend a pragmatic (gradualistic and 'post-skeptical') notion of universal reason, including basic norms, and on the other hand to perform case-oriented 'piecemeal negations' and 'sublations' with the use of arguments from absurdity (including self-referential arguments). So, what is philosophically novel and important can be summarized in terms of a pragmatic meliorism which allows for a universality denied by contextualist positions. At the same time this pragmatic meliorism, emphasizing, as it does, attempts at overcoming the 'negative', avoids some of the problems inherent in universalistic positions which for the main operate with 'positive' goals and ideals.

As a further hint, helping to situate these essays in their proper intellectual landscape, I will add a few remarks on some characteristics of contemporary Norwegian philosophy.

It is convenient to start with Arne Næss. Coming originally from a Spinozist position, the young Arne Næss elaborated a strongly empiricist position during his stay in Vienna in the thirties.[2] But gradually he dissolved this position from within and was thereby led toward a possibilistic and pluralistic position (of a 'holistic' kind later found in Kuhnian philosophy). This skeptical trend finally brought him to his present position, a deep ecology (or 'ecosophy') reminiscent of Spinoza but which, in a Næssian perspective, implies a strong practical commitment. In the fifties and sixties, Næss, together with other philosophers and social scientists, played an active role in discussing and analyzing political topics such as fascism and democracy, non-violence and civil resistance.[3] And all along he held an open discussion with philosophers with other positions, including phenomenological positions, interested in problems related to human actions and intentions.[4] During these debates the parties managed to a large extent to overcome the traditional opposition between analytic and continental philosophy.[5] The result of these and other discussions was a widely held consensus in favor of an analytically and contextually interpreted 'transcendental' pragmatics.

In this intellectual environment – skeptically inclined and with a sensitivity to the urgent political problems of a modern world – some 'mediation' between continental questions and an analytic way of working turned to a large extent into a common heritage. The essays of this book are indebted to this heritage.

*

This collection of essays has the following structure: (1) In the first essay, "Praxeological Reflections", I offer a reflection upon lifeworld activities, in the style of thinking found in praxeological pragmatics. In so doing I indicate the need for an 'overcoming' of contextualist thinking in the direction of epistemic questions of a more universalistic nature. (2) The next essay, "Arguments from Absurdity", addresses these epistemic questions by analyzing various cases of informal 'reductio ad absurdum' arguments. I argue in favor of a gradualist notion of 'contingent necessity' (in harmony with a praxeological pragmatics of late-Wittgensteinian provenance). (3) The following essay, "Pragmatism and Pragmatics", focuses on the transcendental-pragmatic and universal-pragmatic conceptions of these epistemic questions, viz. the Apelian and Habermasian notions of a discourse theory of truth and rightness. Criticizing the idea of an ideal speech situation, and of consensus as a criterion of validity, I argue in favor of a gradualist and melioristic conception of normative and theoretical validation, a conception which focuses on arguments rather than on consensus, a conception which confirms an asymmetric 'primacy of the negative' and asserts a constitutive notion of rationality as a regulative idea. In a slogan we could say that my strategy is that of 'strengthening by weakening'. (4) In "Madness and Reason", with the subtitle *"Reductio ad pathologicum* as a *via negativa* for elucidating the universal-pragmatic notion of rationality?*", I argue along these lines in favor of this 'weak' version of universal pragmatics. (5) In "Contextual and Universal Pragmatics" I discuss the interrelationship between praxeological pragmatics and universal (transcendental) pragmatics; but in this essay my criticism is mainly directed against the former (for its inadequate notion of philosophical reflection and of lifeworld modernization). (6) However, the following essay, "The Pragmatic Notion of Nature", comments critically on the high-level paradigmatic conceptualizations in Habermasian thinking (focusing especially on his dealings with the notion of nature). The point I am making is one that favors gradualism. (7) In "Ethical Gradualism and Discourse Ethics" I discuss discourse ethics in relation to the debate concerning the notion of a 'moral subject' on the borderline between humans and animals. Prior to the 'principle of universalization' interpreted in quasi-utilitarian terms,[6] we must find out who are the 'affected' subjects, entitled to morally relevant interests (and 'advocatory representation' if unable to participate in a discourse). I consider the virtues of a paradigmatic (dichotomic) thinking and of a gradualist analysis of intermediary cases, and discuss the adequacy of the standard ethical positions, arguing in favor of discourse ethics as the final horizon for such a discussion. "Modernization of the Lifeworld" (8) and "Rationality and Contextuality" (9) add to the earlier discussion of universal pragmatics, points of view and arguments from the debate on maturation and modernization, and in this perspective I discuss the recent debate between Apel and Habermas on *Letztbegründung* ('ultimate normative justification') and *Sittlichkeit* ('ethical life'). Once more I argue in favor of my gradualist and meliorist version of pragmatic philosophy.

Even though each essay can be read alone, there is still a fairly tight web tying the various perspectives and approaches together into one overall discussion of the basic issue, viz. that of the 'embeddedness of universal reason'. These essays, as well as the philosophical tradition to which they belong, represent another approach to these problems, a way of thinking which can be distinguished both from the point of view of contextual praxeology and from that of universal pragmatics (i.e. pragmatics either in Apel or in Habermas).[7] Making that approach visible, both theoretically and practically, is the common aim of these essays in philosophical pragmatics.

NOTES

1. It is thus 'post-positivist' and post 'philosophy of consciousness'. Cf. Karl-Otto Apel, *Transformation der Philosophie*, Frankfurt a.M.: Suhrkamp, 1973; and Dietrich Böhler, Tore Nordenstam and Gunnar Skirbekk, eds., *Die pragmatische Wende. Sprachspielpragmatik oder Transzendentalpragmatik?* Frankfurt a.M.: Suhrkamp, 1986.

2. Cf. *Erkenntnis und wissenschaftliches Verhalten* (1936).

3. Cf., e.g., the UNESCO project on the notion of democracy, led by Næss (*Democracy, Ideology and Objectivity; Studies in the Semantics and Cognitive Analysis of Ideological Controversy*, Arne Næss et al., Oslo, 1956); the thesis on Nazism by his colleague Arild Haaland (*Nazismen i Tyskland. En analyse av dens forutsetninger*, Oslo, 1955); and Næss's work on Gandhian ethics (*Gandhi and the Nuclear Age*, N.J., 1965, *Gandhi and Group Conflict*, Oslo, 1974).

4. E.g., Hans Skjervheim, who criticized the Næssian empiricism in the study of man. Cf. *Objectivism and the Study of Man*, Oslo, 1959. (In *The Theory of Communicative Action*, Boston, 1984, Habermas makes this comment: "Wherein consists then the special methodological difficulties of understanding in the sciences that must gain access to their object domains through interpretation? H. Skjervheim already dealt with this problem in 1959. He is among those who reopened the debate concerning social-scientific objectivism, a discussion that has come to a provisional close with the comprehensive examination by Richard Bernstein, *The Restructuring of Social and Political Theory* (1976). Under the spectacular

impression of Peter Winch's book, *The Idea of Social Science* (1958), it was not sufficiently noticed that Skjervheim was the one who had first worked out the methodologically shocking consequences of the *Verstehen* problematic; had worked out, that is, what is problematic about *Verstehen*." in: Vol. I, pp. 111.)

5. One perspective of this 'mediating' process was the following: quite a number of those from the continental tradition were interested in phenomenological descriptions and intentional explanations of human actions, and quite a number of those from analytic philosophy were interested in the analysis of human actions, including along the lines of the Wittgenstein of *Philosophical Investigations*. Both groups were case-oriented and interested in understanding the phenomena. Add to this that both were discussing these problems with the same social scientists, and with each other – in a small society one has to listen to other people and even read what they are writing. As time passed, the importance of *Schulrichtungen* gradually decreased. Through their detailed case studies of contextual preconditions inherent in (speech) acts, the Wittgensteinian philosophers made an important contribution to this process of combining these two traditions (hence supplementing a similar contribution by the phenomenologists).

We could say that Norwegian philosophers (less burdened than their British colleagues by a local tradition) put the late Wittgenstein to proper use at an early stage. Knut-Erik Tranøy, who became acquainted with Wittgenstein in England, analyzed methodological rules in terms of constitutive norms. Jakob Meløe and his 'Jacobins' elaborated a praxeology of basic actions (which in one perspective reminds us of a Heideggerian phenomenology). Ingemund Gullvåg developed an analytic version of a universal pragmatics. Some of the articles from these discussions are now available in three collections, published at the Scandinavian University Press: *Praxeology*, Gunnar Skirbekk, ed., 1983; *Essays in Pragmatic Philosophy I*, Ingemund Gullvåg and Helge Høibraaten, eds., 1985; and *Essays in Pragmatic Philosophy II*, Helge Høibraaten, ed., 1990. Today there is a Wittgenstein archive at the University of Bergen, computerizing his *Nachlaβ*.

6. Cf., e.g., J. Habermas in *Moral Consciousness and Communicative Action*, Cambridge, Mass.: MIT Press, 1990, p. 65: "Thus every valid norm has to fulfill the following condition: (U) *All* affected can accept the consequences and the side effects its *general* observance can be anticipated to have for

the satisfaction of *everyone's* interests (and these consequences are preferred to those of known alternative possibilities for regulation)".

7. For the application of my conception of pragmatic meliorism on practical issues, cf. Gunnar Skirbekk, *Eco-Philosophical Manuscripts*, Bergen: Ariadne, 1992.

Praxeological Reflections[1]

Introductory Remarks on Lifeworld Activities and Validity Claims

> "Teaching which is not meant to apply to anything but the examples given is different from that which *points behind* them".
>
> Wittgenstein, *Philosophical Investigations*, § 208.

In our day-to-day world, each one of us has to know quite a number of things, depending on the varied activities we engage in. There are so many things, for instance, that a housewife *may* know about; but given a certain set of housing conditions and a certain pattern of family life, there are things she must know in order to be a housewife in that particular society. She *must*, for instance, know how to get hold of food, how various dishes are prepared with the equipment at her disposal, how these may be served up to the members of her family, and how to clear the table and wash up in readiness for the next time around. Here we have one type of operation with clear temporal and spatial boundaries – one kind of day-to-day world for one species of housewife.

The housewife we have in mind doesn't necessarily know where the food – or even the money to buy it – comes from, still less the exact chemical composition of the cheese. What she knows is what has to be known if her job is to get done; and, be it noted, in terms of the concepts built into the performance. The handle is what-you-get-hold-of, butter is what melts in the pan, the knife what you cut bread with, and so on. Things crop up as playing their role in that activity, and this applies both to what we work *with* and to what we operate *on*, what is in process of becoming a finished product. The human body, too, like the space in which it operates, enters the picture as a function of what is going on. We can no more account for the things independently of the activity than we can describe

the activity independently of the things. The housewife's knowledge – the knowledge that is essential to her function – can
likewise be described only in terms of things and operations so
conceived.

To do her work, the housewife must be aware when each
included operation is complete – just when, for instance, the cream
has reached the required stiffness for breaking off the whipping
process and switching to the next step (such as spreading the cream
on the cake). She must know, too, when the job is finally finished
– know the proper start-and-stop routines. And this means she must
have a conscious identity – a certain self-awareness through time
– which comprehends the process in its entirety and enables her to
switch from activity to activity.

It is assumed here that the *agent* is aware of what she is doing
(in this case, that the housewife is aware of what it is her work
requires her to know). We assume, moreover, that *we*, reporting on
this activity, share that insight with the agent.[2]

What we are looking for are those features of day-to-day
activities without which those activities could not retain their identity. We are thus in search of something quite different from an
empirical review of diverse activities or the subjection of some
theory about such activities to an empirical test. Our concern is
with the basic structure of these activities. Or, if you please, features seen as constitutive – as a *sine qua non* – of the activities in
question.

The use we make of examples is not intended to lend empirical
support to theories or to illustrate concepts already acquired. Our
examples, already given shape by our preconceptions concerning
what is at issue, provide us with a basis for acquiring and testing
the categories best suited for getting to grips with the matter in
hand.

We could therefore in a sense be said to be engaging in phenomenology, an attempt to spell out the constitutive features of
phenomena by taking activities within well-defined life-
environments as illustrative examples,[3] indeed a sort of
transcendental phenomenology, though such terms yield in

themselves no very precise information.

What emerges as we describe the housewife's activity and function is the *point of view* it constitutes – the close encounter with things and processes, with spatial and temporal dimensions, with one's own body and one's own identity, as well as with other individuals for whom things are done and with whom dealings go on.[4] And the more exhaustively the activity is specified, the finer the distinctions, of which the point of view, that emerges, admits.

The agent in characteristic action affords us double access to the process of concept formation via two interlocking fields of association,[5] viz. those of grasping and of seeing. If we are not to get hold of the wrong end of the stick, we must first focus right, while a good grip on things helps us get them in focus. The one field lies open through getting a hold and manipulating, the other through sighting and focusing, and the two merge in the operation, the activity. The concepts by which we get to grips with an activity's components are at one and the same time definitive of and determined by what is grasped. It might be put like this: point of view and object in sight, means of comprehension and thing comprehended, are conditional upon each other – just as the activity as a whole and its constituent acts and objects are mutually definitive. It is these two fields of association – visual and manual – that afford joint access to the dialectic of concept formation. The notion of an operation-dependent view thus encapsulates an understanding essentially rooted in activity.

Our aim in describing such activities and the views they incorporate is to bring out more clearly what we already know about our own and other people's activities. We want to bring both our own and other people's way of looking at things into better focus. Failure to realize how other people are "making out" is very possibly a more common reason for gratuitously imposing upon or offending others than any real wish to do them an injury. Just think of the problems children can face and of which grown-ups are quite unaware simply because adults are taller. Or think of the ways we unconsciously exploit other people, where an effort to put ourselves in their shoes could awaken us to what we are doing. Key phrases in this connection are "bringing to consciousness" and "confluence of horizons", and the keynote is struck wherever different individual agents, classes, age-groups, sexes or periods can find no shared viewpoint, no common perspective.

Gaining recognition is, we might say, getting oneself seen as a person, one consequence being that others begin to *see the point* of what one is up to; anyone who remains "unseen" in this sense simply doesn't belong to a community, and suffers all the consequences this must have for a person's sense of identity. There is a kind of unimaginativeness which leaves a person imprisoned in his or her own narrow vision, with very little idea of what it is like for the various other people they rub shoulders with. And this stunted awareness of others brings with it a stunted awareness of oneself. For how can I know what I myself am really about unless I have an adequate picture of the dealings of those around me? The housewife's daily doings mesh with those of the rest of the family, as well as with those of the shopkeeper, the bus driver, the teacher, etc. and thus with the whole community in which she lives.

What a person does (and what gives an adequate picture of that person's doings) is thus seen to be correlative with what other people do (and with what gives an adequate picture of *their* activities). There is no understanding an activity (along with the agent's view of things and of herself) in isolation, for self-understanding is understanding oneself-and-others within a common framework.

Deciding what a person is about when engaging in a particular activity – forging horseshoes, say, at the anvil with a hammer – depends in addition on the actions that *precede* and *follow*. In order to discover whether the man doing the forging is a smith, we don't just keep on watching what he does; we take a look at what he does along with the result. It is selling horseshoes to make a living that identifies him as a blacksmith.[6] If, instead, he goes on to exhibit his handiwork to a class of schoolchildren, he could well be a metalwork teacher or an expert on arts and crafts rather than a smith. Thus the greater totality to which the activity belongs, and from which it gets its identity, has its own *temporal* setting.

As we are already aware, then, the identity of an activity is never to be determined in isolation, but only with reference to a wider scheme of things to which it belongs, one involving other people via division of labor and complementarity of occupations, besides the other activities of the agent himself as time goes on.

A blacksmith is a blacksmith within a division-of-labor patterned community while at the same time, simply as human, having both immediate and more remote bonds of kinship. (The smith may be said to have his place within both a productive and a reproductive sphere, whereas the housewife is, as it were, permanently housed in the realm of reproduction.) By just picking on one function – the smith in his smithy, the wife in her kitchen – we are left with loose threads right and left: connections not to be coped with via a single function, but linking inexorably with other roles in a pattern of life. In a given integrated socio-historical setting, this immanent carry-over from function to function culminates in a variety of typical life-cycles.[7]

The stable self-sufficient, self-governing community is in this sense a sort of minimal operational whole, and *ipso facto* a minimal overall perspective. Such worlds compact in their time, were perhaps the tribe, the city-state and the village.

Yet here, too, we encounter diverse agents, each with a "station and its duties" and the viewpoint that goes with them. Can there be found anywhere a bearer of that conspectus, that overview, in which the wholeness wins its own perspective? Each individual view shades over into others, and so into a totality, but how can the individual, from one confined perspective, reach over into comprehensiveness? Once we admit that the view is bound up with the agent, and that the social sum-total finds no agent identity, we seem at a loss to make the total overview do any real work.

Even if the various activities, each having its own perspective, may be said to culminate in a single operational totality – the self-sufficient local community – there is no one agent who acts out the totality role and to whom we can attribute the overview. The comprehensive agent-subject is a composite of things communally done by a multitude of agents.

Religious leaders have no doubt been taken to be bearers of the real conspectus. But how can we think of them as "agents"? And haven't just such claims been under bombardment ever since the Enlightenment?

The idea was once current that the absolute monarch – in full sail – simply *was* the functioning community as overview-endowed agent. We all know how this claim has been unmasked.

The words of the poets no doubt make the world we live in present to us, but what is there to give them agent status? Admittedly, our vision can be poetically sharpened, and revised, too, for that matter. But how is poetry *qua* poetry to *authenticate* its would-be synoptic vision?

The diverse members of a community surely do, in a sense, assimilate it in its entirety. Just as the individual's functions fall in with and have reference to a whole communal network of intermeshing operations, so does the individual's view of things somehow mirror the aggregate's power of seeing. Through the learning of a language, and by being trained to carry out specific operations and to identify with them, each individual is impregnated with a vision in which the corporate overview is, so to speak, printed off at a specialized location. Seen in this light, the transparent society is one in which everyone sees the point of what everyone else is up to.[8]

By no means everything we do is straightforward "agent-activity", a one-way traffic in the processing of concrete objects. Our way of looking at things, our notion of what we are and the sort of things we latch on to – all this takes shape, to no small extent, in the course of the varied dealings we have with others: conversing, passing on information, showing affective concern, putting a whole viewpoint on display through artistic creativity. Our points of view are, then, not fully represented in the notions of agent-and-thing-done: there must be this carry-over into the dialogue of social and cultural interchange. Accounting for the blacksmith in his smithy is not enough. Our picture must take in the putting of children to bed, the ritual, the festivity and the artist's innovation.⁷

But in what sense may the agents in such cases be said to "know what they have to know in order to do what they do"? And in what sense are the agent's outlook and our own coincident? It is now that we really come face-to-face with the validation issue, as concerns both the agent's outlook and our own. Questions of truth and rightness come up naturally for the agents when their actions and interactions run into problems. Doubts and dissensions can then be dealt with in a variety of ways: *force majeure* or ritual, careful inquiry or counting votes. But in describing the agents and their actions we ourselves face the same issues, for we implicitly claim for ourselves the relevant insight, and thus claim to have gained the necessary vantage point. To make this claim good, we are bound to validate our own account of things – if we can.

It may be worth while supplementing these programmatic sketches of a phenomenological approach with an attempt to put our validation problem in its historical setting.

In the Greek city-state, a conspectus was still fairly feasible. Aristotle was therefore on the whole content to describe the good life and the good community, so attaining a model perspective as a guide to action and an elucidation of what every inhabitant knew. Otherwise, he assembled data about various city-states and assigned them to classes. Nothing more seemed to be needed. A little reflection and observation sufficed for a man to know what he was doing when he took action, and the consequences of an action were plain for all to see.

In the larger post-Renaissance societies, with their propensity for continual change, the conspectus has been harder to come by. Shared reflections and simple observations are no longer enough if we want to know what we are doing, and each man's deeds are swallowed up in a vast theater of action no man can survey. Indeed, to the extent that we *are* what we do, not knowing what we are up to means not knowing who we are. It is quite apparent that actions not uncommonly have unintended consequences, or even bring about the very opposite of what was meant. Agents, in short, have all too often lost touch with what is really going on, and the sum-total of all the separate acts points sightlessly in a direction none foresaw. The opaque society has no observation window from which it may be steered.

All this leads to a greater need for systematic scrutiny of what is really afoot, and in the wake of the natural sciences empirically oriented social sciences emerge and take shape. What the housewife never glimpsed from her functionally restricted viewpoint, economics, sociology and psychology can open her eyes to. Enlightened by the sciences, we see more clearly, act more effectively; they pave the way from the microcosmic to the macrocosmic perspective.[10] And as they acquaint us with their overview, much that is obscure in our everyday picture is more deeply and sharply illumined.

The comprehensive overview comes to be identified with the scientific perspective, the outlook shared by scientists as agents who represent the common quest of the questing community.

Phenomena like inflation, unemployment and war are things which no one seems to have aimed at and which cannot be comprehended from the functional viewpoint of the housewife or the blacksmith. The attempt is now being made to get to the bottom of such problems through the sciences, and to get them under control through political institutions that turn to the sciences for assistance.

This makes the community of researchers, taken collectively as investigators in joint action, into the agent-subject endowed with the overview. At the same time, the social embodiment of science in the form of expertise available to employers and administrators has transferred the principal overview-directed agent roles to informed political and industrial leaders. As Max Weber has it, the world has undergone "scientization": rational management and ideological concord are in the driving seat. The sciences tell us the way things are, and how the various means available are more or less well suited to attainment of this or that objective. Yet the ends in view, the values to be served, are beyond the scope of science – final justification is not a scientific issue, and values are chosen, not factually established. Decisionism is the watchword here, not rational consensus based on argumentation. Value questions are decided by the largest vote, not by the strongest argument, and it is in free elections and representative political institutions that the various stands on value find a voice. It turns out, however, that in sanely organized states there actually is a virtual consensus on a number of fundamental political aims. The age of ideologies is past, and politics is seen to be rational management based on democratic decision regarding evaluative matters.

These views concerning science and politics are, however, questionable to say the least.

In the first place, the sciences present themselves as particular disciplines, each defined by its specific concepts and methods and, indeed its own view. How the one Truth is to emerge as an all-embracing synthesis of these dissimilar approaches is no small problem. And how might the variants within socio-economics, sociology, ecology, psychology, etc. be harmonized or unified? Is some categorial frame of a higher order to be found, some meta-science, or is intertranslatability at a given stage the most we can hope for?

Supposing these problems to be solved, what sort of organization is needed to ensure that this total view of things takes control over society? Presumably one that restricts the exercise of power to political institutions and places the comprehensive overview at their disposal. Which would, of course, mean putting such spontaneous mechanisms as the market pretty well out of commission. Yet this would call for a multitude of administrative structures serving to ensure access to crucial insights and to consolidate control, surely just the mechanisms that would again fragment both the perspective and the overall control we were after.

Now let us suppose that these problems, too, are out of the way, and that a unitary collective agent-subject, bringing comprehensive insight to bear, controls and governs everything. What sort of society do we end up with? An optimally enlightened oligarchy, it would seem, in which the privileged few have total insight and total power, the rest being left devoid of either. The Platonic state ideal springs to mind.

We have admittedly got this far on very much of an *ex hypothesi* basis: we have envisaged both a unitary agent at the political level and a synthesis of disciplines yielding scientific unity. A fully Platonic position further requires, in the last analysis, the subsumption of all particular viewpoints and interests under the one overview and the interests common to all – a synthesis comprising not just the view-points of the several sciences, but even in the last resort each and every functionally localized view, whether of class, occupation or individual citizen.

We might call this the Gods-eye view, and find no finite eye to behold it. Let us turn in our tracks and look the way we have come.

Suppose, then, a conflict has arisen about building a nuclear power station. How can the problem be tackled in a way that will finally lead to a sane overall perspective and a rational programme of action? Various disciplines can throw light on the issue, and the corresponding experts must be called in: technicians, economists, lawyers, ecologists; and all these submit their reports to the authorities, whose subsequent decisions reflect the values expressed by the electorate. The special forms of expertise tell us the way things are, leaving no room for disagreement where the facts are concerned. But when we turn to asking what is wanted and what needs to be done, there is no expert consensus to draw on. This is where the counting of votes takes over.

But who is expert on what sort of experts to call in?[11] Each discipline furnishes truths about the matter, derived from its own peculiar concepts and methods, but how are we to decide, in a scientific way, who are the relevant experts on a given issue? The answer would appear to be that none of the particular disciplines in question – physics, sociology, economics, and so forth – can settle the matter. Are we to conclude, then, that there is no rational way of hitting on the right choice of experts, so that there is only decision-making to fall back on – as many contend is the case with values and purposes generally. And does this really imply disagreement on just what is at issue?

However – it was, after all, these disciplines that put us in the picture! What are we in fact doing when *we* take it upon ourselves to bring all this up for *discussion*? What sort of expertise and rationality do we lay claim to, and how are we to validate our own pronouncements?

Well, even admitting our lack of any such meta-discipline as we were canvassing, we have at least succeeded in reflecting on the problem-complex involved. Despite our still having arrived at no criterion for selecting the rightful expert, we have succeeded in focusing attention on this multiplicity-of-experts problem. And if we go on to ask by virtue of what sort of insight we do so, the answer that suggests itself is: through reflective understanding of what is at issue and how the various disciplines relate to it. The whole complex of problems is sharply illumined through a reflective interchange among persons with a genuine commitment to penetrate deeper.

We are thus invoking the possibility of an interpretative, hermeneutic and essentially interdisciplinary procedure. The insight which thus emerges owes its credibility to the way arguments stand up under constant challenge – though only, we may add, where arguments win on their own merits, and gratuitous disturbing factors are eliminated. Such ideal conditions, where only the rationality of the participants is allowed to count for anything, must at least be approximated if a resulting consensus is to be accredited. And, needless to say, the free exchange of views here envisaged promotes the formulation of diverse particular viewpoints and thus a wider recognition of them.

In light of this, the overview is now attributed, not to the individual experts or to the powers that be, but to the communion of participants in open, public debate – in an ongoing, emancipated interchange between all those concerned: expert, politician and layman alike.

Are we drifting again into the fanciful, the Utopian? Let us resume our former track.

We must ask whether the very fact that we engage in talk and dialogue about the building of a nuclear power station does not in itself involve us in the presupposition that our own comments are true and correct, inasmuch as, even if we cannot make good what we say there and then, we at any rate count on being able to do so in a fair debate (where the best argument is bound to win). Surely the very person who plays up the irrational elements in human actions and opinions in order to discredit the notion of such an ideal fellowship-in-disputation is bound to make just such a claim about his own protestations. To the extent to which this is always being taken for granted, the ideal communion of fellowship of arguers is already there and in action – if only as an operative presupposition.[12]

This being so, why then should there be such a decisive distinction between "is" and "ought", between assertions on the one hand and imperatives and value-judgments on the other? No doubt there are differences in the way we go about backing these different kinds of claim to validity; but might it not very well prove possible to meet normative validation requirements in the course of such continuing discussion, and here, too, arrive at rational agreement?

In so far as the facts are shaped and indeed constituted via a social practice or institution, there will in principle be nothing to block an immediate transition from institutional facts to norms. Granted, for instance, a life-pattern which includes the institution of borrowing and paying back, the *obligation* to repay under certain circumstances is already ensured. This we can take account of without ourselves underwriting the institution, so that the point really at issue is to what extent we can find institutions (having norms built into them) to which there is no real alternative.[13] For a kind of universal validity could in this way be claimed for the built-in norms. Yet is not the optimally argument-decided discussion to which we implicitly appeal in claiming to validate our assertions and actions just such an indispensable "institution"? However much we may protest that this publicly paraded rationality is a historically conditioned phenomenon, that it is vulnerable, imperfectly realized and easily undermined, do not our own utterances and actions somehow presuppose that we hold ourselves

answerable to such an ideal standard? And doesn't the very notion
of arguments being judged on their own merits entail the presence
of inbuilt norms – regulative principles – such as freedom, equality
and universality?

Once more, we find ourselves propelled toward the overhead
lighting, and recoil, dazzled. From our humble and down-to-earth
start, picturing the doings of blacksmith and housewife, we
repeatedly soar to vantage points at which our sight grows dim.

Yet as we rest and reflect, rubbing weary eyes, a certain after-
image will not go away – that of reason as a reflected-upon and
continuing argumentative coherence due to the joint efforts of
agent-subjects in pursuit of honest agreement.

Could that image, after all, be illusory? It is time to turn about,
and bring our teasing glimpses into better focus.

The Power of The Example

> "But if a person has not yet got the *concepts*, I shall teach
> him to use the words by means of *examples* and by
> *practice*".
>
> Wittgenstein, *Philosophical Investigations*, § 208.

The point of our example of the housewife (or blacksmith) was to
get a better grasp on the fundamental features of activities within
a life-pattern.

What makes a feature fundamental may be elucidated,
Aristotelian fashion, as what is *essential*. A book, say, may be
either hardback or paperback, but it may not comprise only blank
pages (or no pages at all), since it is an essential property of a
book to have pages on which something is written.

A more Kantian elucidation would be to say that fundamental
features are *constitutive*, founding the very possibility of the thing
in question, much as a nation's constitution is a prerequisite for the
rule of law. Thus the constitutive features of an activity are those

by virtue of which it is that activity, so that for lack of them the activity as such must disintegrate.

In seeking to establish what are the constitutive features of an activity – the outlook, say, necessary to a housewife where there is a certain level of technology and a certain division of labor – we are not trying to specify what, in all its concrete particularity, is empirically accessible (e.g. what such housewives in fact typically think about). We seek, instead, something necessary and universal, at least where that special type of activity is concerned.

We focused on what the agent *had to* know in order to perform her action. Now, if we mark the distinction between what is explicit and what is only implicit, we may look for what is constitutive also in things like language-rules, which a language-using agent must be master of, though without necessarily possessing explicit knowledge *about* them.

The features of an activity we emphasize may, in fact, be of widely varying contextual specificity – our examples gaining in empirical particularity as we become more specific about technological and social structuring. We may therefore say that examples lie along a continuum in terms of universality: at the one end, the example fails to be representative of anything other than itself; at the other, the intended example is general enough to virtually coalesce with the concept rather than exemplify it.

By taking into account the variety of activities and functions and their interplay – using hand-plucked examples of assorted generality or attention to detail – one may bring out the *multiplicity* of functions and outlooks, and hence resist the ever-present temptation to oversimplify by using neat tables and clear-cut distinctions.[14]

The object is not just to arrive at general and necessary requirements (such as the claims to universal validity), but to make out what is the point of *this* particular activity. What impels us to generalize, to argue our case and raise the specter of an overview, is partly the fact that activities are not self-contained but need each other's supplementation, and partly the way an activity can seize up, or doubts and conflicts arise, with the consequent review and discussion in the hope of finding a cure.

We can look in a variety of ways for examples that point up the true multiplicity present in an activity – in, say, a housewife's daily round - and here direct experience in the first person can contribute much both to fullness of detail and to the separation of the essential from the accidental.[15]

We can, too, in a variety of ways stress the general aspects of activities, whether we focus on the internal relations among such concepts as 'agent', 'act', 'viewpoint' and 'thing', or on the way these concepts serve in general as constitutive factors in such activities.

The example is, in fact, of a thought-experimental character, being tailored to suit the sort of fullness of detail or universality that preoccupies us. It is thus vouchsafed only a limited degree of autonomy vis-à-vis our preconceptions. Yet a certain independence can be conceded to it, since otherwise it would be merely a figment of the imagination, suited neither to checking nor to bringing out features of the day-to-day world. What makes the example instructive and lends it its power is just the fact that it can furnish a fresh starting-point and work counter to our preconceptions. And it is this autonomy – the very thing that makes the example accessible to others – that also confers on it its corrective and elucidatory force.

When we discuss examples, we exploit common access to the example *qua* example in order to get our point across to others. We can, moreover, by means of example analysis, open our own eyes to crucial factors we had tended to overlook, as well as correcting our own earlier preconceptions by coming to see what sort of disruption of the activity would result if the presumptive fundamental feature were deleted.[16]

There is, at the same time, always something "custom-built" about an example, irrespective of its generality or particularity. In the first place, the activity-in-itself owes its identity to an internal relation between viewpoint, operation, self-identity, and object as these present themselves to the doer of the actions. And secondly, the activity-as-example is always trimmed to suit the preconceptions of whoever is describing it. When it comes to testing out our anticipations[17] in relation to such "trimmed" activities, there is a reflective shuttling back and forth, a hermeneutic circle, since looking *in between* the "custom-built" version of an activity and "what really goes on" is simply not on the cards. And what is here "really" going on is a reflective validation (following in many instances the *via negativa* of *reductio ad absurdum*) of certain features' constitutive status. (Our categories have typically such a status, being themselves incapable of having truth-values, yet, just in so far as they are appropriate, making possible the truth or falsity of assertions.)

The fact that such a testing procedure can and does work can only be accounted for by the extent to which, when all is said and done, we *share* our day-to-day world. No doubt we orient our lives within a variety of private conceptual horizons of greater or less scope, but nothing prevents us, in principle, from seeing the point of each other's activities. These horizons can to some extent converge, a broadly shared outlook be attained, so that it becomes generally accepted that our concepts – our grasping equipment – do (or do not) furnish a firm enough hold on the example considered.

Seeing that our examples are always somewhat made-to-fit, the autonomy of an example as such must rest largely on the way "loose ends" stand revealed when the given instance is properly thought out, since its relative independence points beyond it, betraying, *ipso facto* what is essential to its exemplary function. To put it Spinozistically, a phenomenon can neither be nor be understood in isolation. Or we might say with Hegel that the power of the negative drives thought from the abstract – from that which is clear-cut, and by the same token cut off from that on which it really depends – towards the concrete totality which can both exist and be understood in its own terms.

We have already seen, in the case of the housewife, how various natural continuations beyond a given framework led over into other activities involving other agents (division of labor), into the given agent's preceding and succeeding activities (transitions between work and recreation and between different phases of the same activity) and so into the whole life-cycle of that individual. The least unit that is really understandable purely in its own terms is neither the particular activity nor the particular agent about her immediate business, but a whole community with a certain extension in time.

The question inevitably arises whether this "ultimate and self-sufficient unit" – the ultimate ratifier of our doings and of our very identity - can be seen, in today's perspective, as anything other than a historically incidental world community, comprehensible if at all only by subordinating separate fields of inquiry to an open and all-embracing use of reason.

The tendency to crossing-over, to transition, gives a pointer to depth presuppositions: man is seen as the opener-of-access, receptive to himself, to others and to his own ongoing activity through a timespan (Heidegger), an agent who, for all the finitude of his placing and perspective, can attain new stature in knowledge, insight and breadth of view. What is being presupposed is a comprehending subject whose identity is altered by learning, while remaining self-continuous, so that present comprehension and anticipatory action alike are shaped by an outlook mediated by the past of that identity. In his finitude, man is thus directed via his perspective-localized activities to work, cooperation and learning.

An activity can be carried on as a mere routine, empty of active reflection or conscious choice. But people can also take action, see their own intervention as *open* to them rather than as locked fast by what is and has to be – as reflecting also what is *possible* (as we acknowledge when we say "things might have been different"). There are, in short, alternatives, and these possibles within the actual are something our efforts can bring about. What is uncompromisingly real – our toil and sweat, for instance – is thus seen as contingent, and as something we can do something about.

The "negative", the non-existing, is in this way "promoted", so as to rank above the "positive" or the way things in fact are, inasmuch as acts of deciding between alternatives lie open to us. And here is a condition for human freedom (Sartre).

This function of the negative comes out clearly in verbal communication, via the human ability to say *no*: over and above the power to react and to adapt with greater or less complexity, there is the capacity to take up a *position* on something or other, to become aware of alter-native viewpoints and conditions, and thus to *contradict*. And here is a unique manifestation of human *individuality*. Once the word "no" has been uttered, the way is open to a *reason*-giving response in which the respective merits of this or that point of view are brought to light. Discussion and argumentation separate out as something institutionally distinct – a polyclinic for the healing of denial-bred dissension.

Conversing and interacting, a human individual is not just (*constitutively*) the unfolder of a world, but also, starting from an already formed personal identity, a *joint* unfolder along with others, possessing indeed the capacity – by virtue of an identity-through-change both in time and function (*plus ça change, plus c'est la même chose*) - to partake in the perspectives of others without losing sight of the private perspective that was entertained earlier. Man is not condemned *either* to see others and their perspectives purely from his own angle (treating the other as object) *or* to be swallowed up in some alien perspective ("go native"), since the self-encounter and the temporally ecstatic identity peculiar to man confer the power to *communicate*. But, we may ask, when someone says "no" and demands reasons, what is then true and correct internally to the several perspectives, and where is the perspective to be found that will yield a universally binding answer to such questions? By virtue of his capacity for setting *validation* requirements and for trying to ensure they are met through inquiry and discussion, man reverts critically to his constitutive-communicative role and to the perspective immanent in it.

NOTES

1. Published earlier in: *Praxeology* (= *P*), ed. G. Skirbekk, Oslo: Norwegian University Press, 1983, pp. 117–133. Translated from the Norwegian by Kenneth Young.

2. Cf. the praxeology in J. Meløe: "The Agent and His World", in: *P*, 1983, pp. 13-29.

3. One of the background philosophers here is Martin Heidegger, cf. *Sein und Zeit* (*Being and Time*), §§ 12-34.

4. "As individuals express their life, so they are. What they are, therefore, coincides with their production, with what they produce and with how they produce it." K. Marx and F. Engels, in: *German Ideology*, 1845-46 (MEGA 1/5, pp. 10-11).

5. Cf. Kjell S. Johannessen on the concept of rules and concept formation in Wittgenstein, *Norsk filosofisk tidsskrift*, 2(1973) p. 61.

6. Professional titles tell us what people do and must know, and what *we* can do together with them.

7. The viewpoint essential to an industrial worker in his job may be more limited than that essential to the housewife who reproduces him – or that of a self-supplied peasant. Cf. the gap between the viewpoint essential to an industrial worker in "Modern Times" and that essential to a revolutionary worker who surveys everything, realizes the forces behind the events, and knows how everything is to be changed and how finally everything is to be organized.

8. Cf. the difference between "coming up through the ranks", e.g., from deck boy to captain, and being given a job directly after school. (This leads us to the topics of "professionalism" and "educative society".) Cf. also the impoverished view of the tourist without personal experience of the activities he is looking at and without the relevant facts and concepts from the social sciences.
   In a transparent society everybody sees the point in what everybody else is doing. Let us think of this as a self-sufficient (self-supplied, isolated) agrarian society. When this society is in full working order, it is not *necessary* (among adults) to *talk* in order for people to understand the point of what is going on (i.e. what one does and who one is). Such explanatory talk - talk in presentation of oneself and the point of what one is doing – is, however, necessary in a society where people do not immediately see the point of what other people are doing. Our image of tacit peasants and talking citizens may well be biased, but it contains a certain insight into what is constitutively necessary in different societies with differing functional differentiation and varying levels of transparency.

9. On praxeology and art, cf. J. Meløe: "The Picture in our World", in: *P*, pp. 89–93.

10. Cf. "Ecological Crisis and Technological Expertise" in Gunnar Skirbekk, *Eco-Philosophical Manuscripts* (= *EPhM*), Bergen: Ariadne, 1992. One interesting approach to this problem is the game-theoretical method elaborated by J. Elster in various works (illuminating both rational collective decisions and counterfactual consequences), cf. e.g. *Logic and Society*, London, 1978 and *Ulysses and the Sirens*, Cambridge, 1979.

11. Cf. "Science and Ethics. Some Reflections on Expertise and Politics", in: *EPhM*.

12. Cf. J. Habermas: "Wahrheitstheorien", in: *Wirklichkeit und Reflexion*, ed. Fahrenbach, Pfullingen, 1973. Cf. also "Pragmatism and Pragmatics" in this collection.

13. See J. R. Searle "How to derive 'ought' from 'is'", in: *The Philosophical Review*, 1964, and K.-O. Apel's criticism in: "Sprachakttheorie und transzendentale Sprachpragmatik zur Frage ethischer Normen", in: *Sprachpragmatik und Philosophie*, ed. K.-O. Apel, Frankfurt a.M., 1976.

14. For instance, one may yield to such a temptation by overemphasizing a distinction between technical action and communicative action: the actual variety of forms of action drops out of sight (cf. e.g. J. Habermas's self-criticism on this point, in: "Nachwort" to *Erkenntnis und Interesse*, 1973, n. 27, p. 382, and in: "Was heißt Universalpragmatik?", *Sprachpragmatik und Philosophie*, ed. K.-O. Apel, Frankfurt a.M., 1976, p. 224). There is, however, an opposite temptation as well – that of falling into a shortsighted concreteness, where no important distinctions are clearly seen (i.e. a very detailed, but philosophically pointless analysis).

15. A personal thinking-through, as well as a discussion with other people, may be useful to strengthen our awareness of various aspects or perspectives of life. Such a personal or public reflection takes place against the background of more or less typical kinds of experiences of our culture and subculture, while at the same time this reflection itself may represent a step in a certain transformation of that very background – as for instance in cases of successful emancipatory, *or* appropriative, reflections. (Cf. critique of false consciousness, and conscious appropriation of a cultural heritage.)

    If we want to penetrate as deeply as possible into some half-known cultural phenomenon, it may be useful, however, to extend one's own experiential basis – not only to reflect upon our given particular and common experience, or to gather more data, but to deepen our own understanding through a process of learning, of experiential self-formation.

    However, to *choose* to go into such a kind of resocializing practice (e.g. a voluntary process of proletarization) is still not exactly the same as to have been implanted in this experiential field from the beginning, without ever having chosen it. Furthermore, despite our various efforts to learn and to change, there still are some subtle *limits* to the sharing of experiences; a man cannot give birth, a youth cannot have the crises of the middle-aged.

Our philosophical point, within this rich hermeneutic and pragmatic field, is to stress the interrelation between (1) personal *experience*, (2) reflection on *examples* (*thought-experiments*), and (3) the explication, as well as the corroboration (rejection and correction, or acception and appropriation) of *concepts*.

16. In order to find out whether some concepts are adequate, we may use a *via negativa*: by breaching some of the constitutive conditions we get a result which is seen by competent observers to be absurd. From the recognition of such meaninglessness we may then reflectively try to formulate the condition that was breached and indicate its constitutive nature in the light of the character and extension of the created meaninglessness.

There are various ways in which a setting "breaks down", and there are various forms of "absurdity", from circumstantial unreasonableness to the "unthinkable" – indicating a continuous transition from the empirical to the transcendental. (Cf. "Arguments from Absurdity" in this collection.) Such "arguments from absurdity" may thus be seen as important instances of philosophical "falsification" (categorial corroboration).

17. Cf. M. Heidegger: *Sein und Zeit* (*Being and Time*): *Vorgriff*.

Arguments from Absurdity

Toward an Epistemic Gradualism

I intend to draw attention to a type of rational discourse which differs logically both from that of the logical and of the empirical sciences. By "differing logically" I mean differing in the nature of the validation and invalidation involved. I do not intend to explore this type of discourse in all its details, nor do I intend to investigate all the subtleties of the overlap between the three types of discourse mentioned; I merely want to focus on some standard cases of such arguments and especially to pay attention to gradual transitions between paradigm cases of empirical falsehood and absurdity.

My criterion for characterizing this third type of discourse is the use of arguments from absurdity as a means of invalidation. By an "argument from absurdity" I mean an argument which consists in showing that a breach of some rule or principle results in an "absurdity", and through this absurdity we become aware of the violated rule or principle as a necessary precondition, in the actual context at least, of meaningfulness. Hence we might possibly talk in some cases in terms of 'contingent necessity'.

A standard example of one kind of such an argument would be the following: if we say "seven is green" we commit an "absurdity", and this makes us aware of the principle that color-predicates cannot be ascribed to numbers; we have become aware of this principle as a necessary precondition of meaningfulness for the use of such predicates, viz. in normal usage (disregarding for instance poetic usage).

In talking about arguments from absurdity, I will use terms like "meaningfulness" and "absurdity" in contrast to "truth" and "falsity", and "conceptual" or "philosophical" in contrast to "empirical" and "analytic". These terms are fairly ambiguous, and it is precisely my intention to call attention to the epistemic gradualism hidden in this verbal ambiguity.

This "third road" of reasoning, differing from empirical and from formal logical validation, is traditionally associated with transcendental reasoning. I will therefore allow myself occasionally to use the term "transcendental", but it is not my intention to enter into the debate about transcendental reasoning in the Kantian tradition.[1] Nor do I intend to enter into the classical discussions of transcendental reasoning in analytic philosophy,[2] related as they are to a semanticist perspective. In this chapter my concern is that of a weak version of transcendental reasoning, operating with "weak absurdities" and "strong falsehoods", a gradualist and contextualist notion of transcendental reasoning suited for praxeological pragmatics. In the next chapter I will discuss the notion of transcendental reasoning in a strictly pragmatic perspective.[3]

Transcendental Reasoning

With the reservations just noted I understand *transcendental philosophy* here as a philosophy that tries to confirm transcendental conditions by means of transcendental reasoning. By *transcendental reasoning* I mean reasoning which starts from something given and tries, by means of philosophical arguments, to indicate conditions for the possibility of the given. The result of such transcendental reasoning, the philosophical condition, is called the *transcendental condition* for the given. (In this perspective, the contingency of a condition is entailed by the contingency of that which is given.)

I here have tried to divide the problems of transcendental reasoning into different domains: (i) the given, (ii) the argumentation, and (iii) the confirmed precondition. We will concentrate on different cases of such reasoning. But first I will simply present some examples of transcendental reasoning in this sense.

Examples of transcendental reasoning

The following piece of transcendental reasoning is presented only in a rough and preliminary form – we shall not try here to enter into the full complexity of this argument:

(1) It is actually the case that we can make true statements about things and thereby inform each other about these things.

(2) There are certainly many different empirical conditions for verbal information. But we have in addition this precondition: information about actual things is possible only because we are able to articulate more than one specific statement about a given thing, e.g. about this book. If I could *only* articulate *one specific* statement about the book, e.g., "the book is black", then you, not having the book in sight, could acquire no information about the book through hearing me utter this sentence, for in asking me the question "what is the color of the book in front of you", you could only get *this* one statement from me, "the book is black", whether the book is black or not. To further questions, you could not get any other answer either, since I am *bound*, by hypothesis, to utter *this* one specific sentence. You would therefore be unable to say whether the book is black or not, you would not have obtained any information about the book. We have here presumed that you are free to ask several questions and that silence on my part has no informative significance.

This shows the "triviality" that our freedom to give more than one specific statement about a given thing is a necessary condition for information. And since it is as a matter of fact true that we can make various true statements about things and thus inform each other, this logical condition must subsist. But furthermore, the denial of this necessary condition implies a kind of self-refutation, since this denial entails that verbal information is impossible at the same time as the denial itself pretends to inform. Here we get another kind of impossibility.

(3) As one logical condition for verbal information we therefore have: "it must be possible for human beings to utter more than one

specific statement about a given thing," or, "man must be free to utter more than one specific statement about a given thing".

What is important here is not the content of this sentence, but its status: it is a kind of logical necessity, a "non-empirical" condition for the possibility of information – and therefore, according to the chosen terminology, a transcendental condition.

This should present one type of transcendental reasoning, and thereby serve as an example of such reasoning. In continuing this chain of thought we may say that the thing "must" in a sense "give itself" *in different ways*. The point is, for one thing, that we cannot talk truly about a thing, *qua* thing, if the thing cannot "show itself" from more than one aspect.

In order to give another example of transcendental reasoning applied to nature, in so far as it is involved in human activity, we shall develop this point.

(i) It is the case that you (who read this) can read English.

(ii) One condition for your being able to read this is that the printer's ink can convey assertions. And when the printer's ink can do this, it has to do for one thing with the fact that the ink on the paper is formed in *different* patterns, namely, in different letters. If it were possible *only* to form *one* pattern, e.g. "a", I should not have been able to communicate assertions to you by means of ink on the paper, given that the constellations of the different a's to each other were without importance. The "text" would then for instance have looked like this: " a a a a ...". The articulation of assertions presupposes variety in the use of symbols. We can generalize and say that when the symbols are material in one sense or another, like printer's ink, acoustic waves or rays of light, etc., this means that symbol material *must* be formed in different ways. The case that the printer's ink can convey assertions has to do with the circumstance that the same forms can be *repeated*. If this were not the case the text would, for instance, have looked like this: "a b c d e .. x y z", where no sign occurred twice. The case that these different, reproducible forms can convey assertions has to do, in addition, with the fact that the putting together of these forms follows certain *rules* which you know and I know, and which you assume that I know and I assume that you know.

(iii) Thus we have, as conditions for your reading this, the following factors. It must be possible to form symbolic material in more than one way. It must be possible to reproduce the resulting different forms. It must be possible to combine these different, reproducible forms in sequences according to accepted rules. *How* this takes place is an empirical question. *That* this must be possible is a philosophical statement.

The point of these examples has been to exemplify transcendental reasoning.

We might moderate this point by looking at some simple examples of transcendental reasoning: (i) It is a fact that this pen in my hand is in front of me. (ii) If I had lost this pen, and if someone told me he had found it, but that it was not found in space, I could conclude that he had not found it at all, for it is inconceivable for me what a pen might be that is not in space. (iii) In generalizing this point, we may say that things *must* be in space – it is a precondition for being a thing that it is in space. We could say, space is a transcendental condition for things to be things.

The structure in such transcendental reasoning

We may sketch the structure of these examples of transcendental reasoning in this way.

A

(1) *Given*: "man communicates".
(2) *Argument*: communication would be impossible if only one specific statement could be uttered in each situation.
(3) *Necessity 1*: man can utter more than one specific statement in each situation.
(4) *Necessity 2*: denial of (3) implies a self-refutation (an absurdity).

B

    (1) *Given*: "you can read this".

    (2) *Argument*: this would be impossible if symbolic material could not be formed, formed in different ways, formed according to rules.

    (3) *Necessity*: symbolic material can be formed in more than one way.

C

    (1) *Given*: this pencil.

    (2) *Argument*: inconceivable that this pencil were not in space.

    (3) *Necessity*: space is necessary in order for there to be things (e.g., this pencil).

It is hard to say what kind of necessity we have in each case. We might be tempted to interpret these necessities as *analytic*: the reasoning is circular, we only point out some property which is already given in the initial description. "Man can utter more than one specific statement in each situation" (A,3) is given in the statement "man communicates" (A,1), and similarly for cases (B) and (C). However, the sense in which (A), (B) and (C) may be called "analytic" is certainly not clear. Does the statement "man communicates" analytically imply "we must be able to utter more than one specific statement in a given situation"? It surely might, but it is far from probable that we somehow "mean" all this when we make the statement "man communicates", in the sense in which we might say that we ordinarily "mean" that a "bachelor" is an "unmarried man". And (B) and (C) are even more doubtful in this respect. In what sense might an expression like "you can read this" analytically imply for instance that "symbolic material must be able to be formed in accordance with rules"? Does the term "pencil" analytically imply (in the same sense?) that "space is a necessity for things to be things"?

In (A) we might perhaps rather talk of a *factual* necessity: it is an empirical truth about human communication that more than one specific statement in a given situation is needed. But it is somehow odd to call this necessity "empirical" or "factual". Does it make sense to carry out experiments to see whether it is right? Nor does this make much sense in case (B), and definitely not in case (C), where the impossibility seems to be an "inconceivability". In (A) we included furthermore a step (4), the self-refutation involved in denying (A,3). This self-refutation represents an absurdity, i.e. a philosophical impossibility, and not some empirical impossibility. It is thus inappropriate to call the resulting necessity "factual".

If we say that this necessity represents a *modal truth*, that since human communication *is a fact*, it *must* therefore be *possible* for there to be human communication, then although formally correct, this does not help us, for our question is how certain *conditions for* human communication are necessary, and not whether human communication "must" be "possible" when human communication "is a fact".

We might then say that these cases represent "*conceptual analyses*" in some sense, and that is vague enough to be correct. We may make this statement somewhat more precise by saying that the necessities in these cases are necessities similar to those we have when we work out so-called category mistakes: it is inconceivable that a pencil should not be in space, as it is inconceivable that a thought is colored. But this works less well for (A) and (B), in which cases we may make the impossibility more specifically philosophical by pointing out some indirect selfrefutation involved in the denial of (3).

I shall now present an attempt at an interpretation of the first step in case (A), that is, the step from (A,1) to (A,3).

s = "man communicates".

s'= "man can utter more than one specific statement in each situation".

The statement s is true if the statement s' is true. That is, the truth of s' *makes* the truth of s *possible*, or, the truth of s' is a "condition for the possibility" of the truth of s.

We have to distinguish between *s' makes s possible*, and *s' does not make s impossible*, for there are many *other* statements than s' which do not make s impossible, e.g., "I wear a brown hat". Only some specific statements are like s': *s' makes s possible*, in the sense that if s' were false, then s *would be* false too, that is, s would then be impossible. It is *given* that s *is* true, and thereby that it is possible, so that *each statement* which *makes s possible* and *whose negation would make s false*, *must* be true.

The necessity of (A,3) – statement s' – is consequently a *relative* necessity: it is necessary *given* that (A,l) – statement s – is true.

Some of the difficulties involved

It is clear that transcendental reasoning, as defined above, involves extremely complicated problems, for instance:

1. How do we know that the description of a given phenomenon is adequate? Are other descriptions of the phenomenon possible as well?

2. What logical force does the reasoning itself have? To what do we appeal if other people do not follow our reasoning?

3. How universal are the preconditions confirmed in this way? How valid are they?

It could be said that we start with some *phenomenon*, e.g., a material thing, and the given is in that sense an empirical fact. On the other hand, it could be said that we start reasoning from a *description* of this given phenomenon. Thus, according to different senses of "start", we may call both the phenomenon and the description of the phenomenon the "given". The first problem is whether our description is adequate to the given phenomenon, and further, when we start with a description of a phenomenon, the result of the reasoning (the confirmed precondition) will be dogmatic if we do not take into account that the reasoning is relative to the point of departure, i.e. to the description.

The description is often empirical, but it might also be the case that it expresses philosophical insight. The reasoning itself, on the other hand, cannot be empirical, for in that case the condition would not be a philosophical condition, but an empirical one. As an example take the description "cognitive communication between men is a fact". Experience teaches us that man cannot live without food and adequate temperature, without which men cannot communicate either. Food and adequate temperature are in this sense "necessary (empirical) conditions" for the described state of affairs. On the other hand, it could be said that the correct use of the categories of quantity and quality is a "non-empirical" condition for linguistic meaningfulness, and in that sense a "transcendental" condition for cognitive communication.

What does it mean then to say that this "non-empirical" reasoning confirms a transcendental condition? Three examples have been given above in order to *show* what this means, and in the following sections I will try to illuminate this by further examples. Different forms of arguments from absurdity will then be dealt with in order to exhibit the transcendental status of the various conditions.

Transcendental conditions as "necessary conditions"

Let us assume that the expression "condition for the possibility of ..." may (sometimes) be interpreted to mean "necessary condition (for a necessary condition) for ...". We then have that "space" (as a form of representation in Kant) is a "necessary condition for spatial things (qua *Erscheinungen*)". Accordingly, an elimination of the form of space is thus a "sufficient condition" for there not being things. In this sense these transcendental conditions seem to fit one kind of modal logic, that of necessary and sufficient conditions.[4] However, this scheme alone does not tell us much about the nature of the necessity, possibility and impossibility in these cases. For, the same formula may be used in different cases where the necessities (impossibilities/absurdities) are not of the same kind. If we use "nc" as "is a necessary condition for", and "sc" as "is a sufficient condition for", we have for example "food nc communication", and "man's openness nc communication", and further, "no food sc no communication", "no human openness sc no communication". But although the *formulae* are the *same*, the kind of *necessity* involved is not the same at all. An analysis of the different "necessities" in the different cases is therefore required.

The expressions "precondition", "transcendental condition" or "condition for the possibility of" are used, as opposed to simply "condition", to indicate that the nature of the necessities with which we are dealing is not that of facts or of pure analyticity. The long expression "condition for the possibility of" (*Bedingung der Möglichkeit*) has often been used. In *some* cases, at least, I take it to mean "necessary condition for a necessary condition for something given", for instance, talking in Heideggerian terms: "man (*Dasein*) as openness is a necessary condition for man's immediate presence with things, man's immediate presence with things is a necessary condition for truth, i.e. for statements' corresponding with things".[5] This is both simple and complex. In a way, it illustrates how Heidegger can be said to re-refer the theory of truth to epistemology, and thereby yields a kind of "transcendental" theory of truth. However, it may also be said that "man (*Dasein*) as openness is a necessary condition for man as uncoverer, and man as uncoverer is a necessary condition for man's immediate presence with things, and man's immediate presence with things is a necessary condition for statements' corresponding with things". Three conditions emerge here. Further, it might be said that "man as openness is a necessary and sufficient condition for man as uncoverer", and therefore "man as uncoverer is a necessary and sufficient condition for man as openness". This expresses the "internal" relation between man's openness and man as an uncoverer, the two are somehow interwoven and they somehow mutually condition each other. It is a sort of Hegelian analyticity: by concentrating on one phenomenon (man as an uncoverer of things), we are somehow "forced" to see that it "implies" the other phenomenon (man's openness).

It is now clear that I use the expressions "transcendental reasoning" and "transcendental philosophy" in a very broad sense.

For instance, I do not suppose that the transcendental conditions are to be located in subjectivity in the strict Kantian sense of the word.[6] It might be objected that the word "transcendental" ought to be reserved for a specifically Kantian philosophy and that the word is here used in such a way as to include an inconveniently large part of philosophy, namely all philosophy that tries to indicate preconditions for the given by means of rational philosophical arguments. However, I still think it is useful to have a common term for all philosophy that uses such arguments and therefore I have chosen this terminology.

The Argument from Absurdity

I have said that arguments from absurdity are often incorporated in transcendental reasoning, and that a better understanding of the nature of these arguments can give a better understanding of the status of transcendental reasoning.

The term "argument from absurdity"

What I here call an "argument from absurdity" has also been called a "reductio ad absurdum" argument, as for instance in Ryle's *Philosophical Arguments*.[7] However, the expression *reductio ad absurdum* is used in logic, designating an argument of the following form:

A > B(-B). > -A

that is, when a statement implies a contradiction the statement itself is false (absurd$_1$). In order to avoid misunderstanding, I will not use the term "reductio ad absurdum" about the kind of unformalized and purely philosophical arguments which I am going to analyze, but instead use the term "argument from absurdity".

This argument from absurdity is distinguished from the *reductio*

ad absurdum arguments of formalized reasoning in so far as the
resultant absurdity is not a contradiction, but meaninglessness in
one sense or another. The argument from absurdity is used in
philosophical reasoning to show that a statement, or its implication,
is nonsensical, i.e. neither empirically false nor logically
contradictory but meaningless (absurd$_2$).[8] The strength of an
argument from absurdity thus depends on the nature of the
absurdity, and as there are different kinds of absurdity, there are
different kinds of preconditions.

Furthermore, the purpose of an argument from absurdity is not
simply to disqualify a statement, but to point out some necessary
precondition by showing the absurdity involved in the breakdown
of the precondition. In other words, the purpose is positive (or
constructive), it is not simply to end up with some absurdity. The
purpose is to recognize or confirm, *through* the absurdity, a
precondition for meaningfulness.

An argument from absurdity can be said to be philosophical, and
not empirical, since only meaningful sentences can be empirically
(or analytically) true or false. The question of the meaningfulness
and meaninglessness of sentences is logically prior to that of
empirical truth and falsity. Pointing out and analyzing
meaningfulness and meaninglessness is in this sense a genuinely
philosophical task. In so far as arguments from absurdity are
genuinely philosophical, the confirmed preconditions must also be
philosophical to the same extent.

Meaningless statements: an example

I will briefly give an example of one way in which statements can
be meaningless in order to illustrate the indicated difference
between falsity and absurdity.

"My dog is the first day of May".

It would be odd to say that this sentence is empirically false,
since no imaginable changes in empirical facts could make it true.
We may illustrate the point by comparing this sentence with the

sentence "my dog has a Ph.D. in metaphysics". However empirically false this latter sentence may be, it is nevertheless in a sense *possible* to imagine a dog with a Ph.D. in metaphysics, in the sense that it is possible to tell a fairy tale about it. But it is not at all possible to imagine a dog which is the first day of May, not even in a fairy tale or in a thriller *à la* "Dr. Jekyll and Mr. Hyde". In other words, for one thing, we could characterize the sentence "my dog has a Ph.D. in metaphysics" as a very serious factual mistake, but this sentence *can* at least be regarded as empirical, in the sense that in this case we know what an empirical falsification would be. On the other hand, in the case of "my dog is the first day of May" it is not clear what could constitute a falsification. Of course, we may investigate the dog first and then the first day of May, just as for the sentence "my dog is a bulldog" we would first have investigated what characterizes a bulldog and would then have investigated what characterizes my dog. But there is an important difference between these attempts at falsification, for whereas in the latter case we *can* compare the two sets of data, in the first case the result is simply that we end up with two sets of data which cannot be compared with each other. The empirical investigation in the latter case will therefore not result in an empirical conclusion, but in the recognition that the two sets of data are incommensurable.

It is also strange to call the sentence "my dog is the first day of May" negatively analytic.[9] A negatively analytic sentence ("my dog is not my dog") gives by negation a positively analytic sentence ("my dog is my dog"). But it is meaningless *both* to ascribe to "dog" the predicate "the first day of May" and its negation "not the first day of May". If the negation "my dog is not the 1st day of May" were to have any meaning, it would be in the sense of "my dog cannot be attributed predicates like 'the first day of May'".[10]

Given these conceptions of empirical and analytic it is artificial both to characterize the sentence "my dog is the first day of May" as empirically false and as negatively analytic. The point is that the logical subject and predicate are not commensurable, i.e. not of the same order or type. Such mistakes are therefore usually called category mistakes. In other words, we have seen an example of one way in which statements may be meaningless, i.e. non-empirically wrong, without being analytic. The point so far has simply been to recall the fact that there are non-analytic statements whose meaninglessness can be settled *a priori* by philosophical inquiry.

Meaningless sentences are involved in arguments from absurdity. It is this type of meaninglessness which guarantees the *philosophical* ("non-empirical") status of the argument, which will now be illustrated.

Examples of arguments from absurdity

Examples of arguments from absurdity have already been mentioned, but they shall now be dealt with more systematically. I have chosen two main groups of arguments from absurdity, namely those involving category mistakes and those involving self-refutation in some sense.

We have previously referred to these two category mistakes:
"Seven is green",
"My dog is the first day of May".

In these cases the argument from absurdity consists partly in generating such meaningless statements (the first step) and partly in our becoming aware of the principle which is violated (the second step). In the first step, the difficulty lies in deciding the nature of the absurdity and in finding its relation to empirical falsity and negative analyticity. In the second step, the difficulty lies in turning the insight about an absurdity into an insight about a necessary condition: the sentence "seven is green" in normal situations is absurd in some sense of the word; something is wrong. But what principle or rule has been violated? What is the precondition? Certainly, "seven" and "green" cannot normally be combined, and we even feel that we are right in generalizing the point "color predicates cannot be ascribed to numbers". Should we even generalize further, "quality cannot be ascribed to quantity"?

These rules may be called the violated principles or preconditions. However, the awareness of the absurdity (category mistake) is not *eo ipso* an awareness of the precondition, therefore we have to *generalize* in a sense, in order to obtain the categories. It can also be noticed that "quality" and "quantity" are *traditional* categories, whereas "color predicate" and "number" ("seven" and "green") are less traditional *qua* categories. At the same time, "quality" and "quantity" demand a *broader* generalization than "color predicate" and "number" ("seven" and "green"). In other words, in this case it can be seen that the more traditional the categories, the more we have to generalize.

As we know, in criticizing Russell, Strawson maintained that definite referring statements (such as "the King of France is bald") do not assert the existence (and uniqueness) of the mentioned singular so-and-so, but they *presuppose* its existence.[11] If the mentioned so-and-so (the King of France) does not exist, the statement is not false, but *meaningless* (absurd). The mentioned so-and-so (such as the King of France) is a presupposition for the meaningfulness of the statement, in the sense that the statement cannot be either true or false without there *being* one such so-and-so.

It is of interest that Strawson, who initiated this discussion of referential presupposition, builds up an admittedly transcendental philosophy on the *related* point about the necessity of common, mind-independent objects for language.[12] Roughly stated, a common language and communication are given. If there were no common objects to which we could refer, we would not be able to judge the truth or falsity of other people's statements, because we would not know what they were talking about: that is, communication would break down. Therefore, common objects of reference must exist and be accessible to us.

The *statement* "the King of France is bald" was said to be odd unless there is one (and only one) person who is the King of France. But *A's making this statement* is odd if A does not *believe* that there is one such person, given a normal situation. This is very roughly what some philosophers have called a contextual implication.[13] When it is assumed in a normal situation that a person believes what he says, this right to assume that A believes *p* when he says *p* is not given by a logical entailment, nor by an inductive inference, but by a rule of communication.[14]

The oddity (absurdity) generated by breaking this rule of communication may be called a contextual inconsistency. There is a conflict between an act of stating and a rule for communication. The argument from absurdity here indicates that the broken rule is constitutive for normal stating situations, and the rule is in that sense a transcendental condition for stating.

Now there are different forms of absurdity related to these contextual inconsistencies. We thus have other cases, too, where the context makes the whole utterance absurd. For instance, this happens sometimes when an "I" talks about "myself" in the present tense in the indicative:[15]

> (1) "I cannot speak".
> (2) "I don't exist".

The absurdity here is an inconsistency between *what* is said and the fact that *this person* says it, given it really is "I" who speaks.[16]

One of the earlier examples of arguments from absurdity might be regarded as a contextual inconsistency:

> (3) "It must be possible to form symbolic material in more than one way".

In this case the necessity of the statement is brought out by showing the inconsistency between a denial of the statement and the fact that this denied statement is expressed, whether written in ink or uttered by sound. As in the sentence "I cannot speak", the absurdity is to be found in the relation between the denied statement and the fact that the statement is made. The difference between (3) and (1) is that in sentence (1) the clash has to do with the human power of speech, whereas in sentence (3) it has to do with the fact that speaking (or writing) occurs through the forming of material objects.[17]

However, contextual inconsistency of types (1) and (3) may also be related to other absurd statements. When NN says (4) "I am completely causally determined", then this statement might be interpreted as involving a clash between *what* is said in the statement and the *contextual rule* that people are supposed to believe that their statements are true *and also to have reasons for their belief.* But in this case the statement denies that the speaker has reasons, which means that there is an inconsistency between the content of this statement and one of its contextual presuppositions.[18]

The inconsistencies (absurdities) so far are not pure *self*-refutations, unless the "self" is interpreted as embracing unverbalized (contextual, pragmatic) factors. However, in cases like (5) "this statement is false" the absurdity is only dependent on *what is said*, and independent of *who* says it. Such cases will be called self-referring inconsistencies.

Concerning the arguments from absurdity which are connected with these various inconsistencies, we have seen the following. The arguments bring out absurdities of quite different types; what is common is a "non-empirical" conflict between the statement and its context, whether the context is the assumption that a speaker believes what he says, that the statement involves a claim of truth, or whether it is the assumption is that the statement is uttered by NN, or by NN in a certain setting. We may roughly distinguish between two groups of absurdities: the contextual inconsistencies, where the absurdity is a clash between what is said in the statement and some unverbalized presupposition for saying this, and the self-referring inconsistencies, where the absurdity results when the statement is taken to refer to itself. The transcendental conditions are all characterized by being necessary for the avoidance of some absurdity, of some breakdown of meaningfulness.[19]

The inconsistencies mentioned here, under the headings of pre-supposition and contextual implication, seem to allow for a reinterpretation in terms of category mistakes. For instance, the uttering of the statement "I cannot speak", where the absurdity *prima facie* is a kind of self-refutation, may also be regarded as a category mistake, effected by a misuse of the concepts of man. The statement "I don't exist", which is contextually inconsistent, may also be regarded as a misapplication of a personal pronoun, and thus as a category mistake. It may also be said that the statement "man cannot re-identify mind-independent things" represents a category mistake, since the concept of man entails a reference to things. At the same time this statement is indirectly a self-refutation, through a denial of a necessary referential presupposition for language as such.

I therefore tend to think that many cases of inconsistency may be reinterpreted and analyzed in terms of category mistakes, and I have chosen to concentrate the following comments on arguments from absurdity related to *category mistakes*. This procedure will, I hope, offer us a grasp of these inconsistencies, at least to start with. However, in doing so we interpret pragmatic inconsistencies in semantic terms, as it were, and this is a point to which we will return.[20]

The point of arguments from absurdity: a *via negativa*.

In the preceding exposition, one of the arguments from absurdity ended with the statement "It must be possible to form symbolic material in more than one way". But why all the argumentation in order to reach this conclusion? Couldn't this have been seen directly? I think it could, at least in this case, but arguments from absurdity nevertheless have an important function in making us able to see.

The use of arguments from absurdity could perhaps be regarded as a pedagogical trick, but this trick still has its function. The pedagogical point of using such arguments could be compared with the function of multiplying big numbers. There is on problem in multiplying small numbers: we see directly what 4 x 4 is, it is 16. We also see directly that "what is colored always has extension" is a valid statement, but this faculty of seeing directly decreases as the complexity of the question increases. Somewhat comparable is the situation for arguments from absurdity. They represent a philosophical "multiplication", as it were. When the question actually becomes too complicated we have to work it out, for instance by a metaphysical fiction, where certain structures are negated step by step until the result is obviously absurd. Then it becomes evident which structures are necessary, and why. The use of arguments from absurdity, where structures necessary for meaningfulness are made to break down, illustrates more clearly what these structures are and their status, because the results of their breakdown are seen. This is why it is worthwhile to stick to this *via negativa*, i.e. arguing from absurdity, instead of merely relying on "direct intuition".[21]

The *via negativa*, arguing from absurdity, has a double function; it may be a way of *finding* categories or a way of *confirming* the status of a category. In this work I am primarily interested in the latter function, i.e. arguments from absurdity are regarded as a way of "falsifying" philosophical statements, by appealing to absurdity and not to empirical falsity nor to contradictions, so that we may see more clearly the philosophical status (and legitimacy) of the various preconditions.

Category Mistakes

In order to illuminate in more detail the way in which different arguments from absurdity function so as to confirm transcendental conditions, I will now rephrase some of the points in the domains of *category mistakes* in terms of arguments from absurdity and transcendental philosophy.

Category mistakes

One example of a category mistake has already been considered, namely "my dog is the first day of May", and I have briefly indicated why this statement is neither empirically nor analytically false. Many philosophers tend to agree on the view that category mistakes are neither empirically nor analytically false, and that category mistakes represent a type of meaninglessness which it is a philosophical task to treat. For instance, an influential analytic philosopher, Gilbert Ryle, has maintained that "category-propositions (namely assertions that terms belong to certain categories or types) are always philosopher's propositions" and even that "philosopher's propositions" are always "category-propositions".[22]

The tendency within analytic philosophy to talk about category mistakes as "grammatical"[23] does not change the fact that the grammatical meaninglessness in "my dog is the first day of May" is philosophically more interesting than the grammatical error in "she love him". And the philosophical relevance of category mistakes is not eliminated because of the interest which modern grammarians such as Chomsky have taken in these absurdities.[24] The interesting problem is therefore not whether we should *call* category mistakes grammatical, but *in what sense* they are grammatical mistakes.

However, even if philosophers tend to agree that statements like "my dog is the first day of May" are *absurd* in a philosophically interesting sense, the question of how to determine the relation between such absurdities and factual mistakes seems to remain controversial. I will refer briefly to this problem since it illustrates the subtleties of trying to define the philosophical nature of preconditions by means of arguments from absurdity which are based on category mistakes.

To say that "Peer Gynt" is written by Ibsen and "Hamlet" by Shakespeare is to classify these two works in accordance with a given frame of classification, in this case "belonging to Ibsen's writings" and "belonging to Shakespeare's writings". If we say that

Ibsen has written "Hamlet", we are making a factual mistake. Classifications are empirical procedures, and the choice of classification frames is dependent upon our present interests. On the other hand, we do not classify by means of categories, but categories are presupposed in classification. We do not take from the shelf books classified in terms of "relation", but we may take those books which are classified in terms of "being written by Ibsen", which is an expression falling under the category "relation".

When category distinctions are supposed to be *philosophical*,[25] and classifications are *factual*, then the problem is how to distinguish between categories and classification frames. One procedure is to use *arguments from absurdity*. "Dog" and "the first day of May" belong to different categories since the sentence "my dog is the first day of May" is absurd. But this procedure only tells us about category differences, not about category similarities, and this raises a problem for proceeding by means of arguments from absurdity.

Ryle, for instance, advocated this procedure, recommending the use of different "proposition frames", e.g., "...was the first day of May", into the open places of which one then puts different "proposition factors", e.g., "my dog", "Thursday", etc.[26] If one of the resulting sentences is absurd and the other is not, we have brought out a category difference between the two "factors" (for instance, "my dog" and "Thursday"). But through this procedure we can only *decide* about category *differences*.

Thus, the use of arguments from absurdity ensures that the philosophical status of the category differences is guaranteed, but this procedure ends up in a strange pluralism of categories, on different levels, so to speak. "I" and "Thursday" are mostly (always?) categorially different; "I" and "he" are often not categorially different, but sometimes they are; that is, "I" and "Thursday" have different logical functions (i.e. are categorially different) in a large field, whereas "he" and "I" have different logical functions in quite a small field.

Just as Ryle could criticize Aristotle for giving too few categories, and for establishing them in an arbitrary way, Smart could criticize Ryle for getting "too many" categories, in the sense that in Ryle the concept of a category seems to disappear.[27] Thompson tried to avoid this pluralism of categories, based merely on "falsification" through arguments from absurdity, by giving a test procedure for categories.[28] Two expressions A and B are said to be categorially different only if we *cannot find* any expression, except "thing", "existent", etc., which is applicable *to both of them*, and we should then be assured of a more traditional result as to what is to be called a "category".

In talking about categories confirmed by arguments from absurdity, we had sentences like "my dog is the first day of May". In this type of sentence we do not get reasonable categories according to a more traditional view of what categories are like, and the categories in this specific case may perhaps be formulated thus: "subject terms which cannot take predicates of the days of the month" and "predicates which cannot be predicated of dogs", but these expressions are somehow too special to count as reasonable categories. However, the categories are in this case given almost *immediately*, together with the absurdity, so that we do not have to generalize much in order to get the categories.

But if we look at the sentence "75 kg are green" it will be seen that the categories involved are not "given immediately" with the absurdity. We may first somehow conclude that predicates of color cannot be ascribed to predicates of weight, and further we may generalize this conclusion, saying that predicates of quality cannot be ascribed to predicates of quantity, which indicates that we have indirectly reached the traditional categories of quality and quantity. In this case the absurdity does not immediately indicate the categories; but on the other hand, the categories are of a more traditional type than those found in the case of "my dog is the first day of May".

The same "distance" between absurdity and categories as in the case of "75 kg are green" is to be found in cases like "mind uses its body". Here too we have to generalize in order to get from the absurdity to the categories.

Categories and language games

The breakdown of meaningfulness in category mistakes such as "my dog is the first day of May" shows that there are limits to the possible interrelations of concepts. To apply an analogy: this reduction to absurdity has not shown us the particles but the possible orbits of the particles; it has shown us where the particles *can* move. In other words, the preconditions which we are shown, have the status of rules for the interrelation of concepts.

A more usual analogy for exemplifying the relation between statements and the conditions of meaningfulness which are violated in category mistakes is the metaphor of language games. Each language game, as a "speech activity", is defined by its rules, just like chess and other games. Some games have a large extension, others are more restricted, and there may be various rules overlapping from one game to another. Just as each move in a game is determined by the rules, so are statements determined by linguistic rules, be they semantic or pragmatic.[29]

In breaking a rule of the game, letting the king jump over the opponent's queen, say, you would not make a move at all, and in breaking a rule of language you would not be making a statement at all, only an absurd "statement" which can be neither right nor wrong.

This Wittgensteinian image of language games indicates the *transcendental* status of the rules in relation to the "moves", that is, to the making of true or false statements. Empirical inquiry is a way of bringing out true statements inside the game. Arguments from absurdity are ways of showing the rules themselves, by breaking them. The insight we get by creating breakdowns, like category mistakes, is an insight into the frame of the language game, i.e. the rules governing the game. The insight is in this sense transcendental, that is, it is an insight into the conditions for right or wrong moves, or for the making of statements.

Most of the time we probably use our terms and statements correctly. This is especially the case when the statements are not abstract but more or less concerned with concrete and practical problems, when the words are not new and unknown, and when we keep away from more peripheral uses. However, language also consists of abstract statements, and it develops due for instance to new conceptual breakthroughs in the sciences, and it adopts new and untried concepts (such as "unconsciousness", "point", "simultaneity"), which often inhabit the old vehicles (words) of the language.[30] In these cases we are often uncertain about the behavior of the concepts, that is, about what relations the concepts *can* enter into and about what relations they *cannot* enter into. In order to map out this "geography" of the interrelations of our concepts,[31] we apply arguments from absurdity systematically.

Arguing from absurdity permits us to check systematically the *limits* of the possible interrelations of concepts, by finding where the uses are impossible (absurd), and this insight into the limits of possible interrelations is indispensable if we are to see our concepts correctly. Thus, by arguments from absurdity we can become aware of category differences, which again may point to conceptual rules in terms of which we think. In other words, we may become aware of transcendental conditions for meaningfulness.

However, there are of course different kinds of rules, and not all of them have what I call a transcendental status. *Normative rules*, for instance, that is, rules which are regulative for behavior, have generally no transcendental status at all. There is nothing absurd in *breaking* the rule "no smoking", nor is it absurd to *change* this rule, neither is it absurd to *say that we can do without* that kind of rule. On the other hand, when we look at *constitutive rules*, that is, rules which are constitutive for the activity for which they are rules, we see that absurdity is only produced in some cases. Take the rule of chess: "*the knight moves two squares in one direction and one square in the other*". What happens when we *break* this rule, for instance by moving the knight three squares ahead and one aside? We do something wrong, but it is strange to call this "absurd". A situation where none of the players is aware of such an error and the play continues as before can easily be imagined, as can be the case where this erroneous move is made intentionally by one of the players – this is highly meaningful for an unscrupulous player who is possessed by the idea of winning the game. However, if this error is made *frequently*, the game will tend to break down. It will at any rate not be the game of chess as defined today. If on the other hand we *once* break the rule: "*each player has to have one king (as long as the game is going on)*", we can rightly say that something drastic has happened. The game has broken down.

The answer to the question whether we can *change* these rules of chess depends on how strictly we hold on to the present definition of the game; but again the rule: "each player has to have one king" turns out to be more fundamental than the rule: "the knight moves two squares in one direction and one square in the other".

As to the question whether we *can do without* any rules of chess, the answer is in one sense affirmative, since it is not necessary to have any game of chess at all. But *if* we want to play chess, there necessarily has to be a set of rules; if we want to play chess or some other board game, we must have some rules for the moves of the pieces and for the number of players. That we have to have some such rules is constitutive for this sort of game; to deny this is absurd.

Let us consider the rule: "*do not violate the principle of contradiction*". This rule is said to be necessary for what is sometimes called cognitive communication. If we *break* this rule, the result is a breakdown of cognitive communication. We cannot *change* this rule, and in contrast to the rules of chess, we *cannot eliminate the rule* either. That is, in so far as we stick to poetry, fairy tales or mysticism, we certainly can do without this rule, but these activities are somehow secondary activities:[32] without a field of so-called cognitive communication, where the rule is valid, we would not know what it means to declare the rule *in*valid. And further, as a matter of fact we have to communicate cognitively, in order to master nature and social organization (in order to satisfy our basic needs). In other words, *if* we want to have this kind of informative language, we have to obey the rule: "do not violate the principle of contradiction". This rule is constitutive for this type of cognitive or informative language; it is a necessary condition for this kind of language. But at the same time we *have no choice* as to whether we want to have this kind of language; this kind of cognitive communication is as a matter of fact unavoidable.

With this in mind we return to the category rules. The traditional categories of quality and quantity may be brought into a category rule of this form: "*quality must not be ascribed to quantity*". As a rule of contradiction, this rule seems to be constitutive for cognitive communication. We cannot *break* it without ("cognitive") absurdity, nor can we *change* it, and neither can we *eliminate* that kind of rule.

If we consider the (possible) category mistake "*mind uses its body*", the first problem is to find and formulate the categories. But whatever we should decide to call the categories in this case, the point is that mind is not a something, with an external relation to its own body. The category rule might in this case be something like this: "*Mind cannot be talked about as an entity that uses its body as an instrument*".

It is to be noticed first that this is *prima facie* a linguistic rule, but it is at least a legitimate question to ask whether it is not also something that has to do with the mode of being of mind (man). Then the ontological approach could be taken: given that man (mind) *is* like this, the adequate linguistic account of this fact will be found in a linguistic rule like the one presented above. If we *break* this rule, it may seem reasonable to say that we get an absurdity (a category mistake). However, this is less certain than in the case of the rule of contradiction, since there are people who, for good or bad reasons, think of mind as an entity. Similar considerations seem appropriate as to the questions of *changing* the rule and of *eliminating* that kind of rule.

The purpose of the preceding remarks about rules is to recall the fact that there are many types of rules, and that only some constitutive rules – such as the category rules – function as trans-cendental conditions. These rules apply to arguments from absur-dity which produce something absurd, i.e. category mistakes. The category mistake indicates (more or less directly) the categories, and the categories are used in the formulation of category rules, and these rules function as transcendental conditions.

Transcendental Insight

I have tried to indicate a distinction between transcendental insight and empirical knowledge. The negative criterion has been the difference between reduction to absurdity and empirical falsifi-cation. It turned out that this difference is not a difference between two sharply divided groups: not only are there different ways in which statements directly or indirectly are empirically falsifiable, but the group of transcendental conditions is also heterogeneous, because the extension and the logical strength of the resulting absurdities differ from case to case. There are even marginal cases where a more precise concept of absurdity is necessary in order to decide to which group the statement belongs (e.g., "my dog reads books").

My conclusion is one in favor of a *gradualist* notion of absurdity and hence of arguments from absurdity and of transcendental reasoning. In this perspective the term "contingent necessity" becomes interesting, viz. for more modest contextualist cases of arguments from absurdity.

The status of the main distinction is that of a difference between (i) empirical statements and (ii) conditions which are necessary for the possibility of meaningful empirical statements, in the sense that a breakdown of these conditions results in meaninglessness. This is the linguistic version of the distinction. However, as meaning is not restricted to language but implied in all human actions and attitudes, this distinction generally applies to the difference between (i) various social phenomena, e.g. to the difference between shaking hands, receiving orders, congratulating, buying, and (ii) to the conditions (social settings) which make these social phenomena possible, in the sense that a breakdown of these conditions results in meaninglessness: to shake hands is no longer to shake hands but just a physiological occurrence.[33] This opens up the possibility of praxeological analyses of preconditions inherent in various human activities.[34]

Transcendental insight is the insight that a specific transcendental condition is necessary for avoiding a certain form of meaninglessness. At this point I would add that it is crucial that the *semantic* perspective, of "category mistakes" (and "frames"), is itself transcended in favor of a *pragmatic* perspective, within which we think in terms of pragmatic competence and tacit knowledge inherent in action and in terms of self-reflection.[35]

NOTES

1. For the recent debate, cf. e.g. Rüdiger Bubner, "Kant, Transcendental Argument and the Problem of Deduction", *The Review of Metaphysics*, 28(1975), pp. 453–467; Reinhold Aschenberg, "Über transzendentale Argumente. Orientierung in einer Diskussion zu Kant und Strawson", in: *Philosophisches Jahrbuch*, 85(1978), pp. 331–358; Gerhard Schönrich, *Kategorien und transzendentale Argumentation. Kant und die Idee einer transzendentalen Semiotik*, Frankfurt a.M.: Suhrkamp, 1981; Marcel Niquet, *Transzendentale Argumente. Kant, Stawson und die sinnkritische Aporetik der Detranszendentalisierung*, Frankfurt a.M.: Suhrkamp, 1991.

2. Cf. e.g. Barry Stroud, "Transcendental Arguments", *The Journal of Philosophy*, 65(1968), pp. 241–256; and Donald Davidson, "On the Very Idea of a Conceptual Scheme", *Proceedings and Addresses of the American Philosophical Association*, 47(1974), pp. 5–20 (reprinted in *Truth and Interpretation*, Oxford: Clarendon Press, 1984, pp. 183–198). Also Richard Rorty, "Strawson's Objectivity Argument", *Review of Metaphysics*, 24(1970–71), pp. 207–244; and "Transcendental Arguments,

Self-Reference, and Pragmatism", in: *Transcendental Arguments and Science*, eds. P. Bieri, R.-P. Horstmann, and L. Krüger, Dordrecht: Reidel, 1979, pp. 77–103; Rüdiger Bubner, "Selbstbezüglichkeit als Struktur transzendentaler Argumente", *ibid.* pp. 304–332.

3. Cf. K.-O. Apel commenting on transcendental reasoning in the analytic debate from Strawson to Davidson, "The Hermeneutic Dimension of Social Science and its Normative Foundation", in: *Man and World*, 25(1992), p. 253.

4. Cf. K. E. Tranøy: *Vilkårslogikk*, Oslo, 1960.

5. Cf. Gunnar Skirbekk, *Truth and Preconditions*, Bergen, 1972.

6. Cf. Strawson's reasons for separating Kant's transcendental arguments from Kant's idealistic epistemology. *The Bounds of Sense*, Part One, London, 1966. Walter Schulz, on the contrary, regards transcendental philosophy as a philosophy about constitutive *subjectivity* and tends to neglect the question about the transcendental status of arguments. (In: *Wittgenstein*, Pfullingen, 1967, pp. 29–39.)

7. Oxford, 1945, p. 6. (*Ibid.*, p. 6, "A pattern of argument which is proper and even proprietary to philosophy is the *reductio ad absurdum*".) Also M. Black: *Language and Philosophy*, Ithaca, 1949.

8. Here I ignore the question whether a "statement" can be said to be meaningless. (Cf. R. Hancock, "Presuppositions", *Philosophical Quarterly*, 1960, and G. Ryle, *Philosophical Arguments*, Oxford, 1945.) See K.-O. Apel's argumentative use of terms like "sinnlos", within his "sinnkritisches Argument" in favor of a transcendental-pragmatic ultimate justification (*Letztbegründung*), e.g. in his article in: *Zwischenbetrachtungen*, eds. A. Honneth et al., Frankfurt, 1989, pp. 15–65.

9. I here use the terminology of A. Næss, in: *Communication and Argument* (Oslo, 1966, p. 74).

10. Cf. A. Pap: "Types and Meaninglessness", in: *Mind*, 1960, p. 54, where he makes a distinction between "limited" and "unlimited" negation. Cf. also G. H. von Wright: *On the Logic of Negation*, Helsinki, 1959.

11. P.F. Strawson: "On Referring", *Mind*, 1950. As to some exceptions, i.e. statements which function meaningfully without fulfilling Strawson's claim of referential presuppositions: (1) Fairy tales, mythology (cf. Hart). (2) Laws of nature, such as the law that all bodies free from impressed force persevere in their state of rest or in uniform motion in a straight line (Hart). (3) "The King of France no longer exists" (Stroll). (4) "The lodger next door bought five of these brushes" – which is not "odd" for the salesman to say, even if there is no "lodger next door" – as long as there are brushes to be sold (Harré).
    Some of the main articles in this discussion are the following: Hart, H. L. A.: "A Logician's Fairy Tale", *Phil. Review*, 1951. Strawson, P. F.: *Introduction to Logical Theory*, New York, 1952. Sellars, W.: "Presupposing", *Phil. Review*, 1954. Strawson, P. F.: "A Reply to Mr. Sellars", *Phil. Review*, 1954. Strawson, P. F.: "Presupposing", *Phil. Review*, 1954. Harré, R.: "A Note on Existence Presuppositions", *Phil. Review*, 1956. Peterson, S.: "All John's Children", *Phil. Quarterly*, 1960. Hancock, R.: "Presuppositions", *Phil. Quarterly*, 1960. Hungerland, I.: "Contextual Implication", *Inquiry*, 1960. Llewelyn, J. E.: "Presupposition, Assumption and Presumptions", *Theoria*, 1962. Strawson, P. F.: "Identifying Reference and Truth-Value", *Theoria*, 1964. Stroll, A.: "Presupposing", *Encyclopedia of Philosophy*, New York, 1967.

12. P. F. Strawson: *Individuals*, New York, 1959, and *The Bounds of Sense*, London 1966. See also S. Hampshire: *Thought and Action*, ch. 1, London, 1959. Cf. notes 1 and 2 above.

13. Cf. I. Hungerland: "Contextual Implication", *Inquiry*, 1960, and P.H. Nowell-Smith: "Contextual Implication and Ethical Theory", *Proc. Aristot. Society*, 1962, and A. Stroll: "Presupposing", in: *Encyclopedia of Philosophy*, New York, 1967.
    There are other situations than stating situations where we have a kind of contextual implication. If A shouts wildly "I am not excited", we shall nevertheless feel that we have some right to assume that he is – again, given normal shouting situations, i.e. that A is not playing in a theater, etc. Cf. Y. Bar-Hillel "Analysis of 'Correct' Language", *Mind*, 1946.
    Cf. I. Hungerland (*Inquiry*, 1960) who tries to point out the factors which constitute a "normal stating situation".

14. I. Hungerland (cf. note 13) argues cogently that the inference from "A says 'p'" to "A believes p" (given a normal stating situation) is not an inductive inference, nor a logical entailment, but a communicative assumption. Cf. also A. M. MacIver, "Some Questions about 'Know' and 'Think'", *Analysis*, 1937/38, pp. 43–50. On the different senses of "assuming", see R. Hall, "Assuming", *Phil. Review*, 1958, and "Presuming", *Phil. Quarterly*, 1961. (The word "believe" is certainly in need of clarification in this case.) As to modifications and reservations in connection with the view that "A says 'p'" *always* gives us the right to assume "A believes p", cf. the critical notes in: H. A. Alexander, "Comments on Saying and Believing", in: *Epistemology*, ed. Stroll, New York, 1967.

C. K. Grant discusses (in: "Pragmatic Implication", *Philosophy*, 1958, pp. 303–324) the nature of implication in existence presuppositions and in contextual implications, arguing for the view that these implications are neither purely empirical, nor strictly logical, but are (for one thing) connected with the notions of rational action and of asserting.

15. Cf. the term "pragmatic paradox", in an article of the same name by D. J. O'Connor (*Mind*, 1948) and "pragmatic self-refutation" in: J. Passmore, *Philosophical Reasoning*, London, 1961. To be sure, the two following examples, (1) and (2), are only absurd when taken literally, in normal situations.

16. These cases may be interpreted as involving category mistakes between personal pronouns, e.g. "he" and "I".

17. We introduced this example of an argument from absurdity, in case (3), in order to show how varied the status of transcendental conditions may be, saying that this example had to do with *nature* (things). We now see the point more clearly, and at the same time we have to add a reservation: nature in itself is not transcendental, but nature functions as a transcendental condition in so far as it is *involved in human actions*. This is so because transcendental conditions have the character of being "necessary *for...*", namely "for" avoiding breakdown in *meaning*, and meaning is always social meaning. But the introduction of nature, or symbolic material, on the level of transcendental conditions is not something accidental, for what are human actions without nature (things)?

In an argument from absurdity mentioned earlier we had: (6) "It must be possible for human beings to utter more than one specific statement about a given thing." The necessity of this statement is shown by pointing out the inconsistency in denying the statement and still claiming that it should be understood. That this is an absurdity, an inconsistency, is not immediately clear. The absurdity may be pointed out in this way: *to deny* this statement is to say that human beings can *only* utter *one* statement about a given thing. This is an ambiguous statement, but this statement is here intended to mean that we are *bound* to utter only one specific statement, in the sense that we always, automatically, answer "X is Y", e.g., "this book is black", when asked a question about X (this book), independently of whether X (the book) has the quality Y (being black) or not. If this were the case, communication would break down, since the statements of other people could in principle never be trusted. In this case it would be *impossible* to *learn* a language, which means that we would be unable to state this very denial. Therefore, the denial of statement (6) indirectly entails that this denial itself is impossible.

The inconsistency in denying statement (6) is thus rooted in a clash between the claim that the denied statement (6) is true (meaningful, possible) and the circumstance that the content of the denied statement (6) indirectly implies that this claim of truth is impossible. This absurdity (in a denied statement (6)) is in that sense a self-stultifying inconsistency: if the denied (6) were true, it would have been impossible to utter the denied (6).

18. Concerning this rule of communication, cf. P. H. Nowell-Smith: "Contextual Implication and Ethical Theory", *Proc. Aristot. Society*, 1962, pp. 5–6.

There are many ways of explaining human behavior. The answer to the question *"why* did he do this?" is in some circumstances rightly given in terms of reasons, and in other circumstances in terms of physiological or psychological causes. (Cf. L. W. Beck: "Conscious and Unconscious Motives", in: *Mind*, 1966, and J. Hellesnes: *Sjølvkunnskapen og det framande medvitet*, Oslo, 1968.) We may therefore say that "determinism" (explanation of man in terms of physiological or psychological causes) is *one* possible language game. However, this possible language game has the disadvantage of being unworkable for some important statements in the first person singular present tense indicative. This is why determinism as a philosophical theory can be said to be absurd.

There is another point, turning on the distinction between cause and reason, which indicates the impossibility of prediction in certain cases: there are, as a matter of fact, *reasonings* the result of which we simply cannot predict. How could we have causally predicted Einstein's theory of relativity *before* he had formulated it? Only by reasoning *faster* than he did.

19. These examples of absurdities show that transcendental conditions are found not only on one level, somewhere in abstract thought, but that transcendental conditions are located "all over" and on various levels, sometimes within language, sometimes in connection with the act of stating and sometimes in social practice.

20. Catchwords for genuinely pragmatic inconsistencies, that deserve special attention, are self-reflective insight and tacit knowledge – as in the late Wittgenstein (praxeological insights) and in Apel (transcendental pragmatics). Cf. "Contextual and Universal Pragmatics" in this collection.

21. In addition we could argue that people seem to agree more easily on what is absurd than on what is necessarily true.

22. Cf. G. Ryle, "Categories", in *Logic and Language. Second Series*, ed. A. G. N. Flew, Oxford: Blackwell, 1953 (1973 ed., p. 65), and also in *Proc. Aristot. Society*, 1937/38 (first and second p.).

23. For instance by Wittgenstein himself, *Philosophische Untersuchungen*, e.g. §§ 90, 110, 111 and 251.

24. E.g. N. Chomsky: *Aspects of the Theory of Syntax*, Cambridge, Mass., 1965.

25. The analysis of the status of a statement is a *philosophical* task, also when the statement itself is empirical. But in the case of category statements, I think the statements themselves may be called philosophical, since the "verification" or "falsification" is carried out by means of *philosophical reasoning* (which is not to say that only *professional* philosophers do carry out these reasonings).

26. Cf. G. Ryle in: "Categories", *Proc. Aristot. Society*, 1937/38, and *Philosophical Arguments*, Oxford, 1945.

.

27. See J. J. C. Smart: "A Note on Categories", *British Journal of Philosophy of Science*, 1953. Cf. also B. Harrison: "Category Mistakes and Rules of Language", in: *Mind*, 1965, and R. C. Cross: "Category Differences", *Proc. Aristot. Society*, 1958/59.

28. M. Thompson "On Category Differences", *Philosophical Review*, 1957. Cf. also J. Passmore: *Philosophical Reasoning*, London, 1961, where he tries to elaborate the Rylean procedure by including the use of certain inferences. (*Ibid.* p. 140).

29. These different linguistic rules are usually not thought of as being as explicit and clear-cut as the explicit rules of chess. Cf. S. Cavell: "The Availability of Wittgenstein's Later Philosophy", *Phil. Review*, 1962, pp. 67–93. (See also P. Winch: *The Idea of a Social Science*, London, 1958, p. 93.)

30. The "relation" between words and concepts is of course a tricky one. I do not want to say, in using the image of a vehicle, that we have two different *entities*, words and concepts, which are somehow related to each other in a one-to-one relation, independent of use and context. (Cf. problems in connection with the vehicle-content model, A. Stroll: "Statements", in: *Epistemology*, ed. Stroll, New York, 1967, pp. 192–201.)

31. G. Ryle: *Philosophical Arguments*, Oxford, 1945, p. 10.

32. I say this without a negative undertone. I do think that the types of discourse mentioned – poetry, fairy tales and religious discourse – may communicate valuable kinds of *insight*. But the question to be answered is: precisely what kind?

33. What happens when the situation of greeting breaks down is probably more a psychological uncertainty: what does it then mean that NN keeps my hand in his? We suppose it means something else. (Is NN trying to find out whether I am nervous?)

34. Cf. "Praxeological Reflections" in this collection.

35. Cf. e.g. "Contextual and Universal Pragmatics" in this collection.

Pragmatism and Pragmatics

Validity Claims and Arguments, in a Melioristic Perspective[1]

Introductory Remarks

When we talk about pragmatism in Apel and Habermas, we do not have in mind the cruder sense of this term which emphasizes "what works" and what is unreflectively taken to be "useful". After all, a critique of instrumentalistic fallacies and ethical shortsightedness belongs to the core of their thinking. The sense of pragmatism at stake here is primarily a conception of scientific investigation and validation, i.e. a pragmatic conception of truth in a broad sense. Its relatedness to pragmatism is realized by its affinity to basic ideas in C. S. Peirce (say, validity by consensus through an unlimited community of investigators).

Both Apel and Habermas have given extended interpretations of Peirce's pragmatism. In connection with the two-volume German translation (1967 and 1970) Apel wrote a long introduction which was later published separately.[2] Here, as well as in various other publications in the early seventies,[3] Apel elaborated Peircean pragmatism in the direction of transcendental semiotics. It especially focused on the community of researchers, conceived as an ideal community engaged in an ongoing interpretative and experimental validation process, for whom a future agreement on the ultimate truth is presupposed as a necessary regulative idea.[4]

These catchwords indicate how a transcendental-pragmatic interpretation of Peircean pragmatism is closely related to conceptions of truth and rationality. They also show how the question of pragmatism in Apel and Habermas is basically a question of pragmatic conceptions of truth – or better, of validity and validation, which depend upon concepts like rational consensus and argumentative validation, unlimited community of investigators, and self-reflective ultimate justification.

I will here delineate the main conceptions of the "transcendental-pragmatic" and "universal-pragmatic" conception of truth and validity worked out by Apel and Habermas, through which the affinity to pragmatism in a Peircean sense will become evident. Before entering the elaboration of pragmatic conceptions of validity in Apel and Habermas, it might be useful to call to mind why validity plays such an important role in the philosophical projects of both Apel and Habermas.

Apel, with his background in the hermeneutic tradition, came to the conclusion that intersubjective and argumentative aspects of validation and validity are insufficiently taken into account in this tradition.[5] This insufficiency shows itself in some self-referential uneasiness (a relativistic tendency) and in an inadequate grasp of the scientific endeavor; and it also implies a premature resignation to the impossibility of ultimate justification of basic norms. The immediate need in our time for ultimate justification of basic norms, and the theoretical obstacles to recognizing its possibility, are both related by Apel to the scientization of the world:[6] on the one hand we live in a civilization based on technology and science, which has created a set of extremely consequential and global problems (e.g. in the field of ecological destruction, military potentials, economic and political inequalities and tensions); on the other hand we possess an overly restrictive conception of scientific rationality, which makes the idea of a rational justification of basic norms seem impossible (and as a result, what is then seen as a struggle between equally a-rational particular interests and preferences gets its pseudo-legitimation). In Apel's view, a rational and just treatment of these problems not only requires scientific insight in a technological or result-oriented sense, but also an open sphere of dialogue and rational formation of will and preferences; and, in the last instance, it requires a compelling justification of a rationally founded universal normative base, over and beyond all particular divisions in nations, races, blocs, and generations. Philosophy cannot implement these norms, but it can contribute positively by uncovering the (often overlooked) possibility of ultimate justification.

Apel's project might be described as an attempt at overcoming, in an Hegelian sense of that term, the prevailing, overly restrictive self-interpretation on the part of science, by showing a deeper sense of rationality, including communicative rationality and possible normative justification, more or less hidden within the presuppositions of the scientific enterprise itself. This is where a transformation of the Peircean pragmatic conception of scientific rationality fits in.

In the case of Habermas similar points can be made.[7] Given his background in the Frankfurt School of critical theory, Habermas was in need of a rationally founded notion of normative validity in order to legitimate the notion of critical philosophy. Without some rationally grounded standard, the programme based on that notion would remain theoretically deficient. In Habermas's view, at least a well-founded notion of procedural natural-rights is required. This goes hand in hand with a critique of a notion of rationality which is ultimately tied to control and domination. Habermas's attempt at elaborating the conception of rationality is well known from the discussion about the three cognitive interests, where communication and emancipation are included.[8] But in this theory of the three cognitive interests and forms of rationality, problems of validity are still not adequately taken care of; not only the validity problems of norms but also theoretical and categorial validity problems are insufficiently treated in the Habermasian position of the mid-sixties.[9] Against this background, an elaboration of the notion of validation – i.e. a pragmatic conception of truth – was a reasonable next task.[10]

The Transcendental-Pragmatic Notion of Validity

Apel generally argues in a hermeneutic-dialectical way, interpreting other philosophers to the point where insufficiencies in their positions become clear. In Apel the overcoming of these insufficiencies points in the direction of an explicitly formulated transcendental-pragmatic conception.[11] A crucial argument in Apel's thinking is an attempt at showing the fallacy of a "semanticist" framework: if one thinks exclusively in terms of semantic categories, overlooking the internal relation between language and subject, important philosophical insights get lost.[12] One tends to regard this relation as an empirical one. Transcendentality becomes at most a question of "constitutive frames", in the sense of the paradigm case of chess where no self-reflective necessity (no strict irrefutability, and therefore no transcendental-pragmatically grounded necessity) is involved. The prescriptive aspects of speech acts are overlooked as an issue for philosophical reflection, and conceived of as an empirical problem to be treated by sciences such as psychology and linguistics. In such a semanticist view there is in this sense a reduction of *validity* (normativity) into factuality. The narrowness of this semanticist conception has to be overcome by a pragmatic conception, but it must be a philosophical, i.e. a reflective and transcendental one, and not merely an empirical pragmatics.

Validity has often been conceived of as *institutionally dependent*, so that change in the institutions would affect the validity of norms. In this case the norms are not valid universally, i.e. for all people, but only *inside* the accommodating institutions, the "language game". A "critical morality", which transcends the various roles and virtues, is here absent. In juridical terms this position is one of positive rights, not of natural rights.

This is the point where philosophical pragmatics becomes important: we do, in our situated speech acts, raise validity claims which in a pragmatic perspective can be shown to transcend the bounds of any particular institution and to presuppose a universal validity.[13] This philosophical pragmatics can be roughly introduced as follows: In social interaction we presuppose that what one says or does can be understood by other people; if not immediately, it can be made so by appropriate translation and explanation. In principle, it is understandable. We also presuppose that people in principle are accountable by virtue of knowing what they say and do, and why. If this were not so, we could not interact. We assume that, as a rule, one means what one says and that one assumes that there are good enough reasons to support it, and to justify why one is acting the way one does. Ultimately, this requires that the institution within which one acts be itself legitimate. When superficial doubt or dissent about these validity assumptions occurs, it can be settled inside the given setting (institution, culture). But if the doubt becomes more profound, its resolution requires special measures in the way of research and argumentation. In an implicit sense this is already presupposed in our pragmatically raised validity claims.[14] In elaborating these implicit, pragmatically given presuppositions, the idea of an unlimited community of researchers emerges. An intersubjectively valid resolution, ultimately settled by discursive consensus, constitutes a pragmatically founded regulative idea.[15]

In this connection Apel finds support in C. W. Morris's semiotics.[16] His semiotic division into semantics, syntax, and pragmatics is for one thing used to stress the intersubjective character of natural language. It is *inter*subjective because sign interpretation necessarily transcends the idea of the methodological self-sufficiency of the individual ("methodical solipsism"),[17] and it is inter*subjective* because it involves persons capable of reflection (not only of semanticist meta-language/object-language thinking), capable of raising validity claims that presuppose intersubjective validation, and capable of communication with each other about something (the "double structure" of communication).[18]

Armed with this transcendental interpretation of Morris's semiotics, Apel works out the Peircean conception of an unlimited community of researchers.[19] Apel interprets Peirce in a Kantian way, so that the resulting transcendental-semiotic conception of Peirce is proposed as a paradigmatic "transformation" of the consciousness-oriented paradigm of traditional transcendental philosophy.[20]

This elaborated version of Morris's semiotics is thus used by Apel to demonstrate the existence of transcendental-pragmatic presuppositions in everyday life/language. A speech act, by virtue of presupposing implicitly mutual understanding, is already an act of reciprocal recognition of the other subjects. It necessarily involves the assumption of a possible vindication of implicitly and explicitly raised validity claims concerning the truth of what is claimed to be the case, the rightness of the norms involved, the general intelligibility of what is communicated, and the truthfulness of the speech actor (following the Habermasian terms).[21] The revised Peircean conception of the unlimited community of investigators – of interpreters and experimenters – is seen as an adequate articulation of the implied presupposition of possible intersubjective vindication. Validity is thus intersubjective, not subjective and relative, and it is not merely founded on data and perception, but established through intersubjective interpretation and argumentation, by the free consensus of all.[22]

Normative validity is found in the procedural norms themselves. They imply reciprocal recognition among the participants and universalization as a normative standard. This is, one may say, a procedural version of the categorical imperative with its mutual egalitarian recognition and validity through universalization. (But an adequate interpretation of needs is part of the evaluation process.)[23]

The central core of this pragmatic conception of rationality is for Apel the unavoidability of argumentative rationality.[24] This is the foundation to which Apel returns again and again (cf. his arguments against the *deductivist* trilemma of ultimate justification: regression, circle, or decisionism):[25] if we are to argue seriously, and thus really seek a valid answer, we have to take the arguments of all actual and possible opponents seriously. At each moment we must accept normative preconditions of argumentation, such as mutual equal recognition and the readiness to accept the better argument. Apel's reference to these preconditions of argumentation is no proof in a deductive sense, but the reflective demonstration of a rational irrefutability. Apel's demonstration shows that all attempts toward seriously arguing against the validity of these preconditions, necessarily presuppose their validity in the very act of arguing against it. This is for Apel the rock bottom, where rationality shows its compelling nature. This binding force of rationality – as irrefutable and already accepted – not only holds for explicit arguing, and counter-arguing, but also for scientific activity in general, as well as for validity claims raised in everyday life, since in the last instance these claims implicitly require argumentative vindication.

Apel conceives this strictly reflective way of arguing as a "criticism of meaning",[26] i.e. as an indication of how the meaningfulness of implicit claims of truth and rightness is presupposed in a way which cannot be denied or neglected without self-defeating implications. When applied to arguing, this "meaning criticism" exhibits pragmatic/semiotic preconditions in the very act of arguing (and of thinking, Apel adds).[27] This implies a self-referential structure. However, when applied to everyday (non-argumentative) communication, the argument for the undeniability of the norms for argumentation itself requires an extended argument. It must show that universal validity claims are really raised in all speech acts, even when not consciously formulated by the actors themselves, and that the meaningfulness of these claims implies that they can be vindicated through intersubjective argumentation resulting in a consensus. When it comes to the elaboration of this transition Apel and Habermas apply different strategies. Apel relies more on arguments from irrefutability while Habermas elaborates a universal pragmatics of communicative competence and extends the application of his views to theories of socialization and historical evolution.[28]

We now have validation of norms on two levels, as it were: the validation of the constitutive, procedural norms themselves and the validation of various normative questions brought into the argumentative checking process. The reflective resolution of the former is in principle definitive; we claim to know that they are valid, here and now. On the other hand, which of the thematized normative validity claims will be found to be valid in a discussion is an open question to be decided in the actual process of argumentation between the persons involved. One cannot predict these results, though one can predict that egoistic and ethnocentric conclusions, such as fascism, are ruled out, because of the egalitarian universalization inherent in the validation process. But beyond this, what will in each concrete case be found to be the right answer, e.g. about hierarchy and authority, is in principle an open-ended question. And there are normative questions, e.g. about taste and style, for which there might never be any rational consensus, so that in these cases the differing views are all legitimate. This is the field of rational tolerance and legitimate pluralism.

What has been said here about the 'unrejectability' of argumentation and the universality of argumentatively settled validity claims does not imply a denial of the historicity of argumentative activity, nor does it imply a guarantee against regression into irrationality. But inherent in our pragmatically raised validity claims, and their presupposition of possible vindication, there is a peculiar appeal for rational thinking and action, and for a practical concern for the improvement of argumentative rationality.[29]

Such argumentative validation implies a right to evaluate the legitimacy of different societies and cultures, even in cases where argumentative rationality has not developed or has been repressed. This right to evaluate others is however no *carte blanche* for autocratic and elitist decisions, since it is based on the possible assent of all persons involved. Furthermore, even when transcultural evaluation in this sense is legitimate, as in cases of ritual homicide, the question remains as to whether such an evaluation (recommendation, criticism) actually ought to be made, and if so, in what form this should be done.[30]

We have delineated, in somewhat free formulations, the main points in Apel's pragmatic conception of validity. In order to bring out its philosophically puzzling aspects more clearly, we shall add a few critical remarks.[31]

If the criterion of validity (truth) is defined by argumentatively achieved consensus,[32] one may ask whether this conclusion applies to itself. In fact, to support his view Apel does not primarily appeal to consensus, but to what he sees as the irrefutability of self-referential arguments.[33] To elucidate the structure of this argument he refers, for instance, to Aristotle's argument for the irrefutability of the principle of contradiction.[34] This is not a case of validation by consensus, or even by an intersubjective procedure.

Here one single person could in principle recognize the validity of the argument. One may certainly point out that all rational beings will in this case reach the same conclusion, and so there will be consensus. But to say that truth implies consensus among rational beings is not to say that consensus is what we understand by truth, or the way we decide what is true. This objection may be met by drawing a distinction between, on the one hand, the self-referential validation of this conception of procedural validation and, on the other, the argumentative validation of disputed issues *within* this validation process. The latter may then, without inconsistency, be described in fallibilistic and melioristic terms, whereas the former is claimed to be definitive. This is a strategy found in Apel.[35]

However, if one still wants to use the term "consensus theory of truth" to characterize this position, one should at least add that in this case there are quite important distinctions inherent in the term "consensus".

The transition from everyday (non-argumentative) interaction to full validating argumentation presents serious problems,[36] which also arise for the transition from actual to pure argumentation.[37] To say that in arguing seriously one has to take arguments seriously, is one thing; to say that we have to take arguments seriously once we take part in some actual but incomplete or even distorted discussion, is something else. There is, to be sure, something compelling in arguments even in distorted contexts. (Try, for example, to defend clearly inconsistent views in a court!) This point supports the view that there is some "driving force" in actual discussions toward pure argumentation that is free from hindrances and distortions. In actual discussions there are, however, various specific institutional standards and rules for what is "sufficient" and "reasonable" in arguing, and these tell us when we have obtained enough clarification and well-foundedness to regard the problem as solved in the sense that we are entitled to claim that we understand and know. In everyday life special reasons are required to go on arguing beyond this point. Even if one accepts that validity claims are raised in everyday life, presupposing some real vindication, one might doubt whether this entails the further presupposition that the only acceptable validation is one carried out intersubjectively under the conditions of an ideal discussion.

In order to uncover such basic presuppositions, an *empirical* analysis of the validity claims raised in everyday speech acts will not do. (For instance, the use of questionnaires – asking people whether in their speech acts they really presuppose validation by rational consensus, obtained through ideal speech situations – will not be successful, since most people do not have these concepts in any explicit sense.) This is the reason why an elaboration of transcendental semiotics or of universal pragmatics is required. This is also the point where a negative strategy is applied: Apel and Habermas both present criticisms of alternative conceptions of truth as an introduction to their own notion of validity.[38] In the case of Apel his transcendental-semiotic interpretation of Peirce is presented as a superior notion of truth, integrating other conceptions.[39] In this notion Apel sees a synthesis which accounts for both the connection to reality and the ongoing intersubjective interpretation, a notion by which "the problem of an adequate explanation of the truth conception that underlies modern empirical science" is reached.[40] The point of this negative strategy is the following: since this transcendental-pragmatic conception supposedly represents a position *superior* to other conceptions of truth, the truth claim inherent in speech acts *must* be interpreted according to this transcendental-pragmatic conception.

Seen from some distance, Apel's version of truth and validation is fairly close to Habermas's conception. Some main points of dispute between the two authors should, however, be pointed out.

The status of *reality* in these intersubjectivist notions of validity presents a source of uneasiness. Apel here sees an ambiguity in Habermas: on the one hand Habermas presupposes that "the abstract facts which are the correlates of true propositions are asserted by us with respect to objects in the world";[41] and on the other hand Habermas makes "a rigorous distinction between the question of truth about *abstract facts* which for him is a question of *reflective validity-claims* to be settled on the level of *argumen-*

tative discourse and the question of *evidence* about *objects of experience* which for him is a question of pre-discursive *information* within the frame of *pre-reflexive communicative* interaction between people".[42] This uneasiness, we shall see, influences the core notions of validity and consensus.

For Apel the answer lies in the Peircean conception of reality as that which is recognizable in the long run, viz. in the conception of "ultimate opinion".[43] This conception defines reality indirectly, i.e. by the notions of an ideal community of research and argumentation: the real is that which all investigators finally would agree upon. However, if reality as recognizability is taken to mean "what all investigators can agree upon", the problem remains as to whether they actually will *reach* such an agreement. Furthermore it is an open question how we should know that some future consensus really is the *final* one. The expression "in the long run" serves to avoid a reduction of the normative sense of the "true consensus" to the descriptive sense of any "actual consensus", but it implies a lack of determinateness as to what the true consensus really is.

Another main point of dispute turns around the question of *transcendentality*.[44] This is partly a question of terminology. Habermas is reluctant to use the term "transcendental", with its Kantian connotations, in connection with preconditions for communication and validation; he therefore prefers to talk about universal (or formal) pragmatics, not about transcendental pragmatics. But it is also a question of methodological emphasis. Apel places emphasis primarily on self-reflective argumentation (and on more traditional philosophical reasoning, especially hermeneutical criticism), whereas Habermas places emphasis on justification through social scientific theory. This methodological difference implies philosophical differences. In Apel's opinion Habermas introduces empirical contingency beneath the transcendental rock bottom. In Habermas's opinion, Apel overstresses the strength and extension of transcendental (self-referential) argumentation.[45]

The Universal-Pragmatic Notion of Validity

I will now delineate some main points in Habermas's so-called consensus theory of truth. Then I will focus on some problems, mainly along the universality-situatedness dimension, namely:

(1)   The question of the external and internal delimitations of a purely discursive theory of validity.
(2)   The question of the unavoidable situatedness of discourse.
(3)   The question of the normativity of actual consensus.

In Habermas (as in Apel) the concept of truth is not analyzed in connection with semantical entities, but in connection with pragmatic entities where the performative aspect implies truth claims (and thus the expression "is true" is rendered non-redundant).[46] The validity of these claims rests on their acceptance, i.e. acceptance for sufficient reasons, as Habermas also puts it.[47] (Here two interpretations are possible: validity through mere intersubjective assent, and validity through good reasons; a consensus theory and a discourse theory.)[48] Habermas takes "institutionally unbound" explicit speech acts as paradigm cases.[49] ("I hereby nominate...." is a case of an institutionally bound speech act in a sense which "I promise you...." is not.[50]) For Habermas there are four universal validity claims: intelligibility, truth, rightness, truthfulness.[51] They are "universal" in the sense, first, that the validity claims are meant to be valid independently of any particular institution or situation, and second, that all speakers are able to raise them. The ability to do so belongs to our common communicative competence. These four validity claims are operative in all communicative speech acts, and in other types of speech acts they are involved in deficient modes. In everyday life there is a basic mutual trust in the implicit validity claims, a background consensus. (In asking for a cup of tea one presupposes that the cup is available and portable, that the other person understands the question and takes the questioner to be serious, and that both persons find it appropriate that this request is made.) Through doubts and disagreements the implicit validity claims may become explicit; then a rational solution can be sought and possibly obtained by various reasons – the extreme case involving a radical switch into fully specialized investigation and argumentation.

Habermas relies on a distinction (developed in Ramsey and Strawson) between facts and objects of experience.[52] Facts are what true statements state, and they are not in the world as things are. You can break a thing, e.g. a glass, but not a fact, e.g. the fact that the glass is fragile. Habermas elaborates this point into a distinction between the validity of fact-stating utterances and the objectivity of object experience,[53] and he brings this distinction to bear on his general criticism of correspondence conceptions of truth: correspondence theory conflates validity and objectivity.[54] However, even if one agrees with Habermas's general criticism of correspondence conceptions,[55] his use of this dichotomy between objectivity and truth – which goes together with similar dichotomies between "action" and "discourse", "constitution" and "validation" – may seem puzzling, since the two factors apparently intertwine (as we shall point out below).[56]

For Habermas, truth and rightness are the two discursively (i.e. argumentatively) redeemable universal validity claims.[57] Truthfulness is tested in subsequent interaction, and intelligibility (language related)[58] is an indispensable condition for discourse (i.e. argumentation).

The further steps in Habermas's presentation of his pragmatic conception of validity will be discussed with reference to his original and most extended exposition, *Wahrheitstheorien* from 1973.[59]

"It belongs so to speak to the nature of validity claims that they can be redeemed".[60]

This is the notion of pragmatically rooted validity claims whose meaningfulness presupposes vindication.

"The bringing about of a consensus under the conditions of a discourse is the 'way of action' by which a discursive validity claim is redeemed...".[61]

This is an interpretation of the pragmatically rooted validity claims from the standpoint of a consensus theory.

However, the concept of consensus is certainly ambiguous. We have a moderate version saying that if a validity claim is found to be valid, then all competent persons of good will should be able to agree upon it. Consensus is an implication of validity. In a strong version of the consensus theory, validity is *defined* by consensus. A view is valid because there is a consensus about it. Furthermore the term consensus may be defined in different ways, e.g. by various requirements for competence and number of participants.

A contingently achieved consensus cannot represent a criterion for the right answer, Habermas says. For that purpose we need a grounded, or rational consensus.[62]

To avoid a circle (by defining rational consensus by another rational consensus) rational consensus is defined by Habermas as "the formal properties of discourse", i.e. as an argumentation in which only arguments count and no irrelevant factors interfere (only "the unforced force of the better argument" determines the conclusion).[63] The notion of discourse is thus tied up with a notion of a free speech situation, where intersubjective obstacles are eliminated (the realm of action and experience is blacked out)[64] and cooperative search for truth is the only motive. (Cf. the notion of an unlimited community of investigators in Apel's transformed version of Peirce, and the notion of communication free from domination in Habermas.)[65]

Discourse is explicated by the notion of an ideal speech situation essentially implying equal chances of discursive participation, and freedom reflectively to criticize and change given linguistic frames – i.e. equality of status, and freedom, as its core. These are supplemented with authenticity, rational motivation, and competence, and with elimination of time limits.[66] (Thus we are confronted both with a discursive-structural notion of an ideal speech situation, and with a notion of an ideal speech situation which embraces individual qualities.) "Language system", historically generated and transmitted by socialization, is a basic notion here. Language system (should we say: horizons, traditions, categorial frameworks?[67]) are not themselves true or false, Habermas emphasizes; they make true or false assertions possible. But their adequacy can be checked and changed, by reflective activity. Such reflection is an essential part of discourse.

Briefly stated, to make reflective-critical activity possible, an undistorted and free speech situation is required. The ongoing argumentation should be free to treat any issue from any perspective. Liberality and equality are in this sense conditions for rationality. The consensus obtained under these conditions is a grounded (rational) consensus, which is said to be a "sufficient criterion" for the vindication ("redemption") of validity claims.[68]

The ideal speech situation is thus primarily determined "negatively", viz. by elimination of all discourse-conditioned and interpersonal hindrances to a free argumentative activity (elimination of harmful inequality among the participants and of deadlines), though with the additional "positive" characteristics of personal authenticity and of motivation for validation (and *only* for validation).

In summary, there are pragmatically raised universal validity claims in communication, presupposing a vindication by consensus, viz. by rational consensus in the sense of discursively obtained consensus; discourse presupposes critical reflection on given frames and perspectives in order to improve them; free discourse requires an ideal speech situation; consensus obtained under these conditions is not merely factual but a criterion of validity. In other words, the implicit validity claims imply the notions of ideal speech situation and discursively obtained consensus, *qua* unavoidable regulative ideas, at the same time as the possibility of vindication is counterfactually presupposed in argumentation and communicative action, and in this sense these notions are constitutive of argumentation and communication. There is, however, no external criterion for whether or not an ideal speech situation is realized (and mostly it is not).[69]

(1) To the thesis that language systems are not true or false, one may object that even when the terms true and false are reserved for assertions, this terminology does not rule out *a kind of validation* of the so-called language systems (or, one may say, a validation of "constitution", since language systems have a constitutive function). This, for one thing, modifies the sharp dichotomy made between validity and constitution.[70] For another, this reflective validation of language systems has to be related somehow to *reality*. At any rate, collective decisions alone – even when carried out in discourse – don't form the paradigm case for solving conceptual problems. Conceptual adequacy requires more than decision. Somehow or other our concepts have to be adequate for the case in hand. Conceptual adequacy, even when it is decided by an argumentative reflection (and not by a "looking in between concepts and phenomena"), must somehow come to grips with *that* which concepts are about. Here, as in any case where a better argument is distinguished from the next best, referring only to the speech situation will not suffice: in a free discussion – where only the better argument counts – that which distinguishes the better argument from the next best cannot itself be part of the inter-subjective setting, since this setting (ideal speech situation, or something less but similar to it) is presupposed to be the *same* in both cases. It therefore has to be something "*in* the argument", which in a sense is its "content", as opposed to the "formal" (i.e. purely intersubjective) characterization of the ideal speech situation, that is decisive for the validation. Granting all difficulties in talking about "correspondence" or "reference", this much of an "objective" element has to be accounted for in a theory of validation. Habermas underlines that he rejects an interpretation of the discursive test of language systems in terms of correspondence theory, but without making it clear how the "*adequacy*" (*Angemessenheit*) of language systems is related to the realm of things and experience.[71]

However, if elements of "content" are necessary in conceptual tests, then the same holds true for both theoretical (empirical) and practical validity claims, since the question of the adequacy of the given language system is part of both kinds of validity claims. And this is to say that a consensus theory, or a discourse theory, cannot be said to be "pure", if that is taken to mean that only consensus (intersubjective assent and no content) or only discursivity (merely structures in the discourse and no content) is sufficient to characterize the notions of validation and validity. In other words, a theory of discourse and of consensus should not be formulated in a way such that the "content reference" is neglected.

We have already seen that Apel points out an ambiguity in Habermas's treatment of the question of "reality". Let us take another look at this problem: At the outset Habermas focuses on the argumentative aspect of validation, somehow leaving aside the more empirical aspect, and in dealing with the sources of failure he tends to concentrate exclusively on the sources of failure located at the intersubjective level. But, we may object, there are sources of failure stemming from the empirical aspect, and there are linguistic (categorial) inadequacies. The latter type of failures is certainly meant to be taken care of by Habermas, partly through processes like therapy, rational socialization, and criticism of ideology, partly through the free, discursive reflection upon language systems. The question is, however, whether Habermas's conception of reflective discourse is sufficient for an elimination of linguistic inadequacies, and whether empirical aspects can be left aside in the way they tend to be by Habermas.

Habermas has declared[72] that a rational consensus obtained in an ideal speech situation is a "sufficient criterion" for the "redemption" of validity claims. Disregarding the difficulties of conceiving and realizing an ideal speech situation and a rational consensus connected to it, one may raise the following question in terms of the logic of necessary and sufficient conditions: Is the ideal speech situation a sufficient condition for validity? Is the ideal speech situation a necessary condition for validity?

In daily life we think we know various things. In some cases we are mistaken, but not in all. In so far as we often possess the truth, without an ideal speech situation, the latter is not a necessary condition for validity. This is a trivial point, which nobody denies.

But if we question a validity claim and ask for a grounded answer, can we then reach such an answer without the anticipation of an ideal speech situation? This question is rhetorical, since there evidently are various culturally dependent or institutionally conditioned ways of getting "sufficiently good" answers, without any ideal speech situation. In this sense, the ideal speech situation is not a necessary condition of taking-something-to-be-true (and sometimes even of having-the-truth).

But what about the case when the answer has to be really certain? Even in this case an ideal speech situation, or even an actually realizable degree of free communication, is not always necessary. Imagine a color-blind person who wants to know with a high degree of certainty whether non-color-blind persons do distinguish things according to objective properties and not only by conventions (as when speaking of "blue sky" and "green grass").[73] He compels some research persons with ordinary color sight to sit in isolation from each other, and they are told (they are given the order, not asked in free communication) to separate a number of scraps, each with a color and an individual number under it, according to their colors. Without going into greater detail with this example, we claim that this color-blind person can in this way arrive at a quite certain answer to his question. In this case neither an ideal speech situation nor any realizable degree of free communication is a necessary condition for obtaining this strongly grounded answer.

The example can of course be commented on in various ways. One can, for instance, point out that the implied compulsory action presupposes a communicative competence among the persons carrying out the experiment, and also among the research persons in so far as they understand the order. However, the question is here satisfactorily settled by looking, without discursive check or change of language. The foundation for validation can therefore most reasonably be said to be located at the level of the phenomena rather than on the intersubjective level – which is not to deny that these phenomena (colored scraps) are already constituted by language and therefore 'mediated' at the intersubjective level. This example does not rule out the possibility of an ongoing discourse, but it denies its necessity, since in this case there is *no point* in going on with a reflective discussion. As a case of validation, it has its relative autonomy over against the discursive demand to question any issue from all perspectives. It indicates a kind of vindication of truth claims in its own right. It does not fit unresistingly into Habermas's paradigm case of validation.

Some of Habermas's own examples illustrate the same point. In the section of Toulmin he refers to the question whether Harry is a British citizen.[74] To settle the question one pays attention to the fact that Harry was born on Bermuda. In addition one refers to British law which says that people born on Bermuda are in general British citizens. This law is a warrant which allows us to assert that Harry is in fact a British citizen, once it is proved that he was born on Bermuda – though one should add a backing to this warrant: "under normal circumstances". If Harry's British citizenship was ever a matter of doubt or dispute, the question would now be settled, i.e. decided beyond reasonable doubt and dispute to the extent that the fact of his birth and the rules of British law are sufficiently well checked. What is explicitly referred to in order to settle the question are facts and rules, both cast in a common language (containing concepts like person, time and place, and membership in a nation). There is no reflection on this language, and no attempt at criticizing or improving it (it may even be pointed out that this question – Harry's British citizenship – is only meaningful inside this linguistic frame). No reference is made to consensus. In fact, no reference is made to the participants in the process of reasoning, or to any community of participants. The question is resolved merely by appeal to facts and rules in the given frame of reference. These facts and rules can be checked by one individual alone, though if doubts occur one may need the help of qualified persons (knowing more about his birth or the given laws).

So far no reference is made to consensus, nor to participants in a validating process. Hence, this is not an example of a piece of discourse in Habermas's terminology (including critical reflection on given frames and validation through a consensus by virtue of an ideal speech situation). This case, too, shows a rational vindication of a validity claim which does not naturally fit into Habermas's conception of truth and validation, with its paradigm in theoretical and universal-political questions:

> "The cognitive paradigms, from the meaning of which truth can be explicated, are not the perceptions or the singular statements by which perceptions are communicated, but general, negative and modal statements".[75]

This paradigm of validity has its great merits (for one thing by capturing validation better than any static subject-object model); and the question whether *all* cases of validation (as, e.g., the legal case of Harry's British citizenship) equally well fall into this paradigm does not imply a denial of its overall importance, but it does situate this paradigm in relation to other relatively autonomous cases of validation.

For the sake of clarity it should, however, be stated explicitly that even in cases like these a reference to possible consensus is necessarily *presupposed*, indeed in a double sense: (i) If it is the case that Harry is a British citizen, then there must exist a background consensus concerning accepted legal rules and notions in the British society. Hence (ii) there is a guarantee that all possible competent speakers in an ideal speech situation should be able to reach a consensus about Harry's British citizenship.

However, our examples show the relative autonomy of the validation process in these cases, implying that it is practically meaningless to enter into a discussion of the actual frames of validity. Such an undertaking is superfluous. But, as we have just pointed out, the status of the notion of an ideal speech situation (or of an infinite community of investigators) as the last instance of validation (and in case of doubt, as a relevant instance of validation) is not thereby denied.

Whereas the question of categorial adequacy indicates an internal element of "content" in this pragmatic conception of validation – thus restricting the possible meaning of the terms "discourse theory" and "consensus theory of truth" – these examples indicate the reasonableness of some external delimitation of this theory over against problems of empirical truth, which have a relatively self-sufficient form of validation where it is pointless to go into a discursive questioning of the frames.

The next question is whether the ideal speech situation is a sufficient condition for validity.

If the rational consensus is said to be a "sufficient condition" in a weak (non-modal logical) sense, it is clear that such consensus does not logically imply validity. We can talk about having good enough reasons for asserting something – a "warranted assertibility" – but then it would be more appropriate to talk about a theory of assertibility than of validity.[76]

If, however, "sufficient condition" is used in a strict modal logical sense, can we then say that *if* we really have acquired an ideal speech situation and reached a rational consensus, then the consensus guarantees the validity of the answer? One may deny this, by arguing for an inescapable, permanent possibility of consensus-modifying innovations both on the conceptual and the experiential level. Even if all discursive-structural hindrances were simultaneously eliminated and we reached a consensus which would therefore count as rational, it is still always thinkable that new concepts and new information might turn up and modify or correct our consensus. There is nothing in the premises, i.e. in the concept of an ideal speech situation, which can rule out this possibility. It is only the elimination of intersubjective and discursive-structural hindrances that is included in the premises. If we have a free, reflective validation in this sense, we may hope that all issues and aspects can be brought into the discursive procedure as time goes on. But it does not follow that we can ever decide *when* the goal is reached (or whether it can be reached). At no definite moment can we really know that from now on nothing that might modify our consensus can ever turn up. Even if the ideal speech situation were realized, and we knew it, we could still never know that we had reached the definite rational consensus which logically implies validity.

Since there is no logical implication between rational consensus (ideal speech situation) and validity, the concept of rational consensus and ideal speech situation do not suffice for a strict definition of validity, nor can they serve as a criterion in a strict sense (even if the ideal speech situation were realized).

However, our pragmatically grounded validity claims (in communication and argumentation) are not thereby denied. They still represent a peculiar obligation to rationality, even if they have to be given a more flexible and pluralistic interpretation. In this sense we may still talk about this conception as being about validity, i.e. first in respect of the claims being pragmatically grounded validity claims, and second in respect of validity as a compelling, regulative idea in argumentative validation.

(2) In this section I will comment on four interrelated points: (a) ideal speech situation, (b) institutionalization, (c) personal perspectivity, and (d) language.

(a) Rational consensus is linked with the notion of discourse and ideal speech situation in order to avoid a regress in the determination of rational consensus.[77] Disregarding the question of how an ideal speech situation can be conceived, or even actualized, one may ask how we could possibly *know* if it *were* actually realized. It is tempting to answer: by a rational consensus. But to the extent that rational consensus is something we reach in an ideal speech situation, we have to actualize that ideal speech situation first, in order to reach a rational consensus about it. Thus we seem to end up in another regress! (And we may add: there is no neutral, discourse-independent way of deciding whether an ideal speech situation is realized or not. Take the case of someone who remains silent in the discussion. Is this silence due to repression, or is it due to an authentic decision of the participant? This we cannot find out "from the outside" without participating in the discussion. The same holds true if we want to know whether an absence of a change in the language frame means unfreedom or just a discursively adequate situation.)

The demand for a possible concrete realization of the ideal speech situation is rooted in the fact that it represents an ideal form of life, not merely a formal principle. But in what sense is this concept realizable, in reality and in thought?[78] To the extent that one conceives of an ideal speech situation as a form of argumentation where all discursive-structural obstacles are eliminated, it can only be as an open-ended concept: one starts by eliminating this and that concrete obstacle, e.g. the social status of the participants determining who is allowed to speak and whom one listens to. Then one may imagine a continuous process of elimination until all obstructions are overcome. But in order to conceive of this in concrete terms, we have to know all possible hindrances and we have to know that they can be eliminated simultaneously. This we have to know here and now. Hence it is evidently not only difficult to decide whether or not an ideal situation obtains here and now,[79] the very concept is problematic.[80] But still, we may often talk meaningfully about our efforts in making the situation better, and about our pragmatically grounded obligation to do so.

(b) If one asks for the conditions under which any discourse may be realized, it is not trivial to note that we always have to apply *one* organizational form, or one material structure, instead of another. One has either to write or to speak, and thus to use specific techniques and rules in each case. We can certainly change and improve the given institutional frames, and we can pass from one to another. But we can never abandon the status of being in one definite setting or another. (This means, among other things, that we have not only constitutive norms on the universal level, but always also particular constitutive norms connected to the particular organizational setting in each case. We can, in this sense, talk about constitutive norms on two levels, the universal and the various particular ones.) Even if discourse may be said to be a "counter-institution" – in the sense that no preconditions are allowed to be sheltered from critical reflection – every possible discourse has to be realized in one organizational form or another.[81] This point is certainly not denied by Habermas, the question is whether he pays sufficient attention to it, and how this affects the relationship between universality and situatedness.[82]

(c) Not only has each one of us a limited amount of knowledge, thus creating the need to rely on others for supplementary information, but our categorial grasps are delimited by our special situatedness or special professional training. Therefore the presentation of other perspectives and views is indispensable for getting us to see our own perspective as a perspective. It is indispensable for the creation of a reflective discussion in which one can try out the relative adequacies of other perspectives, possibly bringing them into some synthesis, possibly agreeing on the legitimacy of some rival perspectives (rational tolerance for legitimate pluralism), and, it is hoped, in realizing a common basis (in communicative competence and pragmatically grounded validity claims). We may sharpen the point by saying that finitude is a precondition for discourse. (If God is omniscient, knowing everything from all possible points of view, in what sense can God take part in a discussion as a genuine participant? If all participants had the same preferences and abilities, should they then count as one or as many? What would be the point of letting more than one person speak?) Thought-experiments indicate that discursive validation presupposes not merely universal communicative and argumentative competence, but also a diversity of finite subjects with different outlooks and differently situated views and interests. In arguing, we recognize each other not only as rational, but also as finite, whereby everybody can learn from everybody, and in a common effort mutually improve our insight.[83]

(d) One may, such as Habermas,[84] distinguish between the legitimation of norms and the justification of individual acts within the frames of an institution, thus thinking in terms of a distinction between justification inside a frame and justification of the frame itself. The problem of the legitimation of norms can be formulated as the question whether the validity claims connected to norms of action can be rationally vindicated by arguments alone. Hence, one apparently has the question of normative validation on the one hand and a question of the appropriate understanding of the various situated actions on the other (the latter implying situational justification of institutional acts, and judgment of their reasonableness in the concrete setting). This distinction may serve to avoid a totalization of merely situational, institution-bound justification, through which the critical potential of free argumentation and validation is overlooked.[85] But even if one holds to this distinction, and hence to the notion of ultimate and universal normative validation, there are still important conceptual interrelations between universal validation and situational concreteness: in order to discuss the validity of a universal norm (e.g. "all persons are born equal"), one has to understand what it means (i.e. that "persons" are "born equal", or "have the same rights"), and for this understanding a learning process through concrete situations in everyday life is required. The same holds true when it comes to the application of this general norm (then, too, one has to be able to judge the various situations where people can be said to have the same rights). One may object that problems of learning and of applying general norms are nevertheless conceptually external to the question of the validation of these norms. This is in a sense correct, but how could one meaningfully discuss the validity of a general norm (e.g. "all persons are born equal") without knowing "what it is about", what it means to follow or to violate the norm in concrete situations (i.e. what it means to be "equal" and "unequal" in various cases)? One does not have to have any complete knowledge (whatever that might mean in this field), but some basic insight into the situational meaning (an insight which can then be further elaborated) has to be present already at the stage of normative validation and agreement. In this sense it is unavoidable that any validation (if it is to be more than empty words) is conceptually related to an understanding of possible concrete cases.[86]

An example here could be found in discussions on human rights in the UN, where representatives from different nations bring with them different historical experiences and codes of interpretation. A possible consensus about such practical questions, in the sense of a generalization, presupposes a mutual understanding of such different perspectives – since what human rights really mean for a national representative (and thereby probably for his or her country) depends on these perspectives. A meaningful agreement on human rights, as general principles, presupposes the formation of some basic consensus about the concrete applications of these principles.

(3) In his criticism of Habermas, Höffe says:

> "The dilemma of these approaches [theories of consensus] is rooted in the fact that they either make truth dependent on historical contingency – i.e. on the distorting relation to rhetorics, suggestion, manipulation, deception, and self-deception – but then the invariance claim of truth is lost – or they introduce normative qualifications for the consensus – qualifications like: unlimited community of researchers (Peirce), critical test by competent observers (Kamlah, Lorenzen), potential or rational consent (Habermas), qualifications which, when regarded more closely, first: do not give any operational criterion of legitimation; second: dissolve the essence of consensus – i.e. making it the result of a historical process of understanding among concrete persons and not among abstract communicators".[87]

Even if one accepts that an *actually* given consensus can be "too weak" and that the notion of an *ideal* consensus implies something unreal and therefore cannot serve as a criterion in a more operational sense, one may still argue for the following points: the notion of an ideal consensus (rational consensus under the conditions of the ideal speech situation) still represents a particular binding force, a necessary regulative idea, which is not arbitrarily introduced but presents itself as the irrefutable result of a reflection on preconditions inherent in argumentation. Further, it makes sense to talk of a third concept of consensus characterized as the continuously improved consensus, in relation to the actual best possible consensus, viz. as the best possible improvement of the consensus obtained at any time. This is a notion of a realistic, realizable obligation to advance toward greater rationality.

This *dynamics* between the actual consensus and the constant formation of a better consensus is not adequately taken into account in Höffe's reflection on actual and ideal consensus.

If one accepts that *"ought* implies *can"*, i.e. that we can only be said to be obliged to do what it is possible for us to do, we shall have to distinguish between the obligation to the ideal consensus and the obligation to the best possible improvement of the consensus actualized at any time. The former is rooted in the reflective recognition of preconditions for arguing, and it represents what we might call our "ultimate obligation". The latter obligation is, in addition, rooted in the recognition of our fallibility, in the sense that fallibility implies that every actual consensus may embrace something that demands correction, every consensus points toward its further improvement. We are obliged to accept as valid what under the best possible conditions until now we have recognized to be valid; and at the same time we know that what we have accepted in this way as the best argument, may still (in various ways, according to the case) be overthrown by an even better argument. What we are ultimately obliged to accept as valid is therefore that which can turn up as the still better argument. Thus, in principle, there is some "call" for constantly transcending the given actual consensus in favor of the even better.[88]

This obligation "forward" – toward the better, in the final instance toward the ideal – is equally directed "backward", against meaninglessness and untruth, what is less well grounded and acceptable. The immediately compelling task in this version of human rationality is the rejection of the *un*acceptable. Take, for instance, the relation between criticizing a given level of scientific expertise as being *in*sufficient to grasp a problem adequately, e.g. a case of building a nuclear reactor where ecological expertise is lacking,[89] and the question about what would be the complete and adequate composition of any scientific body of experts. Often the former, "negative" question is fairly easy to answer, whereas the latter, "positive" question remains unsettled, as for example in the problem of possible future innovations and the possibility of their making new professional perspectives and approaches a reality.

However, at this point it is important to emphasize the primacy of the notion of *argumentation,* or of the *'force of the better argument'*, relative to the notion(s) of *consensus.*[90] The word "consensus" is evidently ambiguous. But if we interpret it in terms of such a dynamics (ranging from that which is actually held to be valid, to the even better, toward that which counterfactually embraces the final synthesis), then we assume that there are *reasons or arguments* at different levels, viz. the best argument here and now, the possibly even-better argument, and the (possibly) final argument. Hence the term "(rational) consensus" should be understood in terms of the notion of the compelling force of the better argument.[91]

Critical Aftermath

Before closing our comments on the transcendental-pragmatic and universal-pragmatic notion of validity we will take a brief look at the reactions in Apel and Habermas to the criticism brought forward against their positions.[92] Broadly speaking, in Habermas we find revisions and changes, in Apel revised formulations. These differences between Apel and Habermas tie in with the recent debate between the two, to which I will return in the two concluding essays ("Modernization of the Lifeworld" and "Rationality and Contextuality"). At the end of this paragraph I will indicate my own position on the question of pragmatically necessary conditions for inquiry and of ultimate normative justification (using arguments from absurdity).[93]

In the early eighties Habermas explicitly talks about the need for a "revision" of his previous analysis.[94] There is a change in perspective and emphasis, from the criteriological notion of a consensus defined by an ideal speech situation toward reconstructions of phylogenetic and ontogenetic learning processes, embracing life-world modernization and modernized "ethical life" *(Sittlichkeit).*[95] Hence Habermas tends even more toward fallible reconstructions, away from (weak) transcendental analyses.[96] However, he sticks firmly to a distinction between *value* questions and questions of *justice*, arguing for the possibility, in modern societies, of universal discursive solutions of questions of justice (whereas value questions are contextual and only apt to be justified within specific settings).[97]

Habermas also argues persistently in favor of *the principle of universalization* as a bridging principle which is supposed to make normative consensus possible. This principle is formulated among other things as follows: "... every valid norm has to fulfill the following condition: (U) *All* affected can accept the consequences and the side effects its *general* observance can be anticipated to have for the satisfaction of *everyone's* interests (and these consequences are preferred to those of known alternative possibilities for regulation)."[98] But this principle, which is supposed to ascertain the validity of universal norms of justice, is certainly problematic; it is vague, pretentious and cast in a quasi-utilitarian language which makes it vulnerable to the objection of being unrealistic.[99]

The universalization principle (U) is different from *the principle of discourse ethics* (D): "Only those norms can claim to be valid that meet (or could meet) with the approval of all affected in their capacity *as participants in a practical discourse.*"[100] However, prior to this definition of (D) Habermas maintains that "... once it has been shown that (U) can be grounded upon the presuppositions of argumentation through a transcendental-pragmatic derivation, discourse ethics itself can be formulated in terms of the principle of discourse ethics (D),..."[101] But this reference to transcendental-pragmatic derivation is immediately modified by a warning against transcendental analysis,[102] and by an explicit criticism of the Apelian idea of ultimate justification through transcendental analyses *(Letztbegründung)*: with the "linguistic turn" (as in Apel's

Transformation der Philosophie) the putative certitude of strict reflection is a possibility well lost.[103] What remains are fallibilistic reconstructions.

Throughout the many discussions on the status of transcendental-pragmatics, Apel has primarily elaborated and consolidated his position rather than revised or changed it.[104] He has elaborated his views on the problem of the application of norms, the "part B" of discourse ethics.[105] On the one hand he has willingly accepted and incorporated Habermas's contributions to a pragmatic analysis of claims to validity inherent in communicative speech acts and Habermas's elaboration of Weberian and Kohlbergian theories of modernization and maturation, while on the other hand Apel remains convinced of the necessity and possibility of an ultimate justification of a minimal procedural ethics.[106] He accepts that any person and any formulation is fallible, also in strict reflection, but he maintains that reflective insight into unavoidable normative preconditions for discursive activities represents an irrefutable *fundamentum inconcussum.*[107] At this top point, and in this sense, there is no fallibility according to Apel. But in other fields (on other levels) fallibilism is an appropriate position.

Hence the core of Apel's position remains unchanged.[108] It is a "transformation of philosophy"[109] based on a "pragmatic turn" in relation to the philosophy of consciousness. To illustrate the unavoidability of reflective insights, he refers persistently to the Aristotelian argument for the irrefutability of the principle of contradiction and to the Cartesian *cogito ergo sum* understood pragmatically.[110] To illustrate the importance of a pragmatic (linguistic) turn, he refers among other things to Wittgensteinian arguments for the impossibility of a private language. This blend of reflective pragmatics and speech act pragmatics is then applied to an interpretation of Peircean pragmatism, viz. the notion of validity as the consensus obtained in the long run under the conditions of an ideal community of investigators. This, as we have already seen, is the architectonic of Apel's position: pragmatics and pragmatism, reflection and speech acts brought together to do justice to both ultimate justification and fallibility.

Habermas does not believe that this construction holds.[111] There is in it, he thinks, an incurable tension between a philosophy of consciousness and strict reflection on the one hand and on the other a philosophy of language and discourse.[112] This objection is part of the ongoing discussion, to which we will return later. It refers to the apparent tension in Apel's position between his monological procedure in reflective justification on the one hand and on the other the dialogical idea of discourse as the procedure of validation: the hard core is one of strict reflection,[113] and his philosophy of discourse apparently represents something different from his philosophy of reflection.[114] However, in arguing in favor of ultimate preconditions, in reflection and/or in discourse, Apel regularly appeals to what he calls "criticism of meaning" (*Sinn-kritik*).[115] His way of arguing often consists in an appeal to the *meaninglessness* which would have come about if we had denied or rejected some basic principle. These arguments, it seems to me, are best understood as *arguments from absurdity*, here applied to pragmatic (not merely to semantic) problems: either self-reference in acts of reflection or self-reference in acts of argumentation.[116] In both cases, the context given is unavoidable for the person performing that kind of activity (whether one is arguing for or against). But a crucial point, it seems to me, is the need for *cautious analyses* of the *different* kinds of "absurdity" and thus of the *different* kinds of precondition, and at this point I still think there is something valuable to be learned from analytically trained philosophers.

I will illustrate the latter point by referring to the work of Knut Erik Tranøy on "methodologies as normative systems".[117] In analyzing "norms of inquiry" Tranøy focuses on what he calls *basic cognitive acts*, namely "(a) the testing and critical examination of truth claims (propositions), and (b) the acceptance and rejection as well as (c) the assertion and denial of propositions so examined". Point (b) is that of the "acquisition of knowledge and insight", and point (c) is "communication of knowledge and insight". The former case, (b), is that of a person related to the truth claim, which he can accept, reject, or toward which he can suspend judgment. The latter case, (c), is that of a person "publicly asserting and denying propositions (truth claims)", that is, he is communicating with other persons in the sense that he can assert or deny or suspend judgment about a truth claim. Tranøy suggests these formulations (among others) concerning the basic cognitive acts of accepting and rejecting propositions (truth claims):

(1)   It is not permitted to accept p if p is known to be false.
(2)   It is obligatory to reject p if p is known to be false.

These norms are supposed to be constitutive for the *acquisition* (acceptance, rejection, suspending of judgment) of truth claims. In that respect, the legalistic terminology is not the best choice, as Tranøy himself admits. A moral terminology would be more appropriate, as for instance: it is wrong to accept p if p is known to be false, and we ought to reject p if p is known to be false. But to the extent that acquisition of a truth claim, as a basic cognitive act, is understood as the relationship between a person and an argument, it is at least questionable whether this relationship is adequately grasped in moral terms. What would it mean to say that a person realizes that the truth claim is false at the same time as he accepts it as true? This would have been inconsistent, so maybe we should rather call it a neglect or disregard of a norm of consistency. If so, we should add that this is not just a semantic inconsistency. It is a case of a personal (pragmatic) inconsistency, maybe a case of madness:[118] the situation is absurd, or pathological. Hence we could call it a case of a *reductio ad absurdum* or *ad pathologicum*. Through such a reasoning around this case, what is shown is the strength of the norm (1), as a precondition which cannot be denied without absurdity in a fairly strong sense. A similar argument can be made for norm (2).

For basic cognitive acts of *communication* (assertion, denial, keeping quiet) Tranøy suggests, for instance, the following norm:

(3) It is not permitted to assert p if p is known to be less
     probable than $-p$

This norm looks more like a moral norm: it is *possible* to lie to
other people, and therefore it makes sense to have a moral norm
that forbids a person asserting (to other persons) what he rejects as
untrue. Briefly, in a research community one should be honest.
Such norms make sense, as moral norms. But in what sense are
these norms of inquiry unavoidable or necessary preconditions for
communicative 'basic cognitive acts'? We disregard here the
question of the status of norms of honesty in communication in
general (in the lifeworld, outside the special case of serious
argumentation), and focus on the question of its status in
communication within the community of investigators. If inquiry
is an activity aiming at well established, interesting and coherent
bodies of knowledge, and if everybody in the community of
researchers has to rely upon other people for a very substantial part
of this knowledge, then it follows that such norms of
trustworthiness play a crucial role in this activity. It is hard to see
how faked findings and fraudulent reports could ever be permitted
in a research community (which is not to say that such rules are
not violated). Granted the clear aim of such activities (inquiry,
research), and given that no human being can ever discover and
ascertain all knowledge that is available in a field of research, it is
indispensable that there be such a norm of honesty for this
activity.[119] In this sense we could speak of this norm as a
"necessary precondition" for inquiry. Given human finitude it is
unthinkable (absurd) that we could do without such a norm of
communication within any field of inquiry. But if this is an
argument from absurdity, it could be seen as a softer kind of
argument than the one above: in what sense is our finitude a
necessary fact and in what sense a contingent one? Does the idea
of a super-being, doing it all by himself, make sense?[120] (To the
extent that it makes sense to imagine such an omnipotent being, we
should talk about this norm of inquiry as a "contingent necessity"
for finite humans.)

The argument in favor of a constitutive norm of honesty in research is based on our need for second-hand knowledge, and hence for confidence since we need each other in this mutual "trade of truths": no single human being can acquire all knowledge by himself, first-hand, since no single human being can actually perform all the experiments and do all the observations. But inquiry also requires the discursive testing of different, competing positions and perspectives. This at least is the case if we have a broader notion of inquiry in mind, that is, not only research within one research programme but the historical development of scientific knowledge. In what sense could we imagine one spirit carrying out all these discussions, for and against the various perspectives and paradigms, for instance from the Renaissance onward? If this development is reconstructed as a learning process in which various actors assert and deny different views, how could such a reconstruction possibly be incarnated in *one* mind alone? At least in the world as we know it, we need each other for such intellectual learning processes. And to the extent that we can formulate norms necessary for these processes, we are not merely talking in terms of norms for one person related to a truth claim (as in case [b] above, of acquisition), nor merely of norms between researchers, since we need to trust in second-hand knowledge (as in case [c] above, of communication), but we are now talking in terms of norms for *free and rational discussions.*

We will not pursue this (theo)philosophical thought-experiment, but just recall that this is the point at which John Stuart Mill declared liberality to be a precondition for rationality, in the sense that a free and open discussion, without censorship, is a prerequisite for one's own confidence in the validity of one's own opinion. (We cannot claim that we are convinced that p is true, at the same time as we are unwilling to learn about any counter-arguments that could undermine this conviction. This is a performative inconsistency and a break of the norm [b] for the acquisition of truth claims.) Once again we face the problem of correctly formulating these norms for discourse (aiming at a rational solution of validity claims). We will not reopen that debate at this stage but merely recall that human finitude is at the bottom of this need for discursive procedures for acquiring well-founded views.

In concluding these remarks on the status of norms related to basic cognitive acts, I will emphasize the following points.

Arguments from absurdity are appropriate for an inquiry into the norms of inquiry. But in using them it does not suffice merely to talk about meaninglessness without qualification. A careful analysis is needed in each case, and then we will see that there are *different* kinds (and strengths) of "absurdity", from what is "thought-impossible" (as in case [b]) to what is "conditionally impossible", indicating a "contingent necessity" (as in case [c]). That is why I chose in "Arguments from Absurdity" to talk of an epistemic *gradualism*. These remarks are relevant for the project of transcendental-pragmatic analyses of the preconditions for reflection and discourse, for the question of the nature of the unavoidability (*Nichthintergehbarkeit*) involved, and hence for the question of the status of these pragmatic preconditions.

In addition to this epistemic gradualism to be found at the core of these pragmatic arguments from absurdity, there is the question of human *finitude* as a precondition for discursive inquiries aiming at the solution of validity claims. Attention to this finitude helps us prevent the idea of a God's eye view. As indicated earlier, our task is the overcoming of *less* well-established views, rather than acquisition of the final truth.[121] It is in this sense that I have spoken of an epistemic *meliorism*.

As to the notion of ultimate justification (*Letztbegründung*), this means that we can accept the project but only when this '*ultimum*' is interpreted as '*the last*', that is, as the best we can get, not as a *fundamentum inconcussum* as an absolute ground from which numerous interesting implications can be drawn.[122]

*

In this perspective it makes sense to talk of universal and transcendental pragmatics in terms of a gradualist and melioristic fallibilism,[123] even though such labels may create more confusion than clarification. Given the courage to use them, one should add that this gradualist and amelioristic fallibilism is based on a transcendental pragmatics of argumentative reason.[124] As some philosophers say: we may say what we like as long as it is clear what we mean. The discussion delineated above indicates that the title "theory of truth", applied to this pragmatic conception of argumentative rationality, is somewhat inappropriate. On the one hand the title seems to promise more than it yields. I refer to the relative neglect of problems of empirical truth and of the "content" element in questions of conceptual adequacy. On the other hand it seems to yield more than it promises. I refer to the procedural conception of natural rights, enabling us (in principle) to give valid answers to basic normative questions.

This pragmatic conception of rationality aims to be more than a piece of theoretical insight. It claims to imply a recognition of an obligation, not only to argumentative-scientific rationality, but to argumentative rationality in society in general. This involves the formation of more adequate views and preferences, for better evaluations and decisions – a more human and rational society. Finally, this obligation expresses the deeper concerns of Apel and Habermas underlying the elaboration of their pragmatic conception of discourse and discursive consensus.[125]

NOTES

1. References

Albert, H. (1975) *Transzendentale Träumereien*, Hamburg.

Apel, K.-O. (1970) "Szientismus oder transzendentale Hermeneutik? Zur Frage nach dem Subjekt der Zeicheninterpretation in der Semiotik des Pragmatismus". In R. Bubner et al. (eds.), *Hermeneutik und Dialektik* Vol. 1. Tübingen. Also in Apel 1973.

Apel, K.-O. (1972) "From Kant to Peirce: The Semiotical Transformation of Transcendental Logic". In L. W. Beck (ed.), *Proceedings of the Third International Kant-Congress*. Dordrecht. Also in Apel 1973.

Apel, K.-O. (1973) *Transformation der Philosophie*, Vols. 1 and 2. Frankfurt a.M.: Suhrkamp.

Apel, K.-O. (1975a) *Der Denkweg von Charles Sanders Peirce*, Frankfurt a.M.: Suhrkamp. Also in K.-O. Apel. *Charles Sanders Peirce, Schriften I und II*, Frankfurt a.M.: Suhrkamp, 1967 and 1970.

Apel, K.-O. (1975b) "Der semiotische Pragmatismus von Ch. S. Peirce und die 'abstractive fallacy' in den Grundlagen der Kantschen Erkenntnistheorie und der Carnapschen Wissenschaftslogik". In J. A. Bucher et al. (eds.), *Bewußtsein. Gerhard Funke zu eigen*, Bonn.

Apel, K.-O. (1976a) "Sprechakttheorie und transzendentale Sprachpragmatik zur Frage ethischer Normen". In K.-O. Apel (ed.), *Sprachpragmatik und Philosophie*, Frankfurt a M.: Suhrkamp.

Apel. K.-O. (1976b) "The Problem of (Philosophical) Ultimate Justification in the Light of a Transcendental Pragmatic of Language". *Ajatus* 36.

Apel. K.-O. (1978) "Transcendental Semiotics and the Paradigms of First Philosophy". *Philosophic Exchange* 2/4.

Apel. K.-O. (1979) *C. S. Peirce and the Question of the Truth-Conception of Modern Science (Toward a Transcendental-pragmatic Theory of Truth)*, Manuscript, Frankfurt a.M.

Apel. K.-O. (1980) "C. S. Peirce and the post-Tarskyan Problem of an Adequate Explication of the Meaning of Truth". *The Monist* 63/3.

Apel, K.-O. (1980/81) *Funkkolleg Praktische Philosophie/Ethik*, Hessischer Rundfunk, Studienbegleitbrief 1, 2 and 8.

Apel, K.-O. (1986) "Grenzen der Diskursethik? Versuch einer Zwischenbilanz", in: *Zeitschrift für philosophische Forschung*, 40.

Apel, K.-O. (1988) *Diskurs und Verantwortung*, Frankfurt a.M.: Suhrkamp.

Apel, K.-O. (1989) "Normative Begründung der 'Kritischen Theorie' durch Rekurs auf lebensweltliche Sittlichkeit? Ein transzendental-pragmatisch orientierter Versuch, mit Habermas gegen Habermas zu denken". In A. Honneth et al. (eds.), *Zwischenbetrachtungen*, Frankfurt a.M.: Suhrkamp.

Beckermann, A. (1972) "Die realistischen Voraussetzungen der Konsensustheorie von J. Habermas". *Zeitschrift für allgemeine Wissenschaftstheorie*, 3:63–80.

Benhabib, S. (1992) *Situating the Self*, Oxford: Polity Press.

Berk, U. (1979) *Konstruktive Argumentationstheorie*, Stuttgart: Fr. Frommann Verlag.

Bernstein, R. J. (1983) *Beyond Objectivism and Relativism*, Philadelphia: University of Pennsylvania Press.

Bertilsson, M. (1978) *Toward a Social Reconstruction of Science Theory Peirce's Theory of Inquiry, and Beyond*, Lund.

Böhler, D. (1983) *Rekonstruktive Pragmatik und Hermeneutik*, Habil. Schrift Philos. Fakultät der Universität des Saarlandes 1981, Frankfurt a.M.: Suhrkamp, 1985.

Böhler, D. (1991) "Menschenwürde und Menschentötung. Über Diskursethik und utilitaristische Ethik", *Zeitschrift für Evangelische Ethik*, 35:166–186.

Böök, L. (1979) "Argumentation och giltighet". In T. Nordenstam and G. Skirbekk (eds.) *Kommunikasjon og moral*, Department of Philosophy, University of Bergen.

Dallmayr, W. (1974) *Materialien zu Habermas' "Erkenntnis und Interesse"*, Frankfurt a.M.: Suhrkamp.

Gadamer, H. G., et al. (1971) *Hermeneutik und Ideologiekritik*, Frankfurt a.M.: Suhrkamp.

Habermas, J. (1967) "Zur Logik der Sozialwissenschaften". *Philosophische Rundschau*.

Habermas, J. (1968a) *Erkenntnis und Interesse*, Frankfurt a.M.: Suhrkamp. Second edition with a postscript 1973.

Habermas, J. (1968b) *Technik und Wissenschaft als 'Ideologie'*, Frankfurt a.M.: Suhrkamp.

Habermas, J. (1971a) "Vorbereitende Bemerkungen zu einer Theorie der kommunikativen Kompetenz". In J. Habermas und N. Luhmann, *Theorie der Gesellschaft oder Sozialtechnologie – Was leistet die Systemforschung?* Frankfurt a.M.: Suhrkamp.

Habermas, J. (1971b) "Theorie der Gesellschaft oder Sozialtechnologie?" In J. Habermas und N. Luhmann, *Theorie der Gesellschaft oder Sozialtechnologie?* Frankfurt a.M.: Suhrkamp.

Habermas, J. (1973a) "Wahrheitstheorien". In H. Fahrenbach (ed.), *Wirklichkeit und Reflexion. Walter Schulz zum 60. Geburtstag*. Pfullingen: Neske.

Habermas, J. (1973b) *Legitimationsprobleme im Spätkapitalismus*, Frankfurt a.M.: Suhrkamp.

Habermas, J. (1976a) "Was heißt Universalpragmatik?" In K.-O. Apel (ed.), *Sprachpragmatik und Philosophie*, Frankfurt a.M.: Suhrkamp.

Habermas, J. (1976b) *Zur Rekonstruktion des Historischen Materialismus*. Frankfurt a.M.: Suhrkamp.

Habermas, J. (1981) *Theorie des kommunikativen Handelns*, Frankfurt a.M.: Suhrkamp.

Habermas, J. (1983) "Diskursethik – Notizen zu einem Begründungsprogramm" and "Moralbewußtsein und kommunikatives Handeln". In J. Habermas, *Moralbewußtsein und kommunikatives Handeln*, Frankfurt a.M.: Suhrkamp. (Engl. transl. in *Moral Consciousness and Communicative Action* [= *MCCA*], Cambridge, Mass.: MIT Press, 1990.)

Habermas, J. (1984) *Vorstudien und Ergänzungen zur Theorie des kommuni-
- kativen Handelns*, Frankfurt a.M.: Suhrkamp.

Habermas, J. (1991) *Erläuterungen zur Diskursethik*, Frankfurt a.M.: Suhrkamp.

Habermas, J. (1992) *Faktizität und Geltung*, Frankfurt a.M.: Suhrkamp.

Hintikka, J. (1967) "Cogito, ergo sum: Inference or Performance?", in: W. Donney (ed.), *Descartes. A Collection of Critical Essays*, New York.

Höffe, 0. (1976) "Kritische Überlegungen zur Konsensustheorie der Wahrheit (Habermas)". *Philosophisches Jahrbuch*, 83. Also in O. Höffe, *Ethik und Politik*, Frankfurt a.M.: Suhrkamp, 1979.

Honneth, A. and H. Joas (eds.) (1986) *Kommunikatives Handeln*, Frankfurt a.M.: Suhrkamp.

Honneth, A., T. McCarthy and C. Offe (eds.) (1989) *Zwischenbetrachtungen*, Frankfurt a.M.: Suhrkamp.

Ilting, K.-H. (1976) "Geltung als Konsens". *Neue Hefte für Philosophie*, pp. 20–50.

Israel, J. (1990) *Sprache und Erkenntnis*, Frankfurt: Campus.

Kuhlmann, W. (1981) "Reflexive Letztbegründung", *Zeitschrift für Philosophische Forschung*, 35.

Kuhlmann, W. (1985) *Reflexive Letztbegründung*, Freiburg/Munich: Alber.

Kuhlmann, W. (ed.) (1988) *Zerstörung des moralischen Selbstbewußtseins: Chance oder Gefährdung? Praktische Philosophie in Deutschland nach dem Nationalsozialismus*, Frankfurt a.M.: Suhrkamp.

Mans, D. (1974) *Intersubjektivitätstheorien der Wahrheit*, Diss. Frankfurt a.M.

MacIntyre, A. (1981) *After Virtue*, Notre Dame: University of Notre Dame Press.

McCarthy, T. (1978) *The Critical Theory of Jürgen Habermas*, London: Hutchinson.

McCarthy, T. (1991) *Ideals and Illusions*, Cambridge, Mass.: MIT Press.

Oelmüller, W. (ed.) (1978) *Transzendentalphilosophie, Normenbegründung*. Paderborn: Schöningh.

Puntel, L. B. (1978) *Wahrheitstheorien in der neueren Philosophie*, Darmstadt: Wissenschaftliche Buchgesellschaft.

Schnädelbach, H. (1977) *Reflexion und Diskurs*, Frankfurt a.M: Suhrkamp.

Schönrich, G. (1981) *Kategorien und transzendentale Argumentation*, Frankfurt a.M.: Suhrkamp.

Skirbekk, G. (1992) *Eco-Philosophical Manuscripts*, Bergen: Ariadne.

Spaemann, R. (1972) "Die Utopie der Herrschaftsfreiheit", *Merkur* 292 (August).

Taylor, Ch. (1989) *Sources of the Self. The Making of Modern Identity*, Cambridge, Mass.: Harvard University Press.

Thompson, J. B. and D. Held (eds.) (1982) *Habermas. Critical Debates*, London: Macmillan.

Tugendhat, E. (1984) *Probleme der Ethik*, Stuttgart: Reclam.

Tranøy, K. E. (1967) "Asymmetries in Ethics", *Inquiry*, 10: 351–372.

Tranøy, K. E. (1976) "Norms of Inquiry: Methodologies as Normative Systems". In G. Ryle (ed.), *Contemporary Aspects of Philosophy*, London: Oriel.

Walzer, M. (1987) *Interpretation and Social Criticism*, Cambridge, Mass.: Harvard University Press.

Watt, A. J. (1975) "Transcendental Arguments and Moral Principles", *The Philosopohical Quarterly*, 25.

Wellmer, A. (1979) *Praktische Philosophie und Theorie der Gesellschaft. Zum Problem der normativen Grundlagen einer kritischen Sozialwissenschaft*. Konstanz: Universitätsverlag Konstanz.

Wellmer, A. (1986) "Zur Kritik der Diskursethik", "Über Vernunft, Emanzipation und Utopie", in: *Ethik und Dialog*, Frankfurt a.M.: Suhrkamp.

Wellmer, A. (1991) *Truth, Contingency, and Modernity*, ms.

2.   Apel (1975).

3.   Apel (1970), (1972), later published in Apel (1973).

4. Cf. also Habermas's extended interpretation of Peirce in Habermas (1968a), pp. 116–78.

5. Apel (1973), Vol. 1, pp. 22–52.

6. Apel (1973), Vol. 2, pp. 359–78.

7. As an introduction to Habermas's earlier development, cf. McCarthy (1978).

8. Cf. Habermas (1968a), also Habermas (1967), (1968b); the main contributions in this discussion are published in Dallmayr (1974).

9. Cf. Habermas (1968a) and his self-criticism on this point in the postscript of 1973.

10. Cf. Habermas (1971a), (1973a); see also Bernstein (1978).

11. Cf. his comments on Searle's shortcomings concerning normative justification and pragmatic undeniability, Apel (1976a), pp. 56 ff.

12. Cf. Apel (1970), or more recently Apel (1978), (1979), (1980).

13. Apel, e.g. in Oelmüller (1978), pp. 162, 165; cf. also Habermas (1971a), (1973a).

14. Cf. e.g. Apel (1973), Vol. 2, pp. 400–401.

15. E.g. Apel (1979).

16. Cf. e.g. Apel (1973), Vol. 1, pp. 138–66, Vol. 2, pp. 178–219.

17. Cf. also the Wittgensteinian argument against the possibility of private rules, often referred to by Apel, e.g. (1973), Vol. 2, p. 399.

18. Cf. Habermas (1976a), pp. 224 ff.

19. Apel (1973), Vol. 2, pp. 188 ff.

20. Cf. Apel's thesis about the "transformation of philosophy", Apel (1973), and Apel (1975b), p. 48 for a programmatic statement on Peirce in this perspective.

21. Cf. the so-called four universal validity claims in Habermas (1971a), (1973a).

22. For an elaboration of the problem of factuality versus normativity in Peirce, leading up to Apel, see Bertilsson (1978).

23. Cf. rational will-formation and need-interpretation, e.g. Apel (1973), Vol. 2, p. 425, and this creates some distance from the Kantian version. Cf. Habermas's discussions of the 'principle of universalization', e.g. Habermas (1983), pp. 75–76. See "Rationality and Contextuality" in this collection; cf. also "Eco-Crisis and the Welfare State" in Skirbekk (1992).

24. Cf. e.g. Apel (1976a), pp. 122–23, "vom methodischen Primat der Selbstbegründung des argumentativen Diskurses".

25. Cf. also Albert (1975) against Apel's transcendental argument.

26. Sinn-Kritik, e.g. Apel (1979), pp. 16 ff., (1973), Vol. 2, p. 173; in Oelmüller (1978), pp. 165–176. See discussion at the end of this essay.

27. See Apel (1979), p. 24.

28. Habermas (1973b), (1976b).

29. Cf. Apel (1973), Vol. 2, p. 429.

30. For the discussion of these problems, and for the discussion of the possibility of motivating those who do not participate in genuine normative discourse to become participants, see Apel et al. in Oelmüller (1978), e.g. pp. 160 ff.; for the relation between the use of argumentation in order to obtain an ultimate validation, and the use of argumentation in order to bring about will-formation and need-interpretation, see Habermas, e.g. (1976b), pp. 280 f., 330–32, 344.

31. From the general objections, see e.g. Albert (1975), Berk (1979), pp.
     160–65, Dallmayr, McCarthy et al. in Oelmüller (1978), e.g. pp. 29 ff.
     and 96, and Wellmer (1979), pp. 49–51.

32. Apel (1979), p. 4.

33. Apel (1976a), p. 123.

34. E.g. in Oelmüller (1978), p. 197.

35. Cf. Apel (1976b), pp. 155 ff.

36. E.g. McCarthy, in Oelmüller (1978), p. 96.

37. E.g. McCarthy, *ibid.* p. 205, and Schnädelbach (1977), pp. 140–72.

38. Apel (1979), pp. 8 ff., and Habermas (1973a), pp. 230–38.

39. Apel (1979), pp. 19–20.

40. Apel (1979), p. 1.

41. See Apel (1979), pp. 18–19.

42. *Ibid.*

43. Apel (1975a), pp. 51 ff.

44. Cf. Apel (1976a), pp. 94 ff., Habermas (1976a), pp. 198–204, and in
     Oelmüller (1978), e.g. pp. 190 ff., 207, and 225 ff.

45. Cf. Habermas (1983), pp. 106–108 (88–93). Cf. also the discussion at
     the end of "Rationality and Contextuality" in this collection.

46. Cf. Habermas (1973a), pp. 213 ff.

47. Habermas (1973a), p. 213.

48. Cf. Habermas (1973a), fn. 33.

49.   Habermas (1976a), p. 223.

50.   Cf. Habermas (1976a), p. 221.

51.   Habermas (1973a), p. 222.

52.   Cf. Habermas (1973a), pp. 215 ff.

53.   Habermas (1973a), pp. 215-18.

54.   Habermas (1973a), pp. 215 ff., pp. 231-34, Habermas (1968a), p. 382.

55.   E.g. Habermas (1973a), pp. 230-38.

56.   Cf. also p. 128 above, as well as critical remarks from Beckerman (1972), Höffe (1976), and Ilting (1976), and cf. Puntel (1978) who comes close to regarding Habermas as a coherence theoretician.

57.   Habermas (1973a), p. 222.

58.   Cf. Habermas (1973a), p. 221, Habermas (1976a), pp. 257-59.

59.   Habermas (1973a).

60.   "Freilich liegt es sozusagen in der Natur von Geltungsansprüchen, daß sie eingelöst werden können..." (my translation) Habermas (1973a), p. 239. ("Redeem" and "redemption" are standard translations of "einlösen" and "Einlösung".)

61.   "Die Herbeiführung eines Konsensus unter Bedingungen des Diskurses ist die'Handlungsweise', durch die ein diskursiver Geltungsanspruch eingelöst wird..." (my translation) Habermas (1973a), p. 239.

62.   Habermas (1973a), p. 239. This is the point from which Mans (1974) develops his criticism: Habermas betrays an intersubjectivist conception by bringing in qualifications.

63.   Habermas (1973a), p. 240.

64. Habermas (1973a), p. 214.

65. For a discussion of this notion, see e.g. Spaemann (1972).

66. Habermas (1973a), pp. 240–59.

67. Cf. his discussions on the notion of a lifeworld, Habermas (1981), and (1992) (Ch. I,ii).

68. Habermas (1973a), p. 255.

69. Habermas (1973a), p. 257. Finally, there is a distinction between discourse and therapy, i.e. between validation and efforts to establish the personal conditions for discourse. Cf. Habermas (1973a), p. 259. Cf. also a distinction between "inquiring (judgmental) discourse" and "forming (pedagogical, therapeutic) discourse".

70. Cf. Habermas (1968a) postscript.

71. Habermas (1973a), pp. 246–53.

72. Habermas (1973a), p. 255. Habermas has later revised his position, admitting that a discursively obtained consensus cannot have the status a criterion of validity, cf. Honneth (1986), p. 352.

73. Example borrowed from L. Böök (1979).

74. Habermas (1973a), p. 242.

75. "Paradigmata der Erkenntnis, anhand deren der Sinn von Wahrheit expliziert werden kann, sind nicht die Wahrnehmungen oder singulären Aussagen, in denen Wahrnehmungen mitgeteilt werden, sondern generelle, negative und modale Aussagen." (My translation) Habermas (1973a), pp. 232 f.

76. Habermas (1973a), p. 240.

77. Habermas (1973a), p. 240.

78. Cf. Wellmer (1979), pp. 44 ff.

79. Habermas (1973a), p. 257.

80. Cf. e.g. Ilting (1976), Schnädelbach (1977).

81. Habermas (1971b), p. 201.

82. Cf. Gadamer's criticism of the ideal speech situation along these lines, e.g. Gadamer (1971), pp. 316–17, and also Böhler (1974), pp. 369 ff.

83. Cf. Gadamer (1971).

84. Oelmüller (1978), p. 126.

85. Cf. Habermas's critical remarks on hermeneuticians of Gadamer's type, concerning the natural-rights issue, in Habermas (1976b), p. 296.

86. Regarding similar arguments (from the perspective of feminism and 'the concrete other'), cf. Seyla Benhabib (1992), e.g. p. 163. On (linguistic) contextuality, cf., e.g., Alasdair MacIntyre (1981); Michael Walzer (1987); Charles Taylor (1989).

87. "Die Aporie dieser Ansätze liegt darin, daß sie entweder die Wahrheit von historischer Zufälligkeit abhängig machen, das heißt dem verzerrenden Zugriff von Rhetorik, Suggestion, Manipulation, Täuschung und Selbsttäuschung aussetzen; dann aber geht der Invarianzanspruch von Wahrheit verloren. Oder sie führen normative Qualifikationen des Konsenses ein, Qualifikationen, die wie: unbegrenzte Forschergemeinschaft (Peirce), kritische Nachprüfung kompetenter Beurteiler (Kamlah, Lorenzen), potentielle oder begründete Zustimmung (Habermas) bei näherem Zusehen erstens kein operationales Legitimationskriterium darstellen und zweitens das Charakteristische von Konsens auflösen: das Resultat eines geschichtlichen Einigungsprozesses konkreter Personen (und nicht abstrakter Kommunikatoren) zu sein." (My translation) Höffe (1976), p. 272.

88. To avoid misunderstandings it should be explicitly stated that these various forms of obligation to rationality do not imply any obligation to seek consensus *tout court* – on the contrary, during the validating process we are obliged to seek arguments, and counterarguments, and thereby promote *dissent*. Only a consensus that emerges through this self-critical process can be said to be sought in a rational discourse.

89. Cf. "Ecological Crisis and Technological Expertise" in Skirbekk (1992).

90. Cf. e.g. Albrecht Wellmer on consensus and argument, Wellmer (1986), pp. 82–112.

91. The term "consensus theory" (and maybe even the term "discourse theory") should perhaps be avoided, in favor of "theory of arguments" or "theory of argumentation".

92. Cf. e.g. the lively discussions in Oelmüller (1978), between Apel, Habermas, Höffe, Kuhlmann, Lübbe, McCarthy, *et al.* Cf. also the contributions in Held/Thompson (1982) with a reply from Habermas. Also Bernstein (1983), Wellmer (1986), McCarthy (1991), Benhabib (1992). Finally the *Auseinandersetzung* between Apel and Habermas in Habermas (1983) and Honneth (1989) and Habermas (1991) [pp. 190 ff.], to which we will return in "Modernization of the Lifeworld" and "Rationality and Contextuality".

93. Cf. the essay "Arguments from Absurdity", but here arguments from absurdity are applied in a *pragmatic* perspective.

94. That is, Habermas envisages a revision of his attempt to "describe the presuppositions of argumentation as the defining characteristics of an ideal speech situation"; though "[t]he intention of my earlier analysis still seems correct to me, namely the reconstruction of the general symmetry conditions that every competent speaker who believes he is engaging in an argumentation must presuppose as adequately fulfilled". Habermas (1983), pp. 98–99; English translation from *Moral Consciousness and Communicative Action*, Cambridge, Mass.: MIT Press, 1990, p. 88.

95. To which we will return in the two closing essays.

96. Hence the difference between Apel and Habermas is broadening. Habermas's move toward comprehensive reconstructive analyses, which are explicitly fallible, prompts a reaction in Apel on behalf of "ultimate justification" through "strict reflection". Cf. Apel already in Oelmüller (1978), e.g. pp. 190 ff.: "Dann hat mich auch der Rückgang auf den sogenannten *objektiven Vorgänge* irritiert" (p. 191). In Apel (1989) the division between the two is directly addressed, provoked ("schockiert", p. 26) by Habermas's incautious remarks about our everyday moral intuitions as being (basically) in order as they are (Habermas [1983], p. 108, transl. *MCCA* p. 98). This is an important point since it is decisive for the question of the relation between politics and philosophy: Whereas Rorty repeatedly refers to the primacy of the former, Apel – referring to the Nazi experience (Apel [1989], p. 27) – insists on the primacy of the latter (cf. e.g. Apel in Kuhlmann ed. (1988): "Zurück zur Normalität? Oder können wir aus der nationalen Katastrophe etwas Besonderes gelernt haben? Das Problem des (welt-)geschichtlichen Übergangs zur postkonventionellen Moral in spezifisch deutscher Sicht", and Rorty, "Der Vorrang der Demokratie vor der Philosophie", *ibid.*). At this point I find that Apel is right, though the question is how the problem of philosophical justification should best be understood, and this is where Apel and Habermas disagree. We will return to this disagreement in the two closing essays.

97. I for one doubt that this distinction is tenable, cf. the discussion in the two concluding essays.

98. Habermas (1983), pp. 75–76, (transl. *MCCA*, p. 65).

99. Cf. e.g. Wellmer (1986), pp. 51–69; along the same lines, Benhabib (1992), pp. 26 ff.
     Cf. the discussion of "interest" in different kinds of "moral subjects" (*Betroffene*): what about the interests of future generations (hypothetic non-existent persons) and what about the different kinds of "interests" or "strivings" in non-human beings? (Cf. "Ethical Gradualism and Discourse Ethics" in this collection; especially to the principle of universalization, see *ibid.* note 14.)

100. Habermas (1983), p. 76 (transl. *MCCA*, p. 66).

101. *Ibid.* p. 103 (p. 93).

102. *Ibid.*, e.g. referring to Schönrich (1981).

103. *Ibid.* 106 (pp. 95–96); Schönrich (1981), pp. 196–200.

104. Cf. e.g. Apel (1986). Also Böhler (1983) and Kuhlmann (1985).

105. Cf. e.g. Apel (1988), also Böhler (1991) with further refinements of the distinctions between justification, hermeneutic application and strategic application.

106. E.g. Apel (1980/81).

107. Cf. Böhler (1991), p. 167. Also Kuhlmann (1985).

108. Cf. the section "The transcendental-pragmatic notion of validity" in this essay.

109. Cf. Apel (1973).

110. Hintikka's analysis is here crucial, Hintikka (1967). Apel's reference to Aristotle, cf. e.g. in Oelmüller (1976), p. 197. His reference to Descartes, e.g. *ibid.* pp. 225–226.

111. Cf. the section "The universal-pragmatic notion of validity" in this essay.

112. Habermas (1983), p. 106 (transl. p. 96).

113. At this point I will not enter into the discussion of whether such a philosophy is possible after the pragmatic/linguistic turn. See the two closing essays.

114. I will not here enter into the discussion of whether there are transitions between reflection and discourse. (See closing essay.)

115. E.g., Apel (1973), II, p. 416: "Daraus folgt m.E., daß der Akzeptierung der moralischen Grundnorm selbst der modale Charakter des *Sollens* zukommt – unter der Bedingung allerdings, daß die Fragen der philosophischen Grundlagendiskussion – ja überhaupt irgendwelche Fragen

– sinnvoll gestellt werden *sollen*. Diese Voraussetzung aber ist – wie wir bereits feststellten – nicht die Bedingung eines hypothetischen Imperatives, denn sie kann gar nicht *sinnvoll* negiert werden, wenn nicht die Diskussion selbst aufgehoben werden soll." Also Apel (1989), p. 20, fn. 7: "Das entscheidende, sinnkritische Argument gegen diese Möglichkeit lautet: Wenn .... dies eintreten würde, könnte man nicht mehr verstehen, was .... überhaupt bedeutet; ...". *Ibid.* p. 21, referring critically to Habermas: "Diese ["Bedingungen der Kommunikation" in Habermas] sind offenbar nur insofern *notwendig* und *universal gültig*, als sie sich bis jetzt als 'alternativenlos' erwiesen hat." "Aus der Sicht der Transzendentalpragmatik muß man hier natürlich die Frage stellen, wie es sinnvoll möglich sein soll, die im Diskursprinzip explizierten *Präsuppositionen* von Begriffen wie *Überprüfung* (qua Falisifikationsversuch) empirisch zu überprüfen." *Ibid.* p. 43: "Der Verweis auf die Möglichkeit der definitiven Beurteilung war ja schon die Pointe des als Sinnkriterium konzipierten Verifikationsprinzips." And p. 49, referring to the importance of the "Verfahren der versuchsweisen Herleitung eines *performativen Selbstwiderspruchs*": "Hier kommt m.E. freilich alles auf die Einsicht an, daß man das gemeinte Verfahren – als solches einer transzendentalreflexiven Letztbegründung durch *reductio ad absurdum* der Bestreitung von Prinzipienaussagen – überhaupt nur auf der höchsten epistemologischen und argumentationstheoretischen Reflexionsstufe – also nur auf der Stufe der *Selbstreflexion des argumentativen Diskurses* -, und nicht etwa auf der Stufe der *theoretischen Aussagen über lebensweltliche Kommunikation* anwenden kann. Nur für den Philosophierenden, der auf die unbestreitbaren Voraussetzungen der Argumentation als solcher reflektiert und darin sozusagen den ersten Zug im transzendentalpragmatischen Sprachspiel begreift, sind die notwendigen Voraussetzungen ('Präsuppositionen') der Kommunikation qua Argumentation *methodisch nichthintergehbar*; ..."

116. Cf. "Arguments from Absurdity".

117. Tranøy (1976).

118. Tranøy (1976), p. 8: "If X knows that *p* is true in the sense that he knows a proof for *p*, it is odd to say that it is obligatory for X to accept *p*. It is, rather, in that case impossible for X not to accept *p*." Cf. the notion of the force of the better argument.

119. Tranøy (1976), p. 8: "It is reasonable, then that it should be second-hand knowledge which is surrounded by methodological norms".

120. Some well-known questions (from theology and philosophy): Would this be the idea of an omnipotent god, obtaining all knowledge and insight first-hand? If this being operated alone, how could he have a private language? If he were not eternal, but born, how could he alone acquire a language and a social identity?

121. On this asymmetry, in favor of the "negative", cf. Tranøy (1967).

122. For the "application" of the position, cf. e.g. Skirbekk (1992).

123. Cf. Apel (1976b), pp. 151 ff.

124. Cf. in the former essay on 'arguments from absurdity'.

125. For further discussions, cf. e.g. Apel (1980–81), Böhler (1983), Habermas (1981), (1983) and (1991), Kuhlmann (1981), Thompson/Held (1982), Wellmer (1986) and (1991).

Madness and Reason

Reductio ad Pathologicum as a *Via Negativa* for Elucidating the Universal-Pragmatic Notion of Rationality?

I shall try here to elucidate the notion of rationality by focusing on cases of irrationality.[1] To be more specific, I shall pursue a kind of *via negativa*, by concentrating on various thought-experiments about mental disorders, in order to illuminate a transcendental-pragmatic or universal-pragmatic notion of rationality (found in various versions in Apel and in Habermas).[2] In other words I will try out "arguments from absurdity"[3] in the form of thought-experiments concerning psychopathological breakdowns of fundamental human capacities. My aim is reflectively to illuminate the status of this pragmatic notion of rationality.[4]

In order to locate the discussion in its wider discursive context three points should be emphasized:

(a) In talking about "arguments from absurdity", or *reductio ad absurdum* arguments, I do *not* have the *formal* versions of such arguments in mind, where absurdities are analyzed in terms of formal contradictions. Rather, the kinds of absurdity I have in mind are substantial ones, like category mistakes, contextual inconsistencies and pragmatic contradictions. I even take it that we can talk about degrees of absurdities, starting from increasingly unreasonable factual mistakes and leading over to clear-cut absurdities (e.g. from cases like "some dogs are by nature green" to "some dogs have an IQ of 65", and further to "some dogs read simple texts", "some dogs read textbooks in philosophy", and "some dogs have a Ph.D. in philosophy").[5]

(b) Instead of elucidating a notion of psychopathology (mental illness) by means of a notion of rationality, I will try *the other way around*, to elucidate a notion of rationality (a universal-pragmatic notion of rationality) by means of a notion of psychopathology. I take it for granted that in our society there is some consensus about what counts as a psychopathological disorder, at least when it is found in its extreme cases. I will rely on such an assumption of some common notion of mental disorder. I go no further in trying to analyze or criticize such a notion of psychopathology, e.g. working out its various hidden presuppositions about rationality and normativity. No attempt at a mutual hermeneutic clarification of notions of rationality and of mental health, or better, of irrationality and of mental illness, is undertaken in this chapter. I deliberately confine myself to the simple task of trying to carry out this *one-way* step, by elucidating a pragmatic notion of rationality through some vague, but, it is to be hoped, commonly used (and acceptable) notion of irrationality in terms of psychopathological disorder.

(c) In doing this I distinguish my discussion of irrationality and mental illness from discussions of historical processes of learning and of rationalization. Some version of *modern* society is my explicit background. I talk about fully socialized individuals in such societies, not of children. In short, I do not want to enter into a discussion of psychopathology in a developmental perspective.

In all its crudeness, the problem is the following: how is the universality of the pragmatic notion of rationality to be understood?[6] First, can this notion of rationality be fruitfully elucidated and somehow supported by a *via negativa*, in terms of arguments from absurdity? Second, can absurdities in this case, as a first step, be elucidated in terms of psychopathological disorders?

As we have seen (in "Pragmatism and Pragmatics"), both Apel and Habermas argue for the universality of a pragmatic notion of rationality.[7] They both share the view that there are universal pragmatic competences related to four differentiated universal validity claims. But they hold somewhat different views concerning the nature of this universality. Apel tends to focus on the universality of argumentative reason and in so doing to stress the self-referential inconsistency inherent in any attempt at argumentatively rejecting what he sees as preconditions for argumentation.[8] However, this self-referential approach is linked to the argumentative activity itself, telling us what is irrefutably given in such situations but without showing how this is related to non-argumentative communication. This is the point where a universal pragmatics based on speech acts comes in, holding that there are, at a fundamental level inherent in standard speech acts, universal validity claims, viz. about meaningfulness, truth, rightness and authenticity, and that there are universal-pragmatic competences enabling the speakers to raise and to redeem these validity claims. But even if some general validity claims might be reconstructively recognized in all kinds of speech acts by philosophers of our culture, these validity claims are certainly not always acknowledged as such by all people in all cultures.[9] The question is then whether empirical and historical relativism can be overcome on a deeper level, i.e. on a universal-pragmatic level.[10]

Let us now approach this universalistic claim, as found in Apel and to some extent in Habermas.

We start with the following case. A police officer presents a report about a car accident, but to the question where the accident took place he says that it just occurred without occurring anywhere – and to the question of its time he says that it just occurred, but not at any definite moment – and finally to the question of possible causes he declares that there were no causes, the accident just occurred. Such a person does not commit merely an empirical mistake; to the extent that he is serious in saying all this, he can be said to be deeply confused. What he says is quite unthinkable. He is out of his mind. This rough "argument from absurdity" indicates some notion of irrefutability or unavoidability: location in time and space, and causes, are conditions for the meaningfulness of any talk about car accidents – they are not merely empirical conditions, but somehow necessary conditions. In this sense, arguments from absurdity are useful for a discussion of the epistemological status of "transcendental preconditions".

In a similar way we can discuss the presumably universal status of the four basic validity claims in Habermas and Apel, i.e.

meaningfulness, truth, rightness and authenticity. A person who speaks has to know the difference between what is meaningful and what is not – viz. in the sense that he implicitly masters this distinction in principle, which is not to say that the person does not make mistakes now and then concerning its correct application. In the same way this performer of speech acts must have a notion of what is reality and what is not, what is right and what is not, and of when he is lying or simulating. If a person not only makes mistakes in applying these distinctions, but simply has not acquired an ability to master these distinctions while speaking, he seems to be mentally impaired or seriously confused.

So far such arguments can in principle provide some clarification and support for the universal pragmatic view. However, this has been achieved only at a relatively vague and general level. To return for a moment to our car accident and the presumed universality of the constitutive nature of the principles of time, space and causality: isn't it possible, i.e. thinkable, that some guru in India, who has not been brought up with Newtonian physics, might claim that certain events occur without causes, or that there is a happy human life beyond time and space? It is, of course, very difficult for us to imagine how this could be conceived as intelligible. But a reference to such counterexamples does indicate the kinds of cases and thought-experiments that have to be handled in order to avoid doubt as to the claimed universality of these principles.

My point is just that we must remind ourselves of how such relativist objections may also be raised against a universal pragmatic conception of necessary basic competences. Even if some distinction between meaningfulness and meaninglessness can be said to be universal,[11] one has not thereby ruled out a possible diversity of opinions as to what characterizes meaningfulness and meaninglessness. The same holds true with regard to the distinction between reality and irreality. This distinction allows for various ontologies, for culturally different conceptions of what is and what is not. One important question here is whether one allows for magic, i.e. whether words and reality are conceived of as differentiated, whether an influence on natural processes is conceived of as requiring more than mere speech.

We may extend this point to the remaining validity claims. Even if notions of being truthful and trustworthy, and of practices and routines being reliable, can be said to be necessarily present in all societies (i.e. for all speakers), the *content* of these notions has certainly varied a lot throughout history. This also holds true as to the way one differentiates between nature and culture, i.e. between laws of nature (causality) and social and moral laws (obligations and institutions), and as to the way the self is differentiated from others, and from nature. The concrete way in which these factors are differentiated is certainly a question of cultural variation, and of historical development.

This leads us to the conclusion that even if one allows for the universality of pragmatically rooted validity claims, as Apel and Habermas do, this does not take us that far, since the actual meaning of these distinctions varies culturally and historically. Despite the self-referential unavoidability of argumentative reason, and despite the general universality of pragmatic competences connected to the four above-mentioned validity claims, there still remains a problem of relativity when it comes to its actual content in each case.

At this point Habermas, in certain contrast to his more purely philosophically oriented colleague Apel, tries to establish *developmental* evidence for the universality of this pragmatically rooted rationality (as we shall see in the closing chapters):[12] the universality of basic pragmatic competences is not merely sought through a cross-cultural comparison on the empirical level; it is argued for in a developmental perspective, both ontogenetically and phylogenetically.[13] Historically (phylogenetically) this means that there are stages in a developmental logic of learning, leading from societies with relatively few institutional and conceptual differentiations toward post-conventional societies with widely developed institutional differentiations and reflective forms of learning and of solving questioned validity claims. This implies that the pragmatic competences for raising and redeeming universal validity claims in modern societies have reached a level where these competences are actualized universally. In this state of modernization – embracing a higher stage in argumentative and communicative competence as well as in scientific and technological problem solving – not only have mythological narratives, but also universalizing worldviews, lost their plausibility. What remains trustworthy is a procedural notion of free and argumentative reason.

Furthermore, there are at this stage various conceptual differentiations, such as that between language and reality (making magic unacceptable), that between nature and society (separating laws of nature from political and moral laws, or *is* from *ought*), and that between tradition and validity (making immanent justification implausible and pointing toward a reflective justification of principles). This is not to deny that irrationality and immorality exist in modern society; they certainly do! But, to the extent that this pragmatic universality can be argued for in this developmental perspective, it does imply that there are some general and irreversible obligations to rationality inherent in modern societies.

This bold attempt at reconciling thoughts in Hegel and the Enlightenment with those of Piaget and Kohlberg, and with classical sociologists of modernity (Durkheim, Weber, Parsons), remains controversial; these are themes which are subject for discussion, even when presented by Habermas as supporting a universal (or "formal") pragmatic notion of rationality. Whether or not they turn out to support this pragmatic theory I leave undecided; I only want to refer to the Habermasian theory of development in order to recall the special status of the universality claim in this theory. It is, for Habermas (more than for Apel), a kind of "conditioned" or historically situated universality.[14] Hence it does not claim that a breakdown in some of the universal pragmatic competences is equally devastating in all cultures, but it does claim that in modern societies a defect in these competences represents a recognized distortion. At least in more extreme cases, a general consensus about such disorders should thus be expected.

My question here is whether or not the status of such generally recognized extreme distortions can fruitfully be analyzed in terms of mental disorders, relying on a "common consensus" concerning the clear-cut cases, even when uncertainty and dissent occur as soon as borderline cases are approached. I want to see whether psychopathological breakdowns can reasonably be said to represent disorders of a generally accepted kind, indicating a consensus in modern societies about the universal nature of the standard use of these competences. For this I must certainly rely on some intuitions as to what works and what does not – or rather, I will have to try out my (our?) notions on this material, opening these for further discussion and criticism. In this sense I enter a hermeneutic process where my own presuppositions play an active role.

A reservation is required, since psychopathological breakdown is only one possibility when something (according to our notions) does not function, the other possibility being underdevelopment, viz. that a certain stage of modernity has not yet been reached (phylogenetically or ontogenetically). In my thought-experiments I will take it for granted that a high developmental level of modernization has in fact been attained. But in any test of the various actual cases the assumption that modernity has been attained certainly remains an open question.

I will proceed in three (overlapping) steps:

(1) Competence of action,
(2) Communicative competence and argumentative competence,
(3) Situational competence.

Competence of Action

In order to act we must certainly have developed various abilities, e.g. related to our body and to things we can move and change, and thereby related to ego identity and to other human beings, with an interwoven net of cognitive, emotive and linguistic skills, embedded in a shared form of life – for one thing, with notions of time and purpose – all this in various cultural versions.

There are different ways of classifying types of action in modern societies (and the classifications may be presented as being more or less analytic or realistic.)[15] In this chapter I would like to align myself with Habermas in emphasizing a differentiation between actions oriented toward effect (purposive action) and actions oriented toward mutual understanding (communicative action). For the time being, I will do this regardless of the question of the deeper nature of this distinction. I merely presume that this broad differentiation makes sense for my present project.

Habermas maintains that both types of action can be rationalized. Actions toward effects are rationalized by improving our purposive capacity, which in systematic form is achieved when science shows us which means can lead us most effectively to our given goals – a knowledge which is highly developed through technology. To the extent that these sciences and technologies make progress, we can talk about a rationalization of these purposive actions. Sociologically, this goes together with the differentiation of economy and politics as social institutions. Actions oriented toward mutual understanding imply that other people are recognized as co-subjects, and not merely as means for "my" projects. These actions, too, can be improved, or rationalized. This takes place when the basic pragmatic competences, viz. the abilities to raise and redeem the universal validity claims of intelligibility, truth, rightness and authenticity, have reached a stage where free and reflective argumentation has become possible. In this sense the highest level of communicative competence, inherent in these actions oriented toward understanding, is related to argumentative competence, and thus to the possibility of argumentative rationalization – as we shall see in the next section.

Since we always have some distinction between co-subjects and things, one might argue that some distinction between purposive and communicative action is (at least tacitly) present in all societies – at least in relatively clear-cut paradigm cases, even when there are uncertainties about various forms of borderline cases. No matter how much a society might be penetrated by magic or animism, there *have to* be *some* (tacit) notions about "what works in work", i.e. about what efforts lead us to results satisfying our vital needs. This is necessarily so, despite the possibly magic nature of the overall frame of understanding in a given society. In short, it is hard to see how one could avoid some distinction between (animated) phenomena with whom one communicates and (nonanimated) phenomena with which this is not the case, even if spirits and some vaguely differentiated parts of nature (such as sacred animals) are conceived of as belonging to the former group.

But whatever might be the cross-cultural universality of this distinction, my point so far is based on the developmental hypothesis of the universality of some such distinction in *modern* societies: in such societies there is at least implicitly some paradigmatic distinction (institutionally and conceptually) between communicative and purposive actions. This is the assumption from which I start.

If, for instance, a peasant or a fisherman seriously tries to *talk to* the storms in order to get them to understand that it is desirable that they leave the area, we take it that the modern reaction would be that this person is out of his mind. If this kind of behavior is permanent and extended, the person will probably be regarded as mad. We, modern man, know that we cannot verbally communicate with natural forces.

If the same person carries out rituals to stop the storms, the overall reaction will probably be the same, though in this case his action can be interpreted as a strategic speech act and not an attempt to communicate with the winds. If a person in a modern society starts to behave in this way, we take it that he will be regarded as crazy or at least irrational. If a group of people behaves in this way, I take it that the general reaction will probably be the same, but in this case one might perhaps ask whether this is a backward subculture which remains unenlightened and undeveloped within a modern society.

When it comes to prayers, I suppose that reactions vary from acceptance to rejection. According to a strict interpretation of Habermas's developmental scheme, prayers are to be classified as intellectualized magical actions, which have gradually lost their plausibility as the modern world has become rationalized: substantial worldviews, in intellectualized religions and in metaphysics, have lost their rational authority; only a scientific and a procedural-argumentative rationality can plausibly be regarded as the final court of appeal.

This Habermasian view, however, can hardly be said to have full empirical support, at least not at the immediately empirical level. As a matter of fact, a lot of people in our modern societies do not regard prayers as crazy or irrational, nor are prayers regarded in this way in our psychiatric institutions (perhaps in contrast to what was the case in Soviet psychiatry).[16]

There is certainly more to be said about this. For instance there is a distinction between what might be called naive prayers, resembling magical speech acts (e.g. with the purpose of obtaining concrete benefits), and what is more like an expression of a religious attitude toward life (without an effect-oriented expectation). To avoid such immediate empirical objections, Habermas may maintain that the developmental thesis delineates the dominant trend which lies underneath the immediate descriptive phenomena: modernity is on its way, but it has not yet reached everyone! Such a move, from a Habermasian standpoint, would be all right, but it would then imply that this (deep level) version of the developmental thesis can be sufficiently supported by other ("non-empirical") arguments.

We have now briefly looked at cases where the communicative form of action invades the effect-oriented form of action. It might also be the other way around: a person acts in a purposive manner in cases where communication is generally supposed to be the adequate form of action. A classical case is the one of pretending friendship in order to obtain personal benefits in terms of power or money. The person might either deliberately manipulate other people, or he might deceive himself as a result of a distorted self-understanding. In its milder versions this kind of behavior raises

moral objections, in its more serious versions we tend to regard it
as pathological. Our reactions in each case may differ according to
our moral principles and to our understanding of the situation. But
as we move toward the extremes, we all tend to regard them as
cases of pathology rather than of moral disgrace. On the other
hand, when we disregard the extremes, which are the more clear-
cut paradigm cases, we have the problem of balancing between
moral and pathological perspectives.

Severe forms of self-deception in this field will be conceived of
as cases of mental illness, not merely as moral problems, nor
simply as a lack of development – though such a mental disorder
may be explained by reference to unsolved problems of individual
development.

If in a society there is a general tendency for the ratio between
these two forms of actions to be distorted, e.g. in the form of a
relative hypertrophy of actions oriented toward effects, this society
itself, and not only its individual members, can be said to be pathological, or abnormally developed.

Before we leave this section on pragmatic competence it may be
useful to emphasize some other points, so that our exposition does
not give too unbalanced an impression. Of course the various abilities which I will here analytically treat in different sections (a, b
and c) are interwoven; there are overlaps between emotive expressi-
vity, co-subjectivity, and lifeworld.

(a) In acting for mutual understanding some appropriate forms
for expressing one's emotions and longings are often required, both
in order to let others experience who one is and in order to get
reactions from others, so that one better understands who one is
(and who they are). Emotions and self-exposition are thus important within the frame of communicative interaction.

(b) The essential role of the others is thereby already indicated.
The other is not only the person to whom one speaks, but also the
person who takes part in correcting and forming one's own self-
understanding. Co-subjectivity is crucial.

(c) This internal relationship to co-subjects is further extended
into the realm of shared dealings, especially those dealings which

are necessary for our common survival, viz. the required dealings of work and reproduction. But here, certainly, there are cultural and historical differences. Typical for modernity are institutions like the economic and the political system, which cannot be adequately grasped with our concepts for everyday dealings but require theoretically developed concepts.[17] We may say that the lifeworld is the realm which in principle is understood or at least can be made understandable by hermeneutic elaboration, i.e. by means of the concepts embedded in our everyday dealings. Our identity in the lifeworld is co-determined by traditional norms and values and by the normative principles related to argumentative reason. The realm where theoretically mediated concepts are required and where socialization takes place by structures of divided labor and of purposive actions on the market, indicates roughly what Habermas calls the "system".[18] However, *de facto* we certainly move across these realms all the time, yet analytically they can be distinguished since they represent differences in institutionalization and conceptualization. "Modern times" are characterized by the necessity of mastering both realms. If we fail we get two kinds of problem. We get problems of governing, related to the realm of the system, and we experience a shrinking of the cultural richness of the lifeworld, through various forms of alienation. In order to live rationally and humanly in modern societies, we have to master reasonably well both these realms and their mutual relationships in a plurality of old and new situations.

I briefly sum up: in order to perform speech acts, a network of competences is required. For one thing we have to master some distinction between acts oriented toward effects and acts oriented toward understanding – mere communication without any acts for useful purposes would be detrimental to our survival, and only effect-oriented acts without any interaction would be devastating for the development of our identity and our mutual understanding. However, a specific differentiation between these two forms of action, each with its typical form of rational progress, belongs to modernity. In modern societies various forms of denial and rejection of this distinction imply unreasonable or pathological results

– as, on the one hand, in cases of assumed communication with inorganic nature, or on the other, in cases of exclusive strategic behavior in the realm of primary socialization. But in saying this I do presuppose a modern notion of reason and of mental normality, i.e. the conception of what is psychopathological is itself culturally situated.

Communicative and Argumentative Competence

In our everyday "doings" and "sayings" there is normally an amount of mutual reliability and trustworthiness. To the extent that we interact with each other as co-subjects we presuppose accountability – which is not to say that lies, unreliable deeds or manipulative attitudes are ruled out, nor is anything empirically said as to the frequency of such phenomena (though somewhere there is some lower level as to what a society can tolerate without itself disintegrating). What I emphasize here is the circumstance that these failures are logically secondary in relation to the mutual recognition of accountability (just as lying is parasitical on telling the truth, since one cannot lie if one does not assume that the other person assumes that one is telling the truth).

A person who is not at all accountable in what he does and says does not participate in society in a human way. Other people may react with moral dismissal, or even with therapeutic attitudes – the latter more and more frequently as the cases become more extreme; at some point the person tends to be regarded as diseased.

Now, I am again talking in a general way and without reference to modern societies in particular. In modern societies, we may say, not only do people (explicitly or implicitly) raise claims of universal validity, they have reached a stage where they conceive of the rational redemption of these claims in terms of argumentative procedures in enlightened freedom. In my discussion I will first focus on communicative competence and then on argumentative competence, even if they mutually refer to each other.

The truth claim may take the form of stating or of presupposing that something is the case, or of supposing that some set of actions will effectively lead to a certain goal. To state or suppose such things without being willing to give the reasons which one takes to be sufficient support, in situations where such a request is appropriate, will normally be seen as strange. If in such situations one is unable to take any adequate step to give such reasons one will normally be regarded as irrational – though it is not irrational to try but fail, i.e. to learn that one was wrong.

For modernity, with its deeply recognized cultural and institutional plurality, the *final* appeal in normative questions is an argumentatively achieved consensus among free and enlightened participants (embracing all those who are touched by the normative issue under discussion, to the extent that these persons are available, physically and intellectually).[19]

Truthfulness and authenticity are normally presupposed in communication as part of mutually recognized accountability, though the correctness of this presupposition is not tested in argumentation but in co-existence over some time, so that possible personal inconsistencies can be experienced. Therapy and improved socialization can correct for a lack of such abilities.

In the same way, meaningfulness, understood as intelligibility of language and of its use in concrete situations, is presupposed in communication – though piecemeal clarification is often required to overcome partial misunderstanding, and reflective discussion of the adequacy of inherent concepts and preconditions can turn out to be necessary in more severe cases.

Habermas speaks not only of communicative competence related to these four universal validity claims. He speaks also of a similar set of 'worlds': the 'objective world', the 'social world', the 'inner world', and even 'language'.[20] It should not be necessary to add that these 'worlds' are *de facto* interrelated.

These so-called worlds are not primarily presented as ontological categories but as world attitudes: the objective world embraces what we grasp in an objectifying (or propositional) attitude. The social world embraces norms and co-subjects conceived in a performative mode, i.e. as valid norms and mutually recognized co-subjects.[21]

With a changing attitude a phenomenon may "change its world": social phenomena seen in a propositional attitude switch over into the objective world. If one by chance becomes an animist, phenomena which earlier belonged to the objective world are now moved over into the social world.

The inner world is that to which the subject itself has a unique access. If language is classified as a world *per se,* it is a 'world' which has to be conceived of in its full pragmatic dimension, i.e. as constituted by action.

I will briefly comment on these four communicative competences and their related 'worlds', emphasizing how these pragmatic abilities can be illuminated through thought-experiments about psychopathological distortions.

The objective world

A person unable to distinguish between what is true and what is not either has not obtained the communicative competence of raising truth claims or this competence has been distorted in his case. Psychopathologically this can be observed in the person's opinions and in his actions.

In his opinion the distinction between reality and illusion has broken down, which in its extreme cases is a typical characteristic of schizophrenia. In actual cases such a blackout may be more or less partial or total, but in all these various cases it is reasonable to interpret the distortions as some kind of breakdown in the pragmatic ability to master truth claims.

Such a distortion may take different forms, e.g. negligence in undertaking what is necessary in order to survive, or illusory acts trying to master illusory problems. Since the validity claims of actions oriented toward effects is one of technological truth, i.e.

about what means lead to what ends, a distortion in the ability to master truth claims will also affect the ability to act adequately in this purposive sense. A distortion in this communicative competence therefore implies a distortion in purposive (or strategic) competence. This can take various forms, e.g. different forms of inability to plan and to carry out necessary work. Such inabilities imply a need for care, whereby the person gets treated as a patient, and the notion of mental illness is close at hand.

This distortion can also take the opposite direction, i.e. overly strategic actions. This, again, shows how a distortion in this communicative competence goes together with a distortion in the competence to act properly concerning actions oriented toward effects, and with a distortion of the relation between these actions and actions oriented toward understanding.

The social world

A person who systematically reduces the social world to the objective world has in a radical sense, no competence in treating normative validity claims. For this person, social phenomena, norms as well as co-subjects, will appear as objective phenomena. This means no communication and no morality. In clear-cut cases this is certainly psychopathological. In its weaker forms, however, it might be regarded as non-pathological, but when gradually moving toward the more severe forms, we get the difficult border-line cases before ending up in the clearly pathological ones.

The competence in mastering normative validity claims is one in which the developmental perspective is especially important since, individually as well as historically, there are stages where normative validity is conceived of as not being differentiated from the realm of facts. Here, however, I am thinking in terms of the Habermasian notion of modernity, in the sense that adults are supposed to have reached a level of pragmatic competence in raising and solving validity claims as potentially valid claims.

The inner world

A person who has no notion of the difference between what is genuinely oneself and what is not has, at the very least, a distorted self-understanding. The distinction between private and public has broken down. This may go either way, as it were, either as an experience of the public sphere invading oneself, e.g. of other people reading one's thoughts, or as an experience of oneself reading the thoughts of other people. This distortion can also take the form of isolation: a feeling of no possible contact between the private sphere and the public one.

Such breakdowns of the sense of what is internal and what is external involve behavioral distortions, either in the form of isolation (autistic tendencies, or fear of being invaded) or in the form of unconstrained behavior.

In these cases there is a lack of authenticity affecting the relation between the self and the other, the internal and the external, which implies a distortion of the communicative competence to express oneself truly, e.g. the ability to know whether one is pretending or not, whether one really means what one says or not. Therefore one's truthfulness is also affected. Whether we focus on authenticity, or on truthfulness, it is certainly distorted in the cases described.

Language

Whereas the distortions treated in the previous section may be regarded as a failure in the linguistic elucidation of biographic material, a general lack of trust in language as a realm of meaning and communication implies a split which is psychopathological, autism being a pure case. Without a linguistic (and pragmatico-linguistic) form of life, the other 'worlds', and the abilities related to them, will suffer as well.

This latter point reminds us of the overlapping character of these competences (and 'worlds'). For instance, a person with no sense for the social world will also have difficulties in carrying out his daily work, and furthermore have difficulties in maintaining a realistic self-understanding.

A person who denies that other people in principle can understand his own ordinary speech acts, e.g. statements about facts and utterances about valid norms, is not only asocial, but irrational. Furthermore, a person in a modern society who refuses to give reasons for his validity claims, in situations where such requests are appropriate, is equally irrational. In mild forms it means that the person is stubborn, in severe forms it means social isolation and is pathological.

This leads us from the realm of communicative competence, where validity claims are raised and 'worlds' involved, to the realm of argumentative competence, where these claims are argumentatively tried out and possibly solved.

I will concentrate on three aspects of this argumentative ability.

(i) In the communication process itself there is mutual recognition, in so far as we speak and listen to each other, and we thereby take each other to be accountable. This mutual recognition takes a special form in argumentation: in arguing, what counts is the better argument. In argumentation the participants together seek valid answers, unrestricted by irrelevant factors. This requires not only sufficient insight into the matter at hand, and communicative competence (e.g. mental health), but also full freedom to speak. In entering such a discussion one has to recognize the other participants as rational, i.e. as persons from whom one can learn – if not, one can teach these other persons or be taught by them, but not discuss with them. Simultaneously the other people have to recognize "me" in the same way. People must thus mutually recognize each other as rational. This is a moral phenomenon, but its status is one of logical necessity: without this reciprocal recognition argumentation is impossible. But this also means that there is a mutual recognition of oneself, and of the other participants too, as fallible; for if one already knew everything, there would be no way of arguing, only of teaching and preaching. So there has to be a mutual recognition of oneself and the other participants as being both rational and fallible – i.e. being able, in principle, to make contributions to the argumentation and to follow the arguments, *and* of being corrected by the arguments put forward by other participants, such that by this shared effort the participants can hope to reach a (more) valid answer. This mutual recognition of rationality and of fallibility indicates a notion of equality and of realistic self-esteem which can be seen as a qualitative notion of mental health.

(ii) Argumentation is thus a shared activity directed toward validation by means of reason. This also implies a personal identity which is at the same time flexible and rigid, as it were. One cannot insist on "one's own opinions", contrary to what the better argument indicates; one's own opinions are those which one sees as the argumentatively best supported ones. Nor can one simply change one's opinion, always in accordance with the latest speaker. One has to be utterly flexible and change opinion in accordance with the arguments. But at the same time one has to be totally resistant to the temptation to give in to views merely because they are held by other (prestigious) participants, without those views being supported by better arguments. This is indeed a precarious identity, not resting on the social acceptance of other people nor on a secured realm of fixed "personal opinions" sheltered from argumentative challenges. This might be seen as an ideal for mental health. Its perfect realization is certainly a hard task. But on the other hand, a complete lack of this reason-oriented identity will appear as something pathological in our societies.

(iii) Finally, it is part of argumentative reasoning to be able to reflect upon given presuppositions, and to change them if there are arguments for doing so. One has to acquire an ability to reflect upon given perspectives, conceptual and methodological, and to try out their adequacy piecemeal in argumentation.

I have referred to three aspects of argumentative competence (in addition to communicative competence and to those of sociopolitical freedom and of professional competence): (i) mutual recognition of argumentative rationality and fallibility, (ii) a simultaneously flexible and rigid attitude (since a better argument is the only factor that counts), and (iii) an ability to reflect upon given perspectives, to test them argumentatively, and to change them if the arguments indicate that they should be changed.

An argumentative change of one's perspective, or linguistic frame, is not merely an external activity. It involves a personal outlook and way of understanding. There is thus some overlap between explicative discourse and reflection upon given perspectives on the one hand and therapeutic and self-formative activities on the other. In both cases there is a need for a process of co-existence with other people in order to see that a common ground is really reached, and not only reached pretendedly or partially. In both cases there is an interrelation between conceptual adequacy/validity and personal identity/understanding.

The relation between discourse and therapy can also be indicated by pointing out that therapy can always turn out to be required inside a discourse, and that discursive virtues, viz. argumentative abilities, are part of what one can hope to obtain in a therapeutic process.

In this perspective therapy is not merely a preparatory activity which goes on before an argumentation can get started. This can be further illustrated by pointing out that argumentation does not merely have the function of validating theoretical and practical questions, and of clarifying linguistic problems. It also has the function of will-formation – one may here compare what has just been said about the personal character of changing frames of reference. In an argumentation which involves will-formation and self-formation, the participants' needs and wishes, or in short their given preferences, are laid open for argumentative improvements, i.e. for argumentative universalization: those preferences are legitimate (valid) that are argumentatively defensible, i.e. are universalizable. (The demand for universalizability is an implication of the circumstance that arguments are not private but valid for all, if valid.)

There is, however, no *a priori* reason to think that all kinds of preferences can be redeemed argumentatively, leading to one clear answer to what is right and wrong to do. In addition to such clear-cut cases, where one solution can be said to be either right or wrong, we have the interesting realm of different rationally possible preferences, i.e. the field of legitimate pluralism.[22]

Situational Competence

There is always a need to judge the appropriateness of embarking on an argument, and to judge the adequate application of the results once an argument is brought to a conclusion. This judgment implies a practical insight. It is an essential part of this practical wisdom to be sensitive to the vagueness of any given situation.[23]

In order to acquire this ability to judge situations of various kinds, a familiarity with one's own culture, and with other cultures, is required. This is an ability which is not fully taken care of by the communicative and argumentative abilities in the form in which we have presented them so far.[24]

To bring in the psychpathological perspective, we may say that this situational competence is part and parcel of any notion of mental health. Without such an ability one becomes a stranger in one's own society.

We may further indicate that a sense of humor and irony is crucial here, not only because laughter prolongs life, but in the sense that humor and irony show that one masters the manifoldness and vagueness of human situations.

We may strengthen this point, about the need for an ability to situate adequately, by referring to the necessity, inherent in argumentation, of understanding the concrete meaning of the issue under discussion, i.e. a necessity which goes further than the need to apply the achieved results in concrete situations, just as in the process of arguing, and in agreeing on the valid answer, one has to know what the general conclusion *means* in concrete terms.[25]

What we might call a hermeneutic effort to reach mutual understanding about the meaning of the words in concrete situations is thus required *within* this kind of discourse. Therefore this sensitivity for the situatedness of language, not only of discourse itself *qua* concrete event, belongs to the full-fledged argumentative ability.

*

In summing up my reflections on the relations between a pragmatic notion of communicative and argumentative competence in modern societies *and* psychopathological perspectives, I would like to remind the reader that Habermas's project is one of grasping scientific-argumentative rationality in a historical perspective, as a developmental theory of society. My present project is an attempt to see whether indications of arguments from absurdity, in the sense of arguments from clear-cut psychopathological cases, might help elucidate the allegedly universal status of these competences within what is called modernity.

My tentative answer is a qualified yes. Such an approach has its virtues. But we should certainly only regard this *via negativa,* using arguments from psychopathology, as one isolated step within a broader discursive field in which a mutually reflective movement between presuppositions and cases is undertaken.[26]

However, the fruitfulness of this approach, say for psychiatry, demands more than a philosophical analysis of thought-experiments concerning pragmatic abilities. In order to try out and find the reasonable borderlines between what is strange, morally blame-worthy or psychopathologically disorderly, an open discussion of concrete cases and empirical material is required, between psychiatrists, psychologists and social scientists, together with enlightened representatives of our society in general.

NOTES

1. References

Apel, K.-O. (1976) (ed.) *Sprachpragmatik und Philosophie*, Frankfurt a.M.: Suhrkamp.
Apel, K.-O. (1988) *Diskurs und Verantwortung. Das Problem des Übergangs zur postkonventionellen Moral*, Frankfurt a.m.: Suhrkamp.
Böhler, D. (1991) "Menschenwürde und Menschentötung. Über Diskursethik und utilitaristische Ethik", in: *Zeitschrift für Evangelische Ethik*, 35(1991) pp. 166–186.
Bernstein, R. (1985), *Philosophical Profiles*, Cambridge: Polity Press.
Gullvåg, I. (1990) "Sanity, Madness, and Perverted Communication", in: *Essays in Pragmatics Philosophy II*, ed. H. Høibraaten, Oslo: Norwegian University Press, pp. 9–55.
Günther, K. (1988) *Der Sinn für Angemessenheit. Anwendungsdiskurse in Moral und Recht*, Frankfurt a.M.: Suhrkamp.
Habermas, J. (1976a) "Was heißt Universalpragmatik?", in Apel (1976).
Habermas, J. (1976b) *Zur Rekonstruktion des Historischen Materialismus*, Frankfurt a.M.: Suhrkamp.
Habermas, J. (1981) *Theorie des kommunikativen Handelns*, Frankfurt a.M.: Suhrkamp.
Habermas, J. (1983) *Moralbewußtsein und kommunikatives Handeln*, Frankfurt a.M.: Suhrkamp.
Habermas, J. (1984) "Überlegungen zur Kommunikationspathologie", in: *Vorstudien und Ergänzungen zur Theorie des kommunikativen Handelns*, Frankfurt a.M.: Suhrkamp, pp. 226–270.
Kuhlmann, W. (1985) *Reflexive Letztbegründung. Untersuchungen zur Transzendentalpragmatik*, München: Alber.
McCarthy, T. (1982) "Rationality and Relativism: Habermas's 'Overcoming' of Hermeneutics", in: J.B. Thompson and D. Held, *Habermas, Critical Debates*, London: MacMillan, pp. 57–79.
McCarthy, T. (1985) "Reflections on Rationalization in the Theory of Communicative Action", in: R.J. Bernstein (ed.), *Habermas and Modernity*, Cambridge: Polity Press, pp. 176–191.
Passmore, J. (1961) *Philosophical Reasoning*, London: Duckworth.
Skirbekk, G. (1987) "La rationalité scientifique comme destin", in: D. Janicaud (ed.), *Les pouvoirs de la science*, Paris: Vrin, pp. 95–108.
Skirbekk, G. (1988) "Politische Kultur – durch philosophische Tiefe oder alltägliche Gewohnheit?" in: (ed.) W. Kuhlmann, *Zerstörung des moralischen Selbstbewußtseins, Chance oder Gefährung? Praktische Philosophie in Deutschland nach dem Nationalsozialismus*, Frankfurt a.M.: Suhrkamp, pp. 290–298.
Skirbekk, G. (1992) *Manuscripts on Rationality*, Bergen: Ariadne.
Wellmer, A. (1986) *Ethik und Dialog*, Frankfurt a.M.: Suhrkamp.

2.   Cf. e.g. Apel and Habermas in Apel (1976). Also "Pragmatism and Pragmatics" in this collection.

3. Cf. "Arguments from Absurdity".

4. Cf. Ingemund Gullvåg (1990) who elaborates notions of mental sanity and madness in the perspective of a pragmatic philosophy of communication and understanding. Also Habermas (1984).

5. More extensively on these issues, cf. "Arguments from Absurdity" in this collection. Also cf. Passmore (1961).

6. For another approach to this question, see "Contextual and Universal Pragmatics".

7. See previous chapter, "Pragmatism and Pragmatics".

8. See "Arguments from Absurdity". Cf. also W. Kuhlmann (1985).

9. This cultural relativism on the empirical level is even more striking when it comes to the way these claims are treated and solved – scientific and philosophical argumentation is a relatively recent historical achievement.

10. If so, this means that modern rationalization and differentiation are counterbalanced by some universal and integrative force at a deeper (universal pragmatic and/or developmental) level. (Concerning the issue 'cultural relativism and universality through cultural modernization', cf. "Modernization of the Lifeworld" in this collection.)

11. In the sense that it is (somehow) unthinkable that we can have a society of speakers without some such distinction.

12. Habermas (1976b) and (1981). See also "Modernization of the Lifeworld" and "Rationality and Contextuality" in this collection.

13. Cf. the discussion of this project, e.g. T. McCarthy's critical remarks on its cross-cultural soundness and on its inherent tension between empirical evidence (at the bottom) and philosophical status (at the top), McCarthy (1982).

14. There are problems in claiming, at the same time, that rationality is a fruit of factual history and that rationality has the status of an unavoidable condition. Cf. "The Pragmatic Notion of Nature", and also "Rationality and Contextuality" in this collection.

15. Cf. e.g. T. McCarthy's critical remarks to Habermasian distinctions [in Habermas (1981)], in T. McCarthy (1985).

16. In such cases the general western attitude is one of moral dismissal. Religion is regarded as belonging to the field of private life and of legitimate pluralism, and to violate this is regarded as ideological and moral obduracy.

17. Cf. Skirbekk (1992), "A Crisis in the Humanities?".

18. Habermas (1981). Cf. critical remarks, e.g. by T. McCarthy (1985) about the status of these terms (e.g., are they only analytic notions or are they realistic?). (Cf. "Modernization of the Lifeworld", note 13.)

19. Cf. e.g. Habermas (1983) and Wellmer (1986).

20. Cf. Habermas (1976) pp. 255 ff. and (1981) vol. I, p. 324. In the first case he operates with four worlds, in the latter with three, leaving out 'language'. This terminological oscillation reflects the fact that all 'worlds' are linguistically constituted.

21. Cf. "The Pragmatic Notion of Nature".

22. Cf. "Pragmatism and Pragmatics".

23. Cf. Skirbekk (1987), and "Contextual and Universal Pragmatics".

24. Cf. Skirbekk (1988). Cf. also K.-O. Apel (1988), e.g. pp. 103–153 on the problem of application, and D. Böhler (1991) pp. 166–186 on the same problem (both in 'part A' and in 'part B' of discourse ethics). Also K. Günther (1988) and Habermas (1991), critically to Apel's distinction (pp. 195–197).

25. For instance in discussing human rights in the international organizations, the agreement achieved will remain vacuous and empty if the different delegates, coming from very different cultures with different historical experiences and codes for interpretation, do not reach a basic common understanding about the words applied in the discussion.

26. Cf. "Praxeological Reflections".

Contextual and Universal Pragmatics

Mutual Criticism of Praxeological and Transcendental Pragmatics

Pragmatics, generally speaking, means theory of action. In its linguistic version pragmatics is concerned with speech acts – and in a philosophically oriented linguistic version, in contrast to an empirically oriented pragmatics, what is at stake is the so-called internal relationship between language in use and the user of language, i.e. an analysis of conceptually necessary or constitutive preconditions of speech acts. Such pragmatically necessary conditions of a speech act may, however, be more or less explicitly verbalized or remain more or less implicit and tacitly inherent in the act itself. One can conceive of such a philosophical pragmatics as being relatively *context-dependent* or relatively *context-independent* as to its conception of language, or relatively *particularistic* or relatively *universalistic* as to its speech-act immanent validity claims.

In this chapter I will discuss the following two kinds of philosophical pragmatics: a praxeology of Wittgensteinian heritage and a universal pragmatics of Apelian and Habermasian heritage; the former being rather contextualistic and particularistic, the latter primarily universalistic as to the conception of language and its inherent validity claims. In discussing these two types of pragmatics I shall focus on the relative strength and weakness of a contextual-pragmatic methodology (based on an analysis of examples) on the one hand and of a universal-pragmatic methodology (based on self-reflection or on a theory of modernity) on the other.

The main references for the universal-pragmatic position are well known (cf. the writings about universal or transcendental pragmatics in Karl-Otto Apel and about universal or formal pragmatics in Jürgen Habermas). My primary references to the praxeological approach are the works of Scandinavian Wittgensteinians, such as Jakob Meløe.[1] A brief introductory remark to this praxeology might be appropriate, before we enter the discussion of these two pragmatic philosophies.

The term praxeology may bring to mind associations with the Polish philosopher T. Kotarbinski, who used just this term in his theories about efficiency in purposive actions.[2] Our use of the term will, however, diverge from Kotarbinski's. Praxeology in our sense is a conceptual analysis and reflective discussion of the way human activities are interwoven with their agents and with the things at which they are directed within our everyday world. It is thus more clearly linked with the early Heidegger and the later Wittgenstein than with Kotarbinski.

In emphasizing the primacy of action in contradistinction to both passive perception and pure cogitation, praxeology thus understood fits in with a persisting modern trend, right from classical pragmatism to the praxis-philosophy of the neo-marxists. From this praxeological perspective, the primacy of practice may be briefly elucidated as follows: (i) Human insight is primarily located in actions; (ii) the articulation of this insight calls for a careful elaboration of described instances of the activities in question. What characterizes this kind of praxeology is thus a certain shared notion regarding method: not all actions are taken to be reducible to purposive performances (*zweckrationales Handeln*), as those theoreticians who take instrumental and strategic moves as their paradigm case have claimed (among them are recent theoreticians of rational action working on decision theory and theory of games). Actions are of different – yet interrelated and overlapping – kinds, ranging from aesthetic responses in daily life to scientific inquiry, from routines and rituals to discussion and creativity. The goal of articulating and enhancing the insights immanent in these varied activities is best served by reflective elaboration of illustrative examples. The common praxeological method is in this way based on an insistence on the careful use of examples, invoking detailed descriptions and thought-experiments.

I

I will discuss sympathetically, though critically, the merits and shortcomings of this praxeology or contextual pragmatics; and I will do so by going straight into a typically praxeological example:

A smith forges horseshoes by means of a hammer and an anvil. In doing this he may well be thinking of remote events or abstract problems, and he may know a lot of different things. But there is something he has to know in order to do what he does. He has to be knowledgeable of appropriate hammering. He has to know how to start and how (when) to stop. He does not have to know all this explicitly, but he has to know it implicitly. And he has to know it in terms of the notions inherent in his work, with its contextually specific grasp and sight. But he does not have to know the chemical formulae for iron, and that kind of thing.[3]

In other words, there are certain insights which the agent must necessarily have, since these insights are constitutive of his activity: "The agent knows what he has to know in order to be able to do what he does". This is the praxeological thesis. Let us say: Doing and knowing are one. Or better: There are necessary, while constitutive, interrelations between action and knowledge.

Praxeology as a philosophical pragmatics represents an explication of such act-inherent preconditions. It represents an analysis of the presuppositions of act-constitutive insight and competence. This is done by minute analyses of examples, such as that of a hammering blacksmith in his smithy.

In so doing it is presupposed that the agent's act-immanent insights are accessible to the describing and analyzing praxeologist, and it is presupposed that the description elaborated by the praxeologist can be appropriate to the actual act.

Through their work, praxeologists thus try to show that the classical problem of the hermeneutic interrelation between language and reality can best be elaborated by carefully analyzing cases of concrete everyday acts. The praxeologist does not thereby deny that all such cases are chosen and linguistically constituted, i.e. that examples are never brute facts, but always "pre-cut". Since any praxeological analysis of preconditions elaborates a special choice of cases, which are linguistically formed in a special way, we therefore encounter the well known problems of the internal relation between that which constitutes and that which is constituted – the interesting point being the way in which praxeologists elaborate these problems in concrete analyses.

Before discussing this issue further I shall briefly make some general remarks on the relation between this praxeological pragmatics and universal pragmatics:

(i) This praxeology is anti-reductionist, like universal pragmatics – in a way it is even more strongly anti-reductionist than the universal pragmatics in Apel or in Habermas, since this case-oriented praxeology tends toward pluralistic contextualism (and, for instance, looks upon the dualistic distinction between instrumental and communicative action, or between understanding and explanation, as far too crude).

(ii) This praxeology is anti-solipsistic, like universal pragmatics, partly because it presupposes the accessibility of other people's actions and of their inherent insights and competence, partly because it tends to accept the reasons given in favor of the argument from private language (in Wittgenstein).

(iii) This praxeology is also anti-skeptical, like universal pragmatics – but according to other premises and in another sense. According to this praxeology, there are adequate insights inherent in our contextual acts, insights that can be explicated by case studies; the idea of overcoming the philosophical problem of skepticism by means of reflective "ultimate justification" (*Letztbegründung*) remains a remote one for the praxeologists.

Proponents of transcendental pragmatics have criticized praxeology for its contextualism, claiming that the praxeological position denies the possibility of a "translation" from context to context, i.e.

that this position implies a problem of relativism and skepticism, which can only be overcome by the universality of a meta-language game. In my view there is in the praxeologist position no such problem of trans-contextual transcendence or innovation; the answer is found in the open possibility of re-socializing processes of learning that can be praxeologically reconstructed and described.[4]

The potential of criticism inherent in this kind of contextual pragmatics arises from its (often implicit) anti-speculative thesis, i.e. from its more or less explicit contextualist conception of language, according to which any use of language not founded in a functioning context of action should be regarded as inadequate or even as meaningless: in asking for its use and function in specific contexts, abstract and airy talk is critically pinned down. However, when this anti-speculative thesis is explicitly claimed as a general thesis, it is self-referentially inconsistent. When the thesis is presented more softly, referring to our manifold experience of the misery of speculative thinking, it does avoid this inconsistency; we then have to demonstrate, from case to case, the nature and extension of the contended misery of speculative thinking – which is an open-ended question. Finally there is the general objection to this anti-speculative thesis based on "functional activities and contexts": what are the criteria for the functioning of an activity, in contrast to idle speculation; and how do we decide the borderline for a truly functional context? Do we not, at least now and then, have "truly functioning activities and contexts" of an argumentative (and philosophical) nature? *Prima facie*, this latter suggestion seems to be based on facts. In addition it leads us, once more, toward the self-referential objection to this kind of anti-theoretical contextualism, viz. it points at the context-transcending nature of this contextualist claim.

In my view the case-oriented and potentially contextualist praxeology suffers from (1) a lack of reflection and (2) a too narrow selection of its cases:

1. Philosophizing is also an activity, an activity in which the participants talk and listen to each other, read and write, in

consequence of which arguments and positions are reconstructed, interpreted, made more precise and evaluated as to their relevance and strength. Discussion and reflection are also activities which can be praxeologically described.

In this perspective we can talk about 'philosophical experience': we learn to know the positions and arguments of, for instance, the Platonic theory of ideas, or the Humean distinction between is and ought, or the general debate between utilitarianism and Kantian ethics. The philosophical experiences of the undeniability of certain presuppositions, such as the principle of contradiction (mentioned already in Aristotle) or the Cartesian cogito, are among the more essential examples. Reflection on self-referential arguments is a typically philosophical activity, and acquaintance with such standard cases is typically a philosophical experience.

2. Artisans, peasants, housewives and fishermen are not the only interesting agents for praxeological analyses. If we want to get a better view of the insight and competence of agents in the modern world, we also have to try to analyze the interwoven activities and contexts of technological experts and of scientists – for certainly, modernity is characterized by scientization (*Verwissenschaftlichung*) and institutional differentiation. Informatics and industrial projects, not reindeer and blacksmiths, are typical for the modern world – in short, robots, not row-boats.

Against this criticism the traditional praxeologist might object, emphasizing the need to start with more simple cases. This objection is fair enough as far as the first few steps in a praxeological project are concerned, but it does not exclude the need for a further elaboration of praxeological projects through more complex cases.

Against this counter-argument a traditional praxeologist might try the contextualist argument once more: "Be careful with idle talk not situated in functional activities!" This, however, is just the question we discussed above; and in this discussion I would further claim, as a point of departure, that modern situations are not, in general, characterized by "notions without functional activities and contexts", but rather the other way around, by "activities and contexts without adequate notions" – in short, the consequences of our modern activities transcend not only our political and administrative control but also, to a large extent, our intellectual survey and thereby our moral ability. In short, we tend to do more than we are aware of; our actions, in their far-reaching consequences, go further and are more intricate than most of our simple notions about what we are doing (the standard case being the ecological crisis). In this perspective contextualist praxeology, with its archaic selection of examples, seems to me to be rather ideological, i.e. concealing and counterproductive.

The context-pragmatic praxeologist might then further object that we ought to distinguish between philosophical analyses of presuppositions on the one hand and sociological or politological analyses on the other. He does the former, not the latter. I do not deny the general possibility and the relative usefulness of such a distinction; in certain contexts it might surely be fruitful and adequate. But when it is defended quite generally by a praxeologist, without contextual references, it looks to me like self-referential carelessness. I might even sharpen my criticism: our praxeologist is a pluralistic contextualist and anti-essentialist; but he does seek to analyze act-immanent insight and competence inherent in elementary simple acts, independently of the historic given characteristics of modernity – that, I assume, is an underlying presumption in his use of the distinction between philosophy and sociology. If that is so, we have here again a self-referential inconsistency; the pluralistic context-pragmatician uncovers himself as a *Fundamentalontologe*,[5] seeking fundamental a-historical preconditions for human acts. In this perspective his narrow selection of archaic cases becomes comprehensible. But the price he pays is that of an inconsistency between his pluralistic-contextualist position and his essentialist search for timeless and general pragmatic preconditions in human acts.

As I am not an anti-essentialist contextualist, I do not deny the possibility of such a praxeological *Fundamentalontologie* – just as I do not deny the possibility of a universal pragmatics. In both cases – in that of general act immanent insight (*Fundamental-*

ontologie) as well as in that of general speech act immanent competence and validity claims (*Universalpragmatik*) – all depends on the various arguments in each case.

However, our praxeologist is perhaps still not satisfied; he would go on defending his contextualism with some further arguments. It all depends on the underlying conception of language, he would say. We should not hypostasize and reify language in a semanticist perspective. Language is fundamentally characterized by use, practice. What he is saying now is not something that should be conceived of as a thesis, but as a praxeological insight that can be shown by means of an elaboration of cases. It can be shown through examples, but not demonstrated and stated as a universal thesis.

At this stage our praxeologist would perhaps defend the primacy of practice against principles (a) and the primacy of concrete instances against discourse and history (b).

(a) Our praxeologist would try to show the general primacy of practice against rules and principles by taking his point of departure in the argument from the primacy of practice and of tacit knowledge in situations of learning and of rule application: using examples he would try to show that an acquisition of the competence to distinguish between what is equal and unequal in different situations depends on socialization and training related to cases in different situations, and that this pragmatic competence is a precondition for the application of rules. (He might also use arguments from absurdity: if we could use a rule X for deciding the correct use of a rule Y, and a rule Z for deciding the correct use of the rule X, we would end up in an infinite regress.[6] Therefore, a precondition for the application of rules is tacit knowledge, based on practice, of how to use the rules.)

I, for one, accept this as a point of departure, but not the generalized thesis. For if it is correct that rules and principles without pragmatic training and tacit knowledge are powerless, it is also correct that practice without any rules or principles cannot even get started. There is no "pure" practice, as a warranted correct standard (over against "rule thinkers" or "principle thinkers").[7] What we have is the tension between practice and principles (rules), a tension which we shall always have to endure and which we should try to elaborate discursively again and again.

(b) By insisting on "concrete instances" in our use of language the praxeologist refers to the "ontological" foundation of contextual speech acts, i.e. to the contextual facts (or constituted states of affair) presupposed in the praxeological analysis. This point itself I would not reject. But these concrete contextual "instances" are not the only decisive factors. The same is true of the intersubjectivity of language, the present intersubjectivity in talking and listening as well as the historically rooted intersubjectivity of language and of linguistically performed discussions. In other words, on the assumption of the basic reciprocity of what is constituted and what constitutes, this insistence on "concrete instances" seems to me to be a kind of objectivistic remainder, in the sense that our pragmatic horizon (that possibly transcends given contexts) as well as our common conceptual history (that certainly transcends given contexts) are both thereby neglected.

These briefly indicated points from the ongoing discussion around contextual pragmatics will suffice for the present – I would just like to add that, in my view, contextual pragmatics, despite the counter-arguments, suffers from a deficit of reflection and relies on too narrowly selected examples.

II

I would now like to present an example taken from our modern world, namely a ("situated") question of energy supply, in order to indicate how, in my view, such an example can be analyzed by a discursive and reflective praxeology. However, in so doing my intention is not to carry out such an analysis in depth but merely to point out the structure of such an analysis.

This case represents an activity situated within a given social, economic and technological context, determined by the goal of securing a sufficiently large amount of cheap energy. The more precise characterization of the actual activity has to be elaborated by taking this goal and the given situation into consideration. Against this background one can try to work out the adequate concepts for a praxeological description. In order to fulfill this goal ("cheap energy now") it is natural, in our modern world, to apply the scheme of normative decision theory: on the background of this given goal we try to make the circumstance of choice clear by elaborating the different alternatives with their various consequences. The goal represents primarily a normative question. The elaboration of the alternative ways of acting and of their consequences represents essentially a scientific task. The point of such a normative decision theory is not to inquire empirically into the facts of our actual attempts at solving problems, but to make clear what it means to choose rationally. This is why we talk of a normative decision theory (in contrast to an empirical one). The well-known scheme of this theory consists in the elaboration of the probabilities of the different consequences and in the quantification of their negative and positive evaluations; the mathematical products of the probabilities and evaluations reached in this way, for each alternative, are summed up; in order to act rationally we should now choose that alternative which has the highest sum of added products (or the lowest, if numbers are negative).[8]

Here I would just briefly emphasize the following points: this case exemplifies a complex modern activity which can be rationalized by the sciences – through scientific work in different disciplines, the various alternatives for action and the probabilities of their consequences can be seen more clearly – and this scientific rationalization (through the effort of groups of experts recruited from various disciplines) makes a (more) rational choice possible for reaching the given goals. First one needs the different disciplines of natural science and technology. But since in this case the human factor plays an important role for the inquiry into the various probabilities, we shall also have to introduce the sciences of man. This is necessary in the light of intended as well as unintended consequences (for possible terrorism as well as for bad routines). As a result the inquiry into the various probabilities becomes even more complicated; for human acts, individual as well as collective, are in principle only partially predictable.[9] This project-inherent need for interdisciplinary pluralism also implies a need for interdisciplinary collocation, since the different scientific reports should preferably be presented for the political agents as an intelligible whole. A hermeneutic and methodological reflection on different disciplinary presuppositions and limits should therefore be undertaken.

In our case, that of energy supply, when the different long-term and partly destructive consequences of this project have been explicated as well as they can be, it is rational to raise the critical question as to whether or not the constitutive goal of the project contradicts some other goals and values, e.g. such goals and values as have to be given even higher priority in the perspective of our socio-ecological survival. For this reason, what we have is a rational need for a critical normative discussion, in which the given project has to be viewed in the light of other goals and other projects.

This is the position for which I am here arguing: it is a matter of an interdisciplinary understanding, i.e. of a communicative rationality, and it is a matter of critical reflection, i.e. of a discursive or argumentative rationality. The decisive point is the rational nature of this overcoming or transcendence: it represents a rationally founded imperative. The technologico-instrumental rationality of the purely decision-theoretical stage is unavoidable, but it can be and ought to be overcome. In this sense we are bound and obliged by the modern discursive and reflective rationality.

In my view, our example does indeed indicate how praxeology could meet the demands of the modern world, viz. through scientifically founded reflection on more complex contexts of action. The example shows that there is a rational need to move toward a discursive rationality, transcending the original context. The question of context-independency and of universality will have to be conceived accordingly.

III

Against this background of modern cases of human activities as well as of unavoidable claims of general validity, issues for discussion in universal pragmatics concerning general pragmatic competence and discursively elaboratable validity claims present themselves with renewed interest to the context-pragmatician of praxeological provenance. I shall therefore change perspective. Having previously questioned contextual pragmatics, I shall now approach the universal pragmatician. This, however, should not be conceived of as an external shift; the philosophical insights and methodical virtues acquired by the praxeologists should not be left in oblivion. The acquired competence should be kept, should be overcome (in a Hegelian sense): *Pragmatic situatedness, tacit knowledge* and *case-oriented philosophizing* are catchwords here.[10]

In this chapter I cannot discuss universal pragmatics in depth;[11] I will only make a few remarks, from a *praxeological* perspective.

From that perspective discussion (discourse) is also an *activity*. The full methodological implications of this apparently trivial statement are neglected by traditional contextual pragmaticians, as well as by universal pragmaticians – the former probably regarding it as far too speculative and ambitious, the latter as far too empirical.[12] From a praxeological perspective the statement implies that case-oriented pragmatic analyses of the different kinds of discourses could and should be undertaken, with regard both to their specific contextual situatedness and their gradual transitions to other discourses and activities and to their inherent transcendence of their very contextuality toward pragmatic competences and claims of a more universal nature.

From a praxeological perspective it is striking that discursive activities do not consist merely of time-limited explicit dialogues between persons who talk and listen to one another. There is more to it. An indication of what is lacking is felt intuitively through an impression of idealized overburdening when it is suggested that very much happens during such dialogues, for instance that people change their views in accordance with the better argument and that they acquire new and exciting insights. But how often does this really occur? How often is it during the discourse itself that we change our views? Is it not rather the case that such changes often take place after the discussion, when we calm down and reflect upon what was said? Is it wrong to say that it is frequently when we think afterwards about what we said, and what they said, that we are struck by the idea that there was something right in what they said or that there was something unclear in what we ourselves said? *Afterwards* one often realizes what one should have said, what one overlooked during the discussion. Then, maybe, one pulls oneself together, sits down and makes some notes, or writes out the problem at some length, in order to get it clear for oneself. In this way it might become clear that the problem was even more complicated than one had earlier imagined, that there are distinctions to be made which were disregarded both by oneself and by the others. Then, maybe, one starts looking into the literature, and one reads with a sharpened awareness of what was discussed; and it then happens that one finds something which one had not seen before, or had not seen in this way.

My point is the following: in this sense former participants might be aware of the circumstance that a discourse, with its talking and listening, is also connected with a greater whole, including reading and writing. Thinking takes place not only during the discussion, but also (not least) afterwards! But this *after* may become a new *before*, for there will be new discussions. In this way we get an afterthought as well as a pre-thought (a re-flection and a pre-flection). And within this afterthought there are reflections of different kinds. We have reflections on what kind of discourse we really had, what preconditions we took for granted and what other perspectives might have been possible.

All in all, such a simple praxeological reminder illustrates that an explicit discourse is only the top of an iceberg, where the real structure embraces pre-thought, discourse and afterthought, and where this spiral rests on four activities, namely speaking, listening, reading, and writing. We may, by contrast (some kind of *via negativa*), indicate how people might "stiffen" in only one of these activities – it is like an intellectual "cabinet of horror": the person who merely speaks, but never listens, nor reads, nor writes. The person who merely listens, but who never talks, never reads and never writes. The person who only reads, never speaks, never listens, never writes. And the person who only writes, without ever speaking, listening or reading. The anomalies are striking! (And even worse, we probably recognize instances of these pure cases in our own intellectual everyday life.)

When the question is raised as to how a discourse should be rightly started or terminated, one should definitely have in mind the idea of this intellectual spiral between the different activities and stages. Then the problem becomes less acute[13], and more pluralistic and exciting: discourses are extended further than specific academic seminars and specific meetings in scientific institutions. A discourse might go on for weeks and months, and even longer.

But praxeologically there is even more to be said about discourses. A discourse is carried out by persons belonging to a certain society. They are socialized into specific traditions, professional and social. In order to make a discourse optimally free and fruitful, many factors should be realized, some rather specific and unpredictable, others rather general and obvious. To the latter belongs the ability to familiarize oneself with different ways of looking at things. Without this ability it is difficult to reflect, by intellect itself (as it were). It therefore helps to have some *experience* of such pluralities of ways of thinking and acting. This ability can be appropriated in various ways, and here we have individual and other variations. But in general we may still say that, for this purpose, it is often quite fruitful to situate oneself in concrete settings dominated by other traditions in one's own discipline. The same holds true for a location in relation to neighboring disciplines. Here we certainly talk of an intellectual relocation, requiring a process of learning, by reading, writing, listening, and talking – but not merely this: one does not become fully acquainted with other traditions of one's own discipline or with other disciplines merely by an intellectual effort. A shared life within a professional community is also often required.

But it goes further, and deeper, as a prolongation of the kinds of socialization required by a competent participant in a scientific discourse. Catchwords here are *praxis* and *tacit knowing*. In some disciplines this kind of competence is primarily 'mediated' by means of shared work with experiments, in the lab or in the field; in other disciplines it is, above all, a question of shared work with texts, and so on. In these various ways a student learns the chosen discipline in a way not totally different from what happens when a ship's mate is taught by a master. One learns to get the right eye and the right grasp. One appropriates a competent estimate. (For example, the screw for a broken finger bone has to be "suitably" tight – and through praxis, under supervision, the student of surgery learns what "suitable" means in this case. Through books alone this competence is not available.) However, since there are differences in professional background within a discipline, it is particularly useful to travel, to go somewhere else, to experience how qualified colleagues, with another professional background, do their work. Through a process of resocialization one then learns concretely how they handle questions, methods and notions. (There is, in this way, an intellectually deep tourism, side by side with superficial tourism.)

The praxeological point is simply that books and articles do not themselves convey all that could and should be learnt. It does not always suffice to read the books and articles of colleagues in neighboring traditions, nor to read about them, nor to talk with them in contexts foreign to them – even if all this might be useful and even necessary. In addition, we also ought to experience them at home, as it were, in order to experience and acquire the "tacit knowing" of their tradition – what is presupposed and not thematized nor commented upon, or, if it is thematized, what is not correctly understood by us until we see it in its proper context. We could add that in reflective and critical activities, as in the sciences, it is not enough to know "one's own" position, without knowing those of the others. This is the old point[14] that one can only know that one is right when one has adequately learnt what one's intellectual adversaries take to be true. It is thus questionable even to claim that one has a thesis or a position of one's own if one has not been sufficiently familiarized with the theses and positions of other people. This, certainly, is a general point, but it does tie in with my praxeological remarks on our situated praxis.

The point is not that such a praxeological notion of "situated discourse" should deliver decisive insight into the solution of the fundamental problems of validity and validation. But it could possibly help us in thinking more adequately of what a discourse might be said to be – for instance concerning the question of its beginning and its end: when does a discourse start, when does it end; when should we enter a discourse, and when should we leave it? This praxeological perspective on discourse, as situated and embedded in everyday life, throws into relief the nature of discourse as something unfinished and always-started; we are "already" and "always" there, between action and discourse in *gradual* transitions.

I will conclude my praxeological reflections on contextual and universal pragmatics with these brief and general remarks:

It is not the case that all contextual-pragmatical points of a Wittgensteinian provenance are incompatible with universal-pragmatics. On the contrary, many contextual-pragmatical points ought to be incorporated into a universal-pragmatical perspective, and there are universal-pragmatical points that ought to be taken care of by a contextual pragmatics. It was the aim of this chapter to contribute to this kind of mutual constructive criticism between contextual pragmatics and universal pragmatics. Such a criticism is itself not a definitely terminable process. Further discussions, concerning our understanding of the various similarities and differences between contextual and universal pragmatics are always required, and this has to take the form of discursive and reflective elaborations of different selected cases. And this again persistently requires renewed versions of a productive process of reading, writing, talking, and listening. Our contribution has itself been a step within this discursive spiral of reflection and criticism.

NOTES

1. Cf. the anthologies: *Praxeology*, ed. Gunnar Skirbekk, Bergen/Oslo: Norwegian University Press, 1983; *Essays in Pragmatic Philosophy I*, eds. Ingemund Gullvåg and Helge Høibraaten, Oslo: Norwegian University Press, 1985; *Die pragmatische Wende*, eds. Dietrich Böhler, Tore Nordenstam and Gunnar Skirbekk, Frankfurt a.M.: Suhrkamp, 1987; and *Essays in Pragmatic Philosophy II*, ed. Helge Høibraaten, Oslo: Norwegian University Press, 1990.

2. Cf. *Praxiology*, Oxford 1965, s. 1: "The praxiologist concerns himself with finding the broadest possible generalizations of a technical nature. His objective is the technique of good, efficient work as such, indications and warnings important for all work which is intended to achieve maximum effectiveness". Cf. also Oskar Lange in *Political Economy*, Oxford, 1971, p. 189.

3. Cf. "Praxeological Reflections" in this collection.

4. Cf. the discussion between Jakob Meløe and Audun Øfsti in *Die pragmatische Wende* (note 1).

5. Cf. Rudolf Haller on Wittgenstein's philosophy as a *praxeologischer Fundamentalismus*, in "War Wittgenstein ein Neo-Kantianer?", in: *Wittgenstein – Aesthetics and Transcendental Philosophy*, eds. Kjell S. Johannessen and Tore Nordenstam, Wien: Hölder-Pichler-Tempsky, 1981 (pp. 32–41, especially pp. 40–41). Cf. Martin Heidegger in *Sein und Zeit (Being and Time)*.

6. Cf. Alice and the tortoise, on deduction!

7. Concerning the mutuality of practice and principles cf. Dietrich Böhler, "Die deutsche Zerstörung des politisch-ethischen Universalismus. Über die Gefahr des – heute (post-)modernen – Relativismus und Dezisionismus", in: *Zerstörung des moralischen Selbstbewußtseins. Praktische Philosophie in Deutschland nach dem Nationalsozialismus*, ed. Wolfgang Kuhlmann, Frankfurt a.M.: Suhrkamp, 1988, pp. 166–216. This article contains an answer to Viggo Rossvær's "Transzendentalpragmatik, transzendentale Hermeneutik und die Möglichkeit Auschwitz zu verstehen", in: *Die pragmatische Wende*, eds. Dietrich Böhler, Tore Nordenstam and Gunnar Skirbekk, Frankfurt a.M.: Suhrkamp, 1987, pp. 187–201.

8. Cf. "Ecological Crisis and Technological Expertise" in Gunnar Skirbekk, *Eco-Philosophical Manuscripts*, Bergen: Ariadne, 1992.

9. Cf., e.g., Popper's argumentation in *The Poverty of Historicism*.

10.   And I add: with the *relative primacy* (i) *of the pragmatic* over the "semantic", (ii) *of the negative* over the "positive", and (iii) *of the gradual* over the "dualistic". (Cf. Gunnar Skirbekk "Praktische Fragen in pragmatischer Sicht. Wissenschaftliche Rationalität als Schicksal", in: *Archivio di Filosofia*, Rome, 1987, Vol. 1–3, pp. 155–165, and also "Die technologische und ökologische Krisenerfahrung als Herausforderung an die praktische Vernunft", in: *Praktische Philosophie – Ethik, Dialoge 1*, eds. Karl-Otto Apel and Dietrich Böhler, Frankfurt a.M.: Fischer, 1984, pp. 402–422, and "Pragmatism and Pragmatics" in this collection.) (i) When our attention is primarily directed toward what is explicitly stated, and what can be stated (semantically), we easily overlook what is genuinely pragmatic. (ii) When our interest is focusing on what is ideal (e.g. the idea of a final consensus), we easily lose the right view of the philosophical importance of the negation of that which is insufficient. (iii) And when our analyses are characterized by schematic dualism we easily disregard the theoretical importance of the gradual passages. (To the latter point, cf. "Arguments from Absurdity" and "Pragmatism and Pragmatics".)

11.   For the more traditional (internal) criticism, cf. "Pragmatism and Pragmatics", "Modernization of the Lifeworld", and "Rationality and Contextuality" in this collection.

12.   Cf., e.g., Steven Lukes, "Of Gods and Demons: Habermas and Practical Reason", in: *Habermas, Critical Debates*, eds. J. B. Thompson and D. Held, London: Macmillan, 1982, pp. 139 ff.; and Michael Walzer, "A Critique of Philosophical Conversation", in: *Hermeneutics and Critical Theory in Ethics and Politics*, ed. M. Kelly, Cambridge, Mass.: MIT Press, 1990, pp. 182–196.

13.   In my view: de-dramatizing this issue in Albrecht Wellmer, *Dialog und Ethik*, Frankfurt a.M.: Suhrkamp, 1986, p. 105.

14.   Articulated, for instance, by John Stuart Mill.

The Pragmatic Notion of Nature

Comments on Habermas

This chapter has a double aim, at different levels as it were. Its primary aim is to discuss the notion of nature, and of natural science, in Habermas, from his early theory of cognitive interests to his present theories of formal (universal) pragmatics and developmental logic. However, in doing so I intend to shed some light on the use of general schemes in philosophy.

Before approaching the Habermasian notion of nature and his use of general schemes, I will briefly present some remarks on the philosophical use of examples, and as a first step I will refer to the test of conceptual adequacy in philosophy and in sociology. The difference between these two disciplines, in this respect, could be said to be the empirical nature of sociology and the non-empirical nature of philosophy. Philosophy has merely conceptual analysis at its disposal. This, however, is certainly too crude. Conceptual analysis is also part of sociology, and through its reflection on empirical sciences, philosophy too relates itself indirectly to the empirical realm. Furthermore, philosophers are intimately related to experience in these two ways:

(1) Philosophers have a relation to experience "in the first person" – that is, to a notion of experience that is etymologically elucidated by the German word *er-fahren*, which means the appropriation (*er-*) of the travelling (*fahren*), just as *er-kennen*, to acknowledge, etymologically means an appropriation or internalization of what we know. This is, in Greek terms, the personal experience of Ulysses, not the objectivated notion of statistical data in the computer! This Ulyssean experience – of different cultures and worlds, cultivated by competent reflection – is in principle open to everyone, but for philosophers, who seek deeper insight into the human condition, it is a unique source.

(2) Philosophers have access to experience through the elabora-

tion of examples.[1] This is a genuinely philosophical relationship to the empirical realm: we try to get a better view of how adequate our concepts are for grasping some aspect of the world by "rubbing" them against examples of various kinds. There is certainly no way of looking in between the concepts and the phenomena, since our examples are always already structured by some concepts – just as our concepts are given to us through situations and situated examples. But from our more or less common practices, in our more or less common world, we still have an experience of what we might call "the power of the examples", viz. that examples are intersubjective, they are common points of reference, and that examples do have some relative autonomy, in the sense that they offer resistance to some attempts at being conceptually grasped. Hence we can learn something from working on the dimension between examples and concepts. And what we can be taught is not restricted to the descriptive level; deep level structures (presuppositions) can be analyzed (e.g. by arguments from absurdity).[2] If this reflective and discursive elaboration of examples represents a kind of empirical base for philosophy, it is certainly far from a safe method. It is fallible. This recognized fallibility means that dogmatic claims are excluded, and that this way of philosophizing is conceived of as a tentative, collective, and meliorating process. Part of the problem is rooted in the circumstance that examples, as always already conceptually structured, can be "cut" at different levels, as it were, from the very concrete and particular to a very general level. Crossing this dimension, from particularity to generality, we have a multitude of different perspectives, related to situations and purposes. This is why a reflective discourse is needed within this elaboration of examples, based on their relative autonomy and availability.

Habermas's project, one might say, is one of 'conceptual adequacy', in the sense of trying to get an appropriate grasp of society, in its development and in its modernity, including its inherent notion of rationality. In carrying out this project Habermas frequently introduces *schemes* of various kinds, such as the schemes about the three worlds, or the four domains of reality, the three basic attitudes, the ontogenetic and phylogenetic stages of maturation, etc.

What is the status of these schemes? In empirical sociology any scheme should in principle be tried out against empirical material; this might at least be the idea when a scheme is introduced without prior conceptual analyses or attempts at justification for the choice of that particular scheme. Habermas, however, does not work like an empirical sociologist. What, then, is the status of the schemes in his work? Do they represent conclusions, end products? Or do they, on the contrary, guide his thoughts? If so, should we interpret their influence as intentional or accidental? Any glance at Habermas's writings will show the relevance of these questions about the methodological status of schemes in this high-level, interdisciplinary project: does he simply take in some scheme, out of the blue – or from traditional philosophy or sociology – in order then to withdraw into a meta-sociology, where neither philosophical argumentation nor sociological tests can reach them? Certainly not. For one thing Habermas has continually exposed himself to discussions; this is really one of the impressive features of his activity. And in so doing, he has gone both into various philosophical debates and into extended textual *Auseinandersetzungen* with the classical theoreticians in sociology. He has, with great energy, tried out his conceptual framework of society and rationality, and as a result of these tests he has often changed his views.

Still, some critics might claim that even his main project, related as it is to society, would have profited from a more extended use of examples in the sense just mentioned, and maybe from a less frequent use of schemes. Be that as it may, our present concern is not with the Habermasian use of examples and schemes in relation to society, but with his use of them in relation to nature and natural science. In this field, which is somewhat remote from the core of his own concern, Habermas makes fewer claims. But here he also carries out much less of a discursive test, either against classical texts or against cases of natural scientific activity. He does, however, make some important claims about nature and natural science, and in so doing applies various schemes. At this point, I would claim, there is a need for further elaboration of relevant cases: any discussion of "fruitful" attitudes[3] or "successful examples of theory formation"[4] in the natural sciences should be carried out by reflective elaboration of case studies – as e.g. in Philip Kitcher's discussion of the relation between Darwinism and creationism (in: *Abusing Science*).

In this chapter, however, it is not my aim to present some relevant examples of this sort. Here I merely want to point out how the need for further elaboration, through examples and cases, emerges. The next step, that of carrying out this job, lies beyond the limits of this chapter.

I here confine myself to some remarks on Habermas's notion of nature and his (literally schematic) treatment of this notion. The lack of example-related discussions in his philosophy of nature illuminates, by contrast, the constructive role of such elaborations of cases.

By way of introduction I would like to summarize Habermas's conception of the three cognitive interests,[5] namely technical interest, practical interest, and emancipatory interest, which, according to Habermas, are related to three attitudes or forms of action, as well as to three kinds of science, what he used to call empirical-analytic sciences, historical-hermeneutic sciences, and critical social sciences based on self-reflection.

In Habermas's terminology, technical interest is the interest in dominating nature, founded in the human need to work in order to survive, and refined and developed into the technological mastering and scientific explanation of nature. Practical interest is the interest in communication, founded in man as a social and verbal being, and refined and developed into the historical-hermeneutic disciplines. Finally, emancipatory interest is directed toward self-reflective liberation from reified and distorted forms of consciousness. Habermas says:[6]

"The conditions of instrumental action arose contingently in the natural evolution of the human species. At the same time, however, with transcendental necessity, they bind our knowledge of nature to the interest of possible technical control over natural processes".

Man constitutes nature, and nature constitutes man. But how can man be constituted by nature when nature is constituted by man? This question has been thoroughly discussed by Thomas McCarthy.[7] Here I will just delineate the main point: the problem is in a sense how one could reconcile quasi-Kantian and Marxian claims in Habermas's theory of cognitive interests. On the one hand we have the claim that our technical interest necessarily discloses nature in objectivating terms, on the other hand we have the claim that man himself is constituted by nature, through evolution.

Taken together these two claims become problematic. If a strong version of the theory of cognitive interests is maintained, to the effect that man cannot grasp nature in itself (since nature is necessarily constituted by man's technical interest), how can we, simultaneously, claim to know what nature itself is like, namely in the form of an evolution that constitutes man?

We may also cast the problem in these terms: nature "in front of us" is constituted by our technical interest and it is to be explained in terms of the empirical-analytic sciences. But which science can then explicate nature "coming from behind", as it were – that is, nature as constituting man, through the evolutionary process?

At first glance, neither the empirical nor the hermeneutic sciences will do. It remains for the so-called power of reflection to do so. However, in his earlier writings, Habermas's concept of reflection is ambiguous.[8] We have to distinguish between (a) critical self-reflection, and (b) reconstruction, the former being a self-liberating activity, with psychoanalysis as its paradigm case, the latter an explication of implicit competences, as in Chomskyan linguistics. Habermas's elaboration of the notion of emancipatory interest and of critical theory takes its point of departure in reflection in the former sense. His elaboration of pragmatics and developmental logics takes its point of departure in reflection in the latter sense, that is, in reconstruction.

If nature, *qua* the evolutionary constitution of man, is explicated in terms of this reconstruction, how does the insight won through reconstruction relate to the empirical-analytic sciences?[9] To the extent that the empirical sciences are involved (and it seems hard to deny that they are), the evolutionary process is conceived as constituted through technical interest, and hence we have the original dilemma of nature constituting man who constitutes nature. To the extent that we allow for a reconstructive approach for the understanding of the evolutionary process, independently of the human constitution of nature in technical terms, grasping nature-in-itself, as it were, we do avoid *this* dilemma, but to the same extent we have abandoned the strict version of cognitive interests *qua* inescapable relations to the world.

Habermas's own solution is rather of the latter kind, that is, an abandonment of the strict version of the theory of cognitive interests in favor of pragmatics and developmental logic.

Habermas says:[10]

"... in the functional sphere of instrumental action we encounter objects of the type of moving bodies; here we experience things, events, and conditions which are, in principle, capable of being manipulated. In interaction (or at the level of possible intersubjective communication) we encounter objects of the type of speaking and acting subjects; here we experience persons, utterances, and conditions which in principle are structured and to be understood symbolically. The object domains of the empirical-analytic and of the hermeneutic sciences are based on these objectifications of reality, which we undertake daily always from the viewpoint either of technical control or of inter-subjective communication."

And he also says:[11]

"There are two versions of this Marcusean idea of a new science. The first, and stronger version, is that there might be a possibility to develop a type of science which is generically different from what we have now; so that due to its very structure this new science could not be applied in the exploitation of nature. This idea is a very romantic idea. I don't want to be impolite to Marcuse, but I'm convinced that this idea has no real base."

How can he at the same time claim that nature is a result of our technical 'objectifications', as he seems to be saying in the first quotation, and that Marcuse's idea of a new science does not fit the real phenomena, which seems to be his point in the second quotation?

This question, widely discussed by Russell Keat, may be cast in these terms:[12] if the cognitive interests are taken in a strict sense, there is no way of speaking about nature-in-itself, knowable to us and independent of nature-as-conceived-of-by-our-technical interest. Nature-in-itself becomes a kind of transcendental postulate. However, at the same time Habermas criticizes Marcuse for talking about nature in inadequate categories, having "no real base", and this criticism presupposes that we do have some access to nature independently of our technical interest. This, at least, is a reasonable interpretation of Habermas's criticism. His criticism seems to rely on an ontological insight which is ruled out by his epistemology of the cognitive interests.

Habermas criticizes those (like Marcuse) who try to relate themselves to *nature* in a *communicative* manner and those who try to relate themselves in *technical* terms to *people and social phenomena*, and in so doing he seems to rely on an independent insight into what natural and social phenomena really are. In this sense the critical aspect of Habermas's critical theory seems to rely on such an independent insight: a technical attitude toward social phenomena is inadequate because it does not grasp those phenomena as they "really are", and emancipatory self-reflection aims at liberating oneself from the illusion that social and mental states of affairs are natural events brought about by natural scientific causes. If there were no way of distinguishing between nature and society independently of the chosen cognitive interest (interpreted in a rather strong transcendental sense), the critical character of critical theory would wither away.

Here again the status of the cognitive interests is at stake. A way out of the problem can be sought either by holding on to a strict constitutive interpretation of these interests and abandoning the critical aspects of the theory, or by holding on to the critical aspects while interpreting the cognitive interests in terms of standard cases for our ways of conceiving the world. According to the latter option, nature is conceived of as paradigmatically disclosed by empirical sciences and technical interest, whereas the social domain, of norms and intentions, is disclosed in a communicative (or morally reactive) attitude, but there may be "gray zones" in between, wherein the "same" phenomena can be disclosed in an objectivating as well as in a communicative and morally reactive attitude (as for instance in cases of alcoholism or of neurotic behavior).

The notion of nature will then *not* be a case of *whatever* is constituted by an objectivating attitude (technical interest), but a matter of *which approach* is found to be *possible and adequate* in each case – a question which has to be resolved through a discursive interpretation, going back and forth between common intuitions of what that realm of reality is like and various conceptual perspectives to it, trying to work out some appropriate view (but without having access to nature independently of all conceptualization, as if we could look in between our concepts and the phenomena *an sich*).

Habermas is well aware of these problems.[13] His reluctance in recent time to stick to a strict (semi-transcendental) version of the theory of cognitive interests and his preference for a pragmatic theory of universal validity claims and for a developmental theory of learning processes can be seen as an attempt to get himself out of the problems delineated above. As we recall Habermas writes:[14]

"... in the functional sphere of instrumental action we encounter objects of the type of moving bodies;..."

It has been argued, for instance by Joel Whitebook,[15] that Habermas's notion of nature is biased in the sense that *physics* seems to be taken as a paradigm for the theoretically adequate approach to nature. Consequently, biology seems to be regarded as reducible to physics. Whitebook states: "... if the entire realm of human cognition can be exhaustively subdivided, as he claims, in terms of the three knowledge-constitutive interests instrumental, communicative and emancipatory then our question becomes: where are the biological sciences to be located within his scheme?"[16] And further: "Habermas is, in short, an anti-reductionist for the human sciences and a reductionist for the life sciences."[17]

I will only make a few remarks. The first concerns biology as a science: the question of the possibility of reducing biology to physics is at least an open one. Habermas, however, does not really go into this discussion, but still he seems to presuppose some sort of reduction of biology to physics. When he talks about nature as constituted by our technical interest (and thus encountered as "moving bodies"), it definitely sounds as if he has physics in mind. However, an evolutionary explanation of animal behavior can be given in game theoretical terms in a functionalist sense, despite the general tendency to reduce biology to molecular genetics.[18]

My second remark is concerned with the problem of sharply delimiting nature from what is not nature: animals do communicate, and we can to some extent decode their communication.[19] Hence, we can, to some extent, 'understand' *nature* in the sense of *animal life*. We should also keep in mind how we communicate with babies, and with mentally retarded or senile persons.[20] These points deserve extended elaboration, but this remark will do here, where our purpose is just to remind ourselves of the intuitive inadequacy of any notion of nature exclusively formulated from the paradigm case of physics.[21]

My third point is that any view regarding all rational actions toward nature as structured by the interest of technical control is too crude, even if we restrict ourselves to the realm of non-animal nature. To make this point intuitively clear I will refer to just one simple example: a sailboat moves along in harmony with winds and waves in a way which a cabin cruiser does not. To be sure, both follow the laws of physical nature. In this sense there is nothing un-natural in either case.[22] The example serves as a reminder of a difference between what has sometimes been called *soft* and *hard technology* and it serves to illustrate the *natural* foundation of such a distinction: if nature is not merely seen in terms of physical concepts – in which case there is no difference between the two vessels – but in terms of concepts of biology, geography and meteorology, then there *is* a difference.[23] If step by step we open our example to the entire ecological environment – with plants, birds, and fish – the difference between the silent, non–polluting, and non-extractive sailboat and the noisy, polluting and extractive cruiser becomes even more striking. In short, the crudeness of the Habermasian notion of technical interest and control tends to blur an ecologically important difference between biologically hard and soft technologies.

My fourth point is closely related to the third. In describing "problems resulting from advanced capitalist growth" in his book from 1973 on problems of legitimation in late capitalism,[24] Habermas offers only a few pages to "the ecological balance". And typically, from his physicalistic position, he ends up here by referring to the physical factor of a possible rise in global temperature as *the* substantial point, leaving aside, as too uncertain and complicated, the various biological and geological factors. Thus Habermas, a theoretician of our time, has relatively little to say about ecology.[25]

Against the background of these sketches of Habermas's notion of nature, mainly from the point of view of his theory of cognitive interests, I will briefly refer to some of his more recent views, based on his pragmatic theory of validity claims and on his developmental theory of learning processes.

In this article "What is Universal Pragmatics?", he ends with the following scheme concerning "the correlations that obtain for (a) The domain of reality to which every speech action takes up relation. (b) The attitudes for the speaker prevailing in particular modes of communication. (c) The validity claims under which the relations to reality are established. (d) The general functions that grammatical sentences assume in their relations to reality."[26]

Domains of Reality	Modes of Communication: Basic Attitudes	Validity Claims	General Functions of Speech
"The" World of External World	Cognitive: Objectivating Attitude	Truth	Representation of Facts
"Our" World of Society	Interactive: Conformative Attitude	Rightness	Establishment of Legitimate Interpersonal Relations
"My" World of Internal Nature	Expressive: Expressive Attitude	Truthfulness	Disclosure of Speaker's Subjectivity
Language	----	Comprehensibility	---

Here, the foundation is not a (semi-)transcendental theory of cognitive interests, but a pragmatic reconstruction of universal validity claims. In *WIUP?*, Habermas talks about domains of reality as relatively independent of our basic attitudes, in the sense that we can relate ourselves both in an *objectivating* and a *conformative attitude* toward society. In the former case, society is turned into the mode of external nature, and in the latter into the "symbolically structured segment of reality".[27]

This brief reminder is relevant for the following quotation, where Habermas defends himself in these words having commented on McCarthy's criticism, which is close to my former remarks:[28]

"Do we have to understand such difficulties as the result of a questionable, too rigidly set out, theoretical programme, as McCarthy thinks? Or do they not simply speak for the view that while we can indeed adopt a performative attitude to external nature, enter into communicative relations with it, have aesthetic experience and feelings analogous to morality with respect to it, there is for this domain of reality only one theoretically fruitful attitude, namely the objectivating attitude of the natural scientific, experimenting observer?

I should like to support this view with the following reflections: The structures of a (in Piaget's sense) decentered understanding of the world that are determinative for the modern period may be characterized by the fact that the acting and knowing subject can adopt *different* basic attitudes towards the same world. We can obtain nine fundamental relations by combining basic attitudes and formal world concepts, as Schema 1 illustrates."

Schema 1
Formal-pragmatic relations

Domains of Reality (horizonal): Basic Attitudes (vertical):	(1) External Nature	(2) Society	(3) Internal Nature
(1) Objectivating	(1,1) Cognitive-instrumental relation	(1,2) Cognitive-strategic relation	(1,3) Objectivistic relation to self
(2) Norm-conformative	(2,1) Moral-aesthetic relation to non-objectivated environment	(2,2) Obligatory relation	(2,3) Censorious relation to self
(3) Expressive	(3,1) Moral-aesthetic relation to non-objectivated environment	(3,2) Self-presentation	(3,3) Sensuous-spontaneous relation to self

Habermas pays special attention to the combinations (1.1), (1.2), (2.2), and (3.2) – which are related to technical interest in nature (1.1), technical interest in society (1.2), practical interest in society (2.2), and emancipatory interest in social self (3.2), though with the reservation that (2.2) is here interpreted in terms more of norms (practical validity claims) than of meaning (communication).

This 'schema 1' shows that Habermas has given up his former semi-transcendental version of the theory of cognitive interests. He now talks of 'domains of reality' ('worlds') and 'basic attitudes' as *two* sets of factors that can be combined in various ways.[29]

We observe, in *scheme 1*, that the basic attitudes are related to the three universal validity claims, whereby *truth claims*, and thereby *all sciences*, are called '*objectivating*'. This concept of objectivation differs from that found in his theory of cognitive interests, where objectivation is related to the technical interest (which is related to domination and control), in contradistinction to the practical-hermeneutic approach to social and human phenomena. However, in this scheme Habermas talks about "cognitive-instrumental relation(s)" to "society". What is meant here? Does he now claim that only cognitive-instrumental relations to nature, and cognitive-strategic relations to society, are possible – i.e. that there is *no* non-strategic cognitive relation to society, or even to culture? – and that there is *no* non-instrumental cognitive relation to nature? There seems to be some confusion here: the old terminology, from the theory of cognitive interests, seems to reappear in this scheme based on universal pragmatics, mixing two different notions of objectivation, the one related to truth claims in general (universal pragmatics) and the other to technical interest (theory of cognitive interests). In this mix-up the practical-hermeneutic sciences seem to have evaporated.

Methodologically, Habermas's emphasis on what we can learn from the development of the sciences implies that each of Habermas's points has to be argued for by an interpretative and discursive elaboration of a set of relevant examples of "successful sciences". In order to carry out this argument, it is certainly not enough just to present a *scheme*. Only through an *elaboration* of relevant *examples* can anything like appropriate support be given for the claims Habermas makes.

I will refer just briefly to the "*theoretical*" aspect (1.1. in the scheme), which is explicated by the vague terms "the objectivating attitude of the natural scientific, experimenting observer"[30] and "cognitive-instrumental relation".[31] What does this really mean? It is far from clear. Does it imply some Hempelian notion of method, or some Newtonian notion of conceptualization? Habermas's allusion to Newton might suggest such a narrow interpretation.[32] But are there not other "fruitful" attitudes and "successful examples of theory formation"?[33]

To sum up:

The notions of nature and of natural science seem to remain ambiguous in Habermas's thought. This is illustrated by the unclarified status of biology within his categorial framework. The problem may be described as an oscillation between an open but vague conception on the one hand and a restricted but unelaborated conception on the other. To the latter belong the allusions to physics, and even to Newtonian physics (which is somewhat astonishing in a project that tries to conceptualize modernity).

Habermas's basic claims, interpreted as saying that nature can be adequately approached (i) by a theoretical attitude, understood strictly physicalistically, (ii) by an aesthetic-artistic attitude, or (iii) by an ecological-moral concern for nature as this physically approachable domain "in front of us", are all too narrow, too narrow both as possible forms of knowledge and as possible human relationships. When interpreted less restrictedly, his scheme avoids this criticism of narrowness, but at the cost of becoming fairly vague. (But despite its vagueness it *does* imply a distinct position in favor of *discursive rationality*, ruling out romanticist attitudes and opinions.)

Finally, to put our general point briefly and bluntly: in order to be able to treat the notion of nature, and of natural science, more adequately, a more reflective and flexible elaboration of case studies, and a less frequent use of great schemes, would be philosophically desirable.[34]

NOTES

1. Cf. "Praxeological Reflections" in this collection (especially the section "The Power of The Example").

2. Cf. "Arguments from Absurdity" in this collection.

3. Cf. Habermaas in: *Habermas. Critical Debates* (= *HCD*), eds. J. B. Thompson and D. Held, London: Macmillan, 1982, p. 244.

4. *Ibid.* p. 245.

5. Cf. *Knowledge and Human Interest* (=*KHI*), Boston: Beacon Press, 1971. German original, *Erkenntnis und Interesse*, 1968, with a new postscript 1973. Also "Erkenntnis und Interesse", in: *Technik und Wissenschaft als 'Ideologie'*, from 1965.

6. *KHI*, p. 35.

7. Thomas McCarthy: *The Critical Theory of Jürgen Habermas*, London: Hutchinson, 1978, pp. 110–125.

8. This is admitted by Habermas himself, cf. "Nachwort" to the second edition of *KHI*. Also, in his "A Reply to my Critics", in: *Habermas. Critical Debates* (= *HCD*), eds. J. B. Thompson and D. Held, London: Macmillan, 1982, p. 233.

9. "What is Universal Pragmatics?" (= WIUP?) in: *Jürgen Habermas. Communication and the Evolution of Society*, Boston: Beacon Press, 1979, pp. 15–20.

10. *Theory and Practice* (=*TP*), Boston: Beacon Press, 1973, p. 8.

11. B. Frankel: "Habermas Talking: An Interview", *Theory and Society*, Vol. 1, 1974, pp. 37–58, quoted on p. 46.

12. Russell Keat: *The Politics of Social Theory. Habermas, Freud and the Critique of Positivism*, Oxford: Blackwell, 1981, pp. 78–93.

13. Cf. *HCD*, p. 233, pp. 238–250.

14. *TP*, p. 8.

15. Joel Whitebook: "The Problem of Nature in Habermas", in: *Telos*, 40(1979) pp. 41–69.

16. Cf. Joel Whitebook *ibid.* p. 59.

17. *Op.cit.*

18. Cf., e.g., Jon Elster's argumentation for *functional explanation* as *unique for biology*, in opposition *both* to the physical sciences and to the social sciences. His position is briefly stated in the preface to *Ulysses and the Sirens*, Cambridge: Cambridge University Press, 1979, p. viii. (Cf. the debate between J. Elster and G. A. Cohen on functional explanations in the social sciences, in *Inquiry* 25(1982), pp. 27–56, and in *Theory and Society*, 11(1982), pp. 453–82 and 483–96.) Cf. also John Beatty in "The Insights and Oversights of Molecular Genetics: The Place of the Evolutionary Perspective" (in *Philosophy of Biology*, ed. Michael Ruse, London: Macmillan, 1989, pp. 209–220), who argues that "the endeavor to explain all biological generalizations in molecular-genetic terms is a fundamentally misguided one,....., evolution matters too." (p. 219).

19. This applies both to their semi-verbal signals, as with singing whales, and to their non-verbal behavior, as with mating and nursing seals. In some cases man and animal may be said to communicate spontaneously, in other cases we can figure out what an animal is doing by indirectly referring to our acquaintance with human behavior. In these cases, some forms of "participant observation" and "hermeneutic effort" can rightly be applied. Cf. "Ethical Gradualism and Discourse Ethics" in this collection.

It is worth noticing that Habermas discusses our ethical relationship to animals in a recent publication (esp. commenting on G. Patzig, e.g. "Ökologische Ethik – innerhalb der Grenzen bloßer Vernunft", in: *Umweltschutz – Herausforderung unserer Generation*, ed. H. J. Elster, Studienzentrum Weikersheim, 1984), cf. Habermas "Erläuterungen zur Diskursethik", in: *Erläuterungen zur Diskursethik*, Frankfurt a.M.: Suhrkamp, 1991, pp. 219–226. But Habermas still thinks of the relationship between man and animal in terms of a paradigmatic difference. In this ethical perspective he speaks of the different animals in gradualistic terms, but he does not approach the touchy and challenging question concerning the moral status of humans with few (or no) communicative abilities, nor does he approach the relationship between these humans and the various higher-order animals. In this respect he remains a "dichotomist".

20. Cf. the problem of defining man (and nature) in bio-medical ethics: questions of defining death, including cases of terminal comas (as in the case of Karen Quinlan), questions of the status of the fetus, and questions concerning the possibility of crossing the man-animal barriers in genetic experiments (e.g. producing offspring from man and chimpanzee).

21. Cf., e.g., Habermas's sharp division between "nature" and the "human world", referring evolution theory either to "a preunderstanding of the *human* world" or to "the empirical-analytic sciences", in: Boris Frankel: "Habermas Talking: An Interview", *Theory and Society* 1 (1974), pp. 44–45: "Since the evolution theory has a methodological status which is quite different from a normal theory in, say, physics, I think that the categorical framework in which the evolution theory has been developed since Darwin presupposes some references to a pre-understanding of the *human* world and not only of nature. The whole concept of adaptation and selection presupposes some elements which are more characteristic for the human sciences than for the empirical-analytic sciences, strictly speaking. So in my opinion, the evolution theory is no example of empirical-analytic science at all. But as far as bio-chemical theories about mutations go into evolution theory, we have, of course, a usual empirical-analytical theory. However, this is not what is characteristic for the design of evolution theory. This is only a component of the evolution theory. Modern genetics is not dependent on the evolution theory framework. Modern genetics is, I propose, a strictly objectifying theory which makes no use of concepts inherently related to our pre-understanding of what social life or cultural life is." – Hence the sharp distinction between nature (physicalistically interpreted) and non-nature prevails.

22. My point here is not one of evaluation – that sailboats are more desirable than cabin cruisers. My point is one about the notion of nature, or rather about the notion of technical control of nature.

23. The sailboat works *with* winds and waves, the cabin cruiser fights its way *against* them.

24. English translation: *Legitimation Crisis*, Boston: Bacon Press, 1975, pp. 41–43. Also T. McCarthy in: *HCD*, pp. 62–78.

25. In talking about these issues it is essential to differentiate between various levels of claims: Habermas's notion of rationality, which also defines modernity, is at the core of his thinking. Ecological questions, on the other hand, belong to the issues that are to be treated discursively, and for which Habermas does not make any privileged claims. Ecological questions belong to those issues that are to be discussed *by means of* this modern discursive rationality.

    As a matter of fact Habermas, a theoretician of modernity, has relatively little to say about ecology. This might be due to a relative weakness in his personal knowledge of these topics. But it might also be due partly to some narrowness in his conception of a natural science. At least the reason given in *Legitimationsprobleme* for not going into substantial ecological questions, namely that these questions are uncertain, does not sound quite convincing when we recall how eagerly he has elaborated social theories that are uncertain and controversial (such as the theories of Piaget and of Kohlberg).

26. In: *WIUP?* p. 68 (Germ. orig. 1976).

    It is worthwhile noticing that the English translation includes some changes in terminology: for instance, the original terms "objectivity, normativity, subjectivity, intersubjectivity" (*Objektivität, Normativität, Subjektivität* and *Intersubjektivität*, cf. *Sprachpragmatik und Philosophie*, ed. K.-O. Apel, Fr.a.M.: Suhrkamp, 1976, p. 259.) are translated by "cognitive: objectivating attitude", "interactive: conformative attitude", "expressive: expressive attitude", and leaving out "intersubjectivity" altogether.

    "Objectivity", as a "cognitive attitude", can be interpreted in a *broad* sense, whereby *both* empirical-analytic and historical-hermeneutic sciences are included (i.e. both technical and practical interest constitute reality in a way which makes true statements possible). But then there is another and *narrow* sense of "objectivating" whereby the empirical-analytic sciences are included and the historical-hermeneutic ones are excluded, and this interpretation seems close at hand in an earlier paragraph in *WIUP?* (pp. 66–67; in the original, pp. 256–257): "By *external nature* I mean the objectivated [*objektivierte*] segment of reality that the adult subject is able (even if only mediately) to perceive and manipulate. One can, of course, adopt an objectivating [*objektivierende*] attitude not only toward inanimate nature but toward all objects [*Gegenstände*] and states of affairs that are directly or indirectly accessible to sensory experience. *Society* designates that symbolically prestructured segment of reality that the adult subject can understand in a nonconformative [*nichtobjektivierende*] attitude, that is, as one acting communicatively (as a participant in a system of communication). Legitimate interpersonal relations belong here, as do institutions, traditions, cultural values, etc [*semantisch gehaltsvolle Objektivationen überhaupt, sowie die sprach- und handlungsfähigen Subjekte selber*]. We can replace the conformative attitude with an objectivating [*objektivierende*] attitude toward society conversely, we can switch to a conformative attitude in domains in which (today) we normally behave objectivatingly for example, in relation to animals and plants." Here "objectivation" definitely seems to designate an attitude toward reality; it is "objectivating" in the *narrow* sense of "reifying", not in the *broad* sense of "thematizing (raising truth claims)".

27. That is, "institutions, traditions, cultural values, etc."
    It should again be observed that *objectivation (objectivating)* is related here to *truth claims in general*, not only to truth claims raised with a *technical* (cognitive) interest in contrast to truth claims raised with a *practical* (cognitive) interest. (In his essay "Knowledge and Human Interest", Habermas says, with reference to the empirical-analytic sciences, that they are related to "the cognitive interest of technical disposition over objectivated processes". Cf. p. 157 in: *Technik und Wissenschaft als 'Ideologie'*, Fr.a.M. 1968; German original: *vergegenständlichte Prozesse*. In this essay, based on the earlier theory of cognitive interests, we thus find a more restricted sense of the term "objectivation" than the one used in the scheme just referred to. At the same time, Habermas emphasizes, as he does in the book *KHI*, that *both* the technical and the practical interest are preconditions for "objectivity".)
    In the actual scheme, historical-hermeneutic sciences apparently have no natural place: either there are *truth*-claims, which are then related to "the world of external nature", or there are *normative* validity claims, related to "our world of society" (cf. the validity claim of rightness in the scheme). Hermeneutic sciences (e.g. *verstehende Soziologie*), which do raise truth claims, but which are not within a horizon of "objectivation"

in the restricted sense referred to above, thus seem to have been left out. However, there is an alternative interpretation, according to which the term "objectivation" is taken in a very broad sense (just as the term "the world of external nature" is interpreted in such a broad sense that social phenomena are included); in that case the (cognitive) "*practical* interest" falls *within* the former category, viz. that of truth claims and of "cognitive: objectivating attitudes".

28. *HCD* pp. 243–244. Also fig. 10 in: *Theorie des kommunikativen Handelns (= TKH)*, I, p. 324. However, Habermas has later declared this scheme, related to the question of nature, misconceived (at a conference on *TKH* at ZIF/Bielefeld June 1985).

29. However, the notion of *nature* ("external nature") is still not clearly defined (cf. again the difficulties in defining the limit between man and nature in bio-medical ethics), and the term *objectivating* allows for interpretations of a *narrow* kind, related to *technical interests and physics*, as well as of a *broader* kind, related to *truth claims*, embracing both practical and technical perspectives (but in this case the terms "cognitive instrumental" – 1.1 – and "cognitive strategic" – 1.2 – become a problem).

30. *HCB* p. 244.

31. *Ibid.*

32. *HCD* p. 249.

33. *HCD* pp. 244–245. Habermas does make an important distinction between moral attitudes and theoretical attitudes (*HCD* p. 247, and *Vorstudien und Ergänzungen (= VE)*, Fr.a.M.: Suhrkamp, 1984, p. 518): we can feel compassion for nature (a *moral attitude*), but we cannot have anything other than an "objectivating" knowledge of nature. In other words, we can extend and develop our ecological awareness in a moral sense without necessarily claiming that there is anything but natural scientific *knowledge* to be obtained of nature. But again, what does "objectivating" knowledge mean? If it is taken to cover all attitudes based on truth claims, it is vague, but *prima facie* not controversial. If, on the other hand, "objectivating" is understood in a strictly physicalistic sense, it is a more questionable claim, containing a reductionism which has to be

argued for.

Along the same lines, Habermas distinguishes between a possible *theoretical* approach to nature and a *sociopsychological* approach (*HCD* pp. 247–248, *VE* p. 518): we cannot have anything but an "objectivating" *knowledge* of nature, but in the realm of ecological crisis we can change (and improve) our *attitudes and practices*. My answer will be the same as above: the notion of "objectivating" knowledge is ambiguous, and if it is understood in a strictly physicalistic sense, it has at least to be argued for.

34. For illustration of this desideratum, cf. Philip Kitcher's contribution to the discussion of scientific rationality and progress (based on an analysis of the controversy between Darwinism and creationism), in: *Abusing Science*, Cambridge, Mass.: MIT Press, 1983.

Ethical Gradualism and Discourse Ethics

Paradigmatic and Gradualist Moral Thinking

The realm of ethics is most often restricted to man and the human world: only humans can act morally or immorally, only humans can be morally praised or blamed, only humans can have a worth or a value in themselves, only humans can be holders of rights; all other beings can merely be ascribed rights or values indirectly, relative to man.[1] In short only humans can be moral agents and only humans can be moral subjects. To what extent is this ethical anthropocentrism tenable? In this chapter I will consider arguments, especially in discourse ethics, in favor of such a paradigmatically unique ethical standing for humans, and I will look into arguments in favor of an ethical gradualism between humans and other mammals and between man and nature.

In our ethical thinking we tend to have some special cases in mind, sometimes without being fully aware of it, sometimes more consciously or even explicitly. I assume that we tend to argue either in terms of typical cases or in terms of degrees of similarity between related cases. The former way of arguing leads to paradigmatic thinking, the latter to gradualism. Each way of arguing has its virtues. The former makes us see differences, the latter makes us see continuities. In philosophy both are required.

I

I will begin by looking at some of the arguments which first come to mind in favor of ethical gradualism, but prior to that I will briefly recall the apparent strength of ethical anthropocentrism.

Morality is located in the socio-cultural world of acting and thinking human beings, and so are other norms and values, be they juridical or aesthetic. Nature can be the object of aesthetic attitudes and evaluations. She can also be the object of legal regulations, e.g. in terms of the right to own and to use natural resources. And nature can be the object of moral considerations, at least as far as biological nature is concerned: the extinction of endangered species is currently conceived as a moral concern, and the unnecessary infliction of suffering upon sentient non-human beings is in general seen as morally wrong. Sentient animals, at least, are thus the subjects of human moral considerations. But these animals cannot themselves take part in these considerations. Nor can they act freely and rationally like human beings. They cannot act morally, nor immorally, only amorally, without responsibility or obligations of any kind. Animal rights are therefore asymmetrical, that is, the rights of animals entail obligations for man, without any obligations on the animal's side. Not even a chimpanzee is taken to be morally responsible for its deeds.

Ethical anthropocentrism is therefore *prima facie* a reasonable position: morality belongs exclusively to man and the human world. Even when we go through a certain repertoire of cases, from physical nature to plants and sentient animals, this conclusion seems safe. Also in the more touchy case of the chimpanzee the same conclusion seems plausible.

However, there is an intensive discussion, especially in medical ethics, on the moral status of borderline cases. We have thorough discussions of the ethical status of a fetus and of people with severe brain damage (such as anencephaly). To what extent do they have the moral status of persons? To what extent do they have human rights? There are academic discussions, there are public debates focusing on such cases as abortion and euthanasia, and there are various initiatives on behalf of those who are not able themselves to participate in such discussions and debates.[2]

In these borderline cases we have members of the human species, such as fetuses or severely brain-damaged people, who do not perform like the paradigm case of a human being. The question concerning their moral status and their moral rights is therefore discussed by somebody else. This kind of *advocatory repre-*

sentation is the standard case for minors.[3] The parents are generally the first to be responsible for their behavior, for their upbringing, and for defending their interests, but other people or institutions might also be entitled to assume this role. This advocatory responsibility and representation is supposed to be reduced gradually in accordance with the process of maturation; it formally ends at the time when the child reaches full legal age.

The cases of advocatory representation in medical ethics are more extreme, as it were; they take place further away from the paradigm case of a mature and morally responsible human being than in the case of rearing children. We have fetuses at different stages, and we have those human beings who are still alive, but who at the end of their lives are no longer able to participate in a discussion about their own situation. We have people who are severely senile and people with severe brain damage. We have babies born with anencephaly who will never be able to participate in any such discussion.

Along the same lines, perhaps transcending the realm of medical ethics, we have the cases of an advocatory concern for the dignity of the recently deceased, and for the values and wishes they expressed while alive. And we have the cases of advocatory concern for coming generations and thus for hypothetical people, that is, for those who are not yet individualized, but who are statistically recognized, even though there are different scenarios with different numbers of people in the future.

To the extent that medical ethics and our ethical concern in general tend to include all such cases within the realm of human morality – giving each of these human beings thereby the status of a person with moral rights – we have taken a major step away from the paradigm case of human morality. In this expansion we include everyone who belongs to the human species regardless of his or her capabilities. We tend to include everybody who can become a mature human being. We include everybody who has been a mature human being. And we include everybody who once could have become a mature human being.

There are certainly great differences between these different cases. And in quite a few cases there is no unanimity about the moral status of the human being concerned; the debates on abortion and euthanasia illustrate this point: membership in the human species is in one sense a biological question and in another sense a normative question, and there is an open debate concerning potential and full membership in the human species in a normative sense. When is a member of *Homo sapiens* a person, with full moral standing? A fetus is a potential person, but in what sense *is* it a person? The same goes for past membership in the human species. A terminal patient with severe brain damage has been a person, but in what sense is he still a person? There is a tendency to proceed from the paradigm case of a normal human being toward cases where morally relevant capabilities are increasingly absent, the limiting case being mere membership in the human species.

These are important questions in a practical sense, since we run into the moral distinction between murdering humans and killing non-humans, the former being morally unacceptable, the latter regarded for the most part as morally acceptable, at least when it is done without undue infliction of pain.

These moral questions are to some extent forced upon us, since the development of modern technology has made it increasingly possible to intervene medically in these borderline cases of human existence.

When these kinds of human existence are taken into account, we are forced to adapt a certain gradualism, namely a gradualism within the human species. So far it is primarily a question of an ontological gradualism, not an ethical gradualism, i.e. it recognizes the biological and psychological continuity between different individuals of the human species, but still insists on the recognition of a moral status for them all. Their characteristics differ, but they are all human beings, with human dignity and human rights. This is a position of ethical anthropocentrism based on an awareness of the borderline cases from medical ethics.

So far we have not questioned the distinction between *Homo sapiens* and other species. However, at this point we ought to look carefully into borderline cases on the other side of the species border.

Everybody is aware of the fact that chimpanzees can act and communicate, and that they can also experience pain and pleasure. Genetically chimpanzees are close relatives to man, and they have well-developed brains and nervous systems.

Nevertheless, a chimpanzee does not possess the higher capabilities delineated above. It is not a moral agent, it is not a morally responsible being. Its use of language is neither reflexive nor creative. It is doubtful whether it can be said to have a social identity based on mutual recognition and verbal communication. But it does act, feel and communicate. It probably has some self-awareness and sense of identity. And it clearly has higher mental capabilities than some of the members of the human species represented advocatorily for the sake of their moral status as human beings.[4] The latter is a disturbing fact.

In self-defense we, the humans, could add that we do take the pain of sentient non-human beings into moral consideration. It is regarded as morally wrong to inflict unnecessary pain on sentient animals; in most countries it is even forbidden by law (although the decision as to what is necessary and unnecessary pain in each concrete case leaves room for considerable and corruptible judgment).

It is more controversial whether we have some kind of moral duty to promote well-being among sentient non-humans, in this case among higher mammals. And there seems to be little support for the view that we ought to help these animals to have a long life – the main exception being special pets (who have their hospitals, and even their own cemeteries). On the contrary, it is for the most part considered, morally, perfectly all right to kill any non-human sentient being, high-ranking mammals such as chimpanzees included. The painless killing of animals is regarded as morally acceptable, an underlying assumption being that none of these animals has any awareness of its own death, except when a higher animal is threatened by death (and that is one of the painful experiences which humans should try not to inflict on animals).

What started as human self-defense here ends in embarrassment: some of our patients, as well as early human fetuses, do not have any awareness of their own death. Even worse: they would probably experience even less of a trauma by being killed than most higher mammals probably experience when we kill them.

If there is a moral difference between two cases, there must also be some morally relevant difference in properties between the two. The decisive difference between the "deviant" cases of *Homo sapiens* and the higher cases of other mammals can hardly be found on the level of *actual properties*: in some cases the non-human mammals rank higher in this respect than some members of the human species. In these cases we will have to argue in terms of past and of potential competence and characteristics in order to find a relevant difference: a member of the human species did have, or can develop, or could have developed such and such competence and characteristics.

These arguments *from potentiality* are partly reasonable. This, for instance, is how the usual catholic (Aristotelian) argument goes, in favor of the moral status of the fetus from the moment of conception. But biology is gradual and nature boundless.[5] Arguments from potentiality are therefore only partly reasonable. Arguments from potentiality have to be balanced against arguments from actuality: how can we consider it moral to kill a vital chimpanzee when we strictly condemn active euthanasia for terminal patients with severe brain damage and hardly any neurophysiological activity?[6]

This is a field of deep emotions. These emotions can easily be explained, just as our discrimination against other species can be explained and understood in various ways, psychologically and sociologically. But the same is true of most acts and attitudes, some of which we would hardly defend morally – such as racial discrimination.

Despite the gradualist arguments from borderline cases between humans and higher mammals, we uphold the unique paradigmatic position of humans: man is a moral agent, not in the sense that human beings *de facto* act morally, but in the sense that they are able to do so. Man does not act, or react, merely from instinct. Man acts in accordance with socially determined norms and values, and he is aware of doing so. He has the ability to reflect upon these norms and values, and to argue for or against them; and he can more or less consciously change them. Man hereby shows his freedom in relation to nature. This freedom, which sets him off from nature, is tied to his status as a social being. He communicates on the basis of his socialization into a community. He communicates with a whole spectrum of linguistic speech acts, and he can therefore reflect and discuss, reject and improve, in short, acquire better insight and knowledge. Humans are agents, they are conscious and thinking beings, they are social beings living in a community. They do not have only material needs, they do not live socially only in a way which requires law and order; they also have personal identity acquired through a vulnerable process of socialization and individuation.

I will leave it at that for the time being. These remarks I hold to be true, as claims within a phenomenology of man as a moral being. They are true of man. And in the universe known to us it is hard to see for whom else they might be said to be true. So evidently man is paradigmatically a moral being.

But then we have the difficult borderline cases: to help justify a moral distinction between human fetuses and infants on the one hand and higher mammals like chimpanzees on the other, we might choose, once again, to stress the notion of *potential* properties rather than that of *actual properties*.

(i) As an analysis of the *actual properties* of borderline cases has shown, arguments from actuality are not conclusive for a sharp distinction between man and other mammals. To begin with, there is a problem as to what actual properties should be considered. What are the relevant properties? Some major candidates are: an ability to act rationally and freely, an ability to make interest claims, and self-consciousness.[7] But even if we should come to agreement on a clear and consistent notion of such actual properties, it is unlikely that such a notion would support a moral difference between all mammals that genetically belong to the human species and all other mammals. For whatever actual properties we choose there will most probably be cases of humans who fail to have these properties, and for quite a few such properties there will be some highly developed non-humans who have more of them than some defective or less developed humans do. If, for instance, we choose conscious self-identity as such an ethically relevant property, we cannot include newborn human infants (thus we open the door for a legitimation of painless infanticide). If we choose some basic brain functions as a morally decisive actual property, we will have a problem in making a moral distinction between a human fetus and a chimpanzee fetus, and we will have to recognize that normal chimpanzees have this actual property to a higher degree than some humans with brain damage. If we include human infants or people with severe brain damage we will have to include adult chimpanzees as well. It is therefore hard to see how any actual property could do the job of providing a sharp demarcation between humans and non-humans.

(ii) For this purpose arguments *from potentiality* are more promising, though not quite conclusive. If, for instance, we take the potentiality of a future self-conscious life to be the morally decisive property, we will certainly have cases of severely defective human infants with less of this potentiality than we find in normal chimpanzee infants. However, at this point we could introduce the notion of a potentiality of a second order, i.e. a potentiality to have potentialities, and on this basis we could argue in favor of a morally relevant distinction between these two cases: a brain-damaged human infant could have had a potentiality to become a self-conscious being in a sense in which the normal chimpanzee infant could not. This is clearly an interesting point. But the twist of the argument consists in a change from considering the real potentialities of an individual to considering the potentialities of the species to which this individual belongs.[8]

Summing up, I would say that arguments from potentiality might give some support to a notion of ethical speciesism, though not unconditionally.

(iii) There is also a theologically grounded anthropocentrism, claiming (for instance) that all humans and only humans are created in the image of God, this giving them a unique ethical standing. In this paper I choose to leave this theological version of ethical speciesism aside.[9]

(iv) There is, however, a sociological version of the anthropocentric position which I will briefly comment upon. This argument does not defend genetic anthropocentrism, or speciesism in the strict sense, but a social anthropocentrism. The argument is one in favor of personhood and moral rights, not as individually given independently of society, but as a moral status inherently ascribed to members of a community. Any being included in this community has moral rights in accordance with his role and function within this community (either egalitarian or hierarchical). By seeking a notion of a socially embedded moral standing, we avoid a notion of individual rights connected to actual or potential properties in the individual. According to such a societal notion, all that matters is whether a being is included in a community, to a large extent regardless of individual properties. If a being is included, this being enjoys a moral status with certain rights (depending on the society and its internal differentiations). Beings that are not included have no such rights, regardless of their actual and potential properties. For instance, a society may include a severely brain-damaged human being as a member with a basic moral standing (as a moral subject, if not as a moral agent), and the same society may choose to exclude a chimpanzee with higher actual (and potential) properties. If such a society decides to make a sharp distinction between those who are merely genetically humans and all other mammals, we have a case of a socially based anthropocentrism (or speciesism). In short, by tradition or by decision, a society can posit an ethical anthropocentrism.

However, the price paid is ethical contextualism. We are at the mercy of a given tradition or of a given form of decision making as to the inclusion and exclusion of community members. The demarcation line between insiders and outsiders might in a given context be one that excludes groups of genetic human beings, regarding them as sub-human. An open discussion of the legitimacy of the given tradition and the given form of decision making is therefore required. Only to the extent that these conditions are freely discussed and agreed upon by everybody concerned could we rightly claim that these conditions are legitimate. Through such an attempt at legitimating or criticizing a given tradition, we transcend ethical contextualism and move toward discursive ethics.

(v) Discourse ethics, as a meta-ethical procedure, implies a certain anthropocentrism since all actual participants, in the world known to us, are humans.[10] But this is merely an empirical fact; in principle any speech-acting sentient being could be a candidate for participating in a discourse. There is also a demarcation problem for humans (defined genetically, theologically or socially) concerning the competence requirements for participation in ethical discourse, and we have the problem of how to represent humans who are themselves unable to participate. All in all, this means that discourse ethics there are borderline problems between humans and non-humans, and the discourse-ethical support for ethical anthropocentrism is therefore conditional.[11] I will just add a few comments on some aspects of these problems: we have to reconsider the conditions for actual and advocatory participation in a moral discourse. Should speech-acting and intelligent Martians participate? According to the basic assumptions of discourse ethics the answer must be affirmative.[12] Should only mentally undeveloped humans be advocatorily represented, and not higher mammals who actually are mentally more developed? According to the assumptions of discourse ethics the answer must be negative. All moral subjects should be advocatorily represented, each in accordance with its moral status (which opens for an ethical gradualism, e.g. from more sentient to less sentient moral subjects).

At this level of meta-discourse we face intricate interrelationships between the conditions for being a *moral agent*, for being a *moral subject*, and for being a *moral discussant*. When we discuss actual and advocatory participation in moral discourse, the distinction between humans and non-humans once again becomes blurred.

II

There is more to be said about morally relevant continuity and discontinuity between humans and non-humans. There are various basic views on what count as ethically relevant properties; here I will just recall the major theoretical positions located around utilitarianism, the deontological position, and discourse ethics.

A classical passage from Jeremy Benthan gives the core of the utilitarian position:[13]

> "The day *may* come when the rest of the animal creation may acquire those rights which never could have been witholden from them but by the hand of tyranny. The French have already discovered that the blackness of the skin is no reason why a human being should be abandoned without redress to the caprice of a tormentor. It may one day come to be recognized that the number of the legs, the villosity of the skin, or the termination of the *os sacrum*, are reasons equally insufficient for abandoning a sensitive being to the same fate. What else is it that should trace the insuperable line? Is it the faculty of reason, or perhaps the faculty of discourse? But a full-grown horse or dog is beyond comparison a more rational, as well as a more conversable animal, than an infant of a day, or a week, or even a month, old. But suppose they were otherwise, what would it avail? The question is not, Can they reason? nor Can they *talk*? but, *Can they suffer?*"

At this point I will briefly summarize my own opinion by saying that the utilitarian focus on suffering (sentience), is conceptually too narrow to grasp the borderline problems between humans and non-humans with sufficient subtlety. This does not mean that the descriptive analyses of the utilitarians are wrong. On the contrary, I think that utilitarian arguments about suffering and sentience (in humans and non-humans alike) have a normative strength which cannot be ignored. But still I regard their perspective as conceptually insufficient:[14] for one thing, utilitarians underplay the paradigmatic difference between humans and non-humans since they disregard the morally relevant aspects of the acquisition and maintenance of a social identity.[15]

I also assume that quite a few of the proponents of individual rights operate with a conceptual scheme which is too narrow to grasp the realm of socialization and of reflective and discursive justification with sufficient subtlety.[16]

In my opinion, the idea of a paradigmatic difference between humans and non-humans is most adequately conceived by the theorists of social identity and of discursive rationality. The gradualist arguments, as in utilitarianism, are thereby not denied, only sublated (*aufgehoben*), as it were.

In my view there are two major advantages to discourse ethics relative to utilitarianism and to classical theories of individual rights:

(a) These two latter positions presuppose socialized individuals, without themselves questioning and elaborating the implications of human socialization for the interrelationship between individuals and communities, for the human need for a mutual recognition of one's vulnerable social identity, and for the discursive interpretation of needs in general.[17]

(b) In the current discussion the emphasis is often given to detailed analyses of actual and potential properties in the various creatures. But then there is still the problem of a possible naturalistic fallacy once such properties are used for normative conclusions. In my view, the best way out is that of a reflection on the constitutive conditions for a normative discussion, in short that of a discourse ethics. Discourse ethics focuses on the self-reflective insight of argumentation, using the undeniability of its constitutive preconditions as its foundation, supplemented with arguments from universal pragmatics and developmental theory. As an ethics based on the self-reflective insight of argumentation and on speech-act inherent preconditions, discourse ethics includes universalization in terms of general role taking and presupposes mutual recognition among the discussants, thus underlining socialization as a core element. Utilitarianism and classical deontology do not reflectively justify their own presuppositions in the same sense; they remain pre-critical by presupposing or positing their basic normative positions.

Both social identity through socialization and normative justification through self-reflection and discourse are essential elements in discourse ethics.[18] Even if discourse ethics has its inherent problems, for instance the problem of the exclusion and inclusion of participants (be they humans or non-humans), and even if this problem is extended to advocatory representation for humans and non-humans (including future generations and future moral subjects of a non-human kind), it still remains, in my view, the best proposal for a fundamental ethical theory. The concepts of justice and solidarity, critical universalization and embeddedness in a form of life, are all important aspects of discourse ethics.[19] Since an act of justification can transcend a given context, thus enabling free criticism (even though any application is context-bound), every given form of solidarity can in principle be questioned discursively. And by including the interrelationship of socialization and individuation, discourse theory avoids abstract individualism and naturalism (concerning rights and properties).

In addition to its post-metaphysical robustness, rooted in self-reflective criticism and in attempts at intersubjective procedural solutions through argumentation, discourse ethics entails the decisive point that it talks in terms not only of utilities or of rights, both of which can be seen as distributed by degrees between humans and non-humans, but of socialized individuals with an identity based on mutual recognition through communication. This kind of identity is hardly found in non-humans. To the extent that morality is not only a question of resources or of rights, but of communicative recognition (social identity), we have here a decisive argument in favor of the claim that humans have a paradigmatic moral status.

We do not thereby claim that social identity is equally well presented in all members of the human species, nor that social identity can in no way be achieved by non-humans, be they mammals or Martians. I merely claim that social identity is paradigmatically human, more so than biological reactions and psychological characteristics. I claim that social identity in this respect is a more adequate notion than that of abstractly conceived individuals and their posited rights.

III

I will end these reflections on the ethical borderline between man and higher mammals by discussing some conceptual distinctions concerning the notion of a moral subject.

In discussing the moral status of humans and non-humans it is helpful to make a distinction between *moral agents* and *moral subjects*. The former are capable of acting morally, the latter are capable of being harmed in a morally relevant sense. Moral obligations are connected both to the interrelationship between moral agents and to their relationship to moral subjects. But moral subjects who are not moral agents are unable to have obligations (either to each other or to moral agents).

If we were to work out a concept of an agent capable of acting morally, we would include notions about capabilities to understand a situation and to evaluate the moral importance of what one does or doesn't do, and to act in accordance with that understanding and evaluation. In trying to make such a concept of a moral agent more precise we move into current philosophical debates on the nature of action, of rationality and of accountability. I assume, however, that the crude distinction between moral agent and moral subject makes enough sense for the time being. At this point I will approach these philosophically controversial issues by introducing the concept of a *moral discussant*, and consider the interrelationship between moral discussants, moral agents and moral subjects.

It could be claimed that the concepts of *moral agent* and of *moral discussant* are co-extensive: those who are able to act morally are able to discuss moral actions, and those who are able to discuss moral actions are also able to act morally. But even if this were empirically true, it does not imply that the two concepts converge into one. However, it is reasonable to assume that those who are able to act morally should normally be able to talk about their evaluations and actions, and even be able to explain why they think their actions were morally right in a given case. That would be the first step toward a moral discussion. In this sense it is reasonable to think of moral agents as potential moral discussants.

This is an important point, and I assume that the claim of an interrelationship between moral agency and moral discourse can be philosophically elaborated along the lines of a universal pragmatics (as in Apel and Habermas) and of a theory of socialization and of modernization (as in Kohlberg or Weber). But these are tricky problems, and we should at least be aware of the various levels involved: even if moral agents paradigmatically are moral discussants, that does not mean that all are. Even if moral agents are potentially moral discussants, that does not mean that they always actually are. It is possible to think of cases of moral agents who are relatively unable to discuss the moral aspects of their actions. The ability to discuss moral questions requires considerable intellectual skills. It presupposes a certain intelligence and a certain training. The required social and intellectual training comprehends an ability to step back and reflect upon a case from different perspectives, an awareness of the possibility of applying different concepts, and an ability to discuss their strengths and weaknesses in a given case. This kind of conceptual and hypothetical reflection requires not only mature (and sane) individuals, but also a certain cultural development, that is, a certain degree of modernization.

This means, all in all, that in claiming an interrelationship between the concept of a *moral agent* and the concept of a *moral discussant*, we are not talking in empirical terms, but in terms of presuppositions and idealizations, that is, in terms of a universal pragmatics concerning competences inherent in speech acts and in terms of a theory of modernization and socialization concerning conceptual development and the development of social identity. Only if we are willing to argue for some such presuppositions can we talk about moral agents as moral discussants, *tout court*. If not, we cannot claim that being a moral agent is sufficient for being a moral discussant.

Could we claim, the other way around, that being able to participate in a moral discourse is sufficient for being able to act morally? The answer depends on the presuppositions built into the concept of a moral discussant. We could try to spell it out in a thought-experiment (and a pretty weird one at that). Let us imagine a robot and a god, both having adequate intelligence, knowledge of all relevant facts, and an ability to speak and to listen.[20] In short, we assume that both are capable of participating in scientific (theoretical) discourses. I also assume that they are able to intervene in worldly affairs. But are the requirements for participating in a theoretical and in a practical (moral) discourse the same? If the answer is affirmative, then these theoretical discussants are moral discussants, and we could ask whether they are also to be regarded as moral agents.

But could discussants without a biological body (like our robot or a bodiless god) count as moral agents? A being without a biological body has no biological needs, no experience of biologically rooted pains or pleasures, no biological birth and growth, no biological aging or mortality, no biological vulnerability. Such a being could, according to our presuppositions, discuss all morally relevant facts concerning moral subjects, be they humans or non-humans. Such a being could also apply legal and formal principles, such as the principle of treating equal cases equally. But how could this being possibly be in a position to understand and evaluate biological life, with its vulnerability and death? It could get information about these facts, but without acquiring through experience the notions necessary to understand these facts. In what sense could this being understand what these facts were about? He could get information about people's reactions toward these facts of life, but how could he understand these reactions? This robot or bodiless god has no experience rooted in life processes from the psychological and social world, including socialization and learning based on bodily existence and interaction. This being could only register people's actions mechanically, without understanding what the passions and interests were all about. The problem here is that of how an observer might acquire act-constitutive notions when he is excluded from participating in the activities for which the notions are constitutive:[21] as a non-participant in the biological world, and in the social world that is based directly or indirectly on biological existence, this being would not be able to participate in all the role taking which is supposed to take place in a practical discourse, and which again opens the way to universalization and to solidarity.[22]

I am not here discussing the old question of whether the devil could participate in practical discourse, i.e. whether good will is a prerequisite of being a moral discussant. (Nor am I discussing whether good will is a prerequisite of being a moral agent, since the concept of a moral agent is understood in terms of the ability to act morally, not of the willingness to do so or of the frequency of morally good actions.) My thought-experiment is focused on the importance of bio-bodily existence for the concept of a moral discussant. The robot, I assume, has no body, that is, no biological body, but merely a mechanical one. The god has no body, or he has a body that is invulnerable and eternal, never born and immortal.

My suggestion is that a biological bodily existence is necessary for a competent moral discussant. Those who cannot be morally harmed, since they lack vulnerability, cannot be moral subjects, and therefore they cannot be moral discussants, even if they have the intelligence, the information, and the semantic competence required: one has to be a moral subject in order to be a moral discussant.

If this argument is tenable it means that discourse ethics has a biological foundation, as part of the competence requirements for being a participant in practical discussions (maybe in contrast to the requirements for being a participant of theoretical discussions). It means that biologically rooted learning and vulnerability represent a shared foundation for moral discussants, moral agents and moral subjects.[23]

To sum up: (i) the notion of a moral discussant and that of a moral agent are not co-extensive, even though they are inter-connected, and (ii) the notion of a moral subject is interrelated to that of a moral discussant: not all moral subjects are moral discussants, but all moral discussants are moral subjects.

It may be that there is a graduality of obligations along the scale from humans to non-humans of various kinds. But gradualism is not relativism. There are, clearly, things we ought to do, and things we should avoid doing. And there are huge areas where our moral intuitions are unclear or inconsistent. Therefore we need an ongoing ethical discussion. We have a clear obligation, as moral discussants, to keep this discussion going.

NOTES

1. Cf., e.g., I. Kant, "Duties to Animals and Spirits", in *Lectures in Ethics*, transl. Louis Infield, New York: Harper and Row, 1963, pp. 239–241.

2. Cf. the German debate on Peter Singer's views on euthanasia, *Zur Debatte über Euthanasie*, eds. R. Hegselmann and R. Merkel, Frankfurt a.M.: Suhrkamp, 1991, and Peter Singer, "On Being Silenced in Germany" in: *The New York Review*, 15. Aug. 1991, pp. 34–40.

3. On the notion of advocatory representation related to discourse ethics, cf. K.-O. Apel: *Diskurs und Verantwortung*, Frankfurt a.M.: Suhrkamp, 1988, e.g. pp. 123 and 143, and D. Böhler: "Menschenwürde und Menschen-tötung. Über Diskursethik und utilitaristische Ethik", in: *Zeitschrift für Evangelische Ethik*, 35(1991) No. 3, pp. 166–186.

4. The point I am making can also be strengthened by a look at the relationship between man and chimpanzees. Two species, we say. But according to zoologists, man and chimpanzee can interbreed, and might already have done so. The offspring would probably not be fertile. But even so, what could not future geneticists be able to achieve by ingenious cloning? What should we have done with such an interbreed between man and chimpanzee? Not to mention possible further interbreeds, producing three-fourths man and one-fourth chimpanzee, or the other way around, etc. Should they be ascribed the status of moral agents with human rights?

5. One can always go further. What about the potentialities of all human eggs and of all human sperms? (What about the potentialities of the genes these cells are made up of? And the other way around: potentially we are all dead. But nobody would argue in favor of his own actual moral status as being equivalent to his future status as a corpse.)

6. Imagine the following scenario: From behind the veil of ignorance Rawls could, hypothetically, be confronted with his daughter being raped by a chimpanzee, and subsequently giving birth to a grandchild who is half human and half animal; and still worse, this grandchild could later be "raped" by some ingenious bio-technicians, artificially interbreeding him with another chimpanzee, thus producing a great-grandchild which is three-fourths ape and one fourth human. If this is a theoretically possible world, which could be envisaged from behind the veil of ignorance, and if Rawls is supposed to care for his offspring three generations ahead, how would this possibility influence his choice of a future world? Would the treatment of animals, at least of chimpanzees, still be excluded as morally irrelevant, or would he include some considerations about animal rights and animal welfare? (On Rawls and environment, cf. e.g. M. S. Pritchard, "Justice and the Treatment of Animals: A Critique of Rawls", *Environmental Ethics*, 3(1981), pp. 55–61; R. Manning, "Environmental Ethics and John Rawls' Theory of Justice", *Environmental Ethics*, 3(1981), pp. 155–165; B. G. Norton, "Intergenerational Equity and Environmental Decisions: A Model Using Rawls' Veil of Ignorance", *Ecological Economics*, 1(1989), pp. 137–159; J. Penn, "Towards an Ecologically-based Society: A Rawlsian Perspective", *Ecological Economics*, 2(1990), pp. 225–242; R. K. Turner, "Environment, Economics and Ethics", in: *Blueprint 2: Greening the World Economy*, eds. E. Barbier et al., London: Earthscan Publications, 1991, pp. 209–224.)

7. The use of language (and its relationship to consciousness) is still a hot issue in this debate. Cf. e.g. R. G. Frey arguing in favor of the uniqueness of man in this respect, in *Interests and Rights: The Case against Animals*, Oxford: Oxford University Press, 1980, and Bernard Rollin arguing (more convincingly, I think) in favor of gradualism, in *The Unheeded Cry*, Oxford: Oxford University Press, 1989. The latter also on animal pain (*ibid.*).

8. And once we introduce the notion of potential potentiality we get a problem in defining its limitations. *Could* chimpanzees have acquired bigger brains? In what sense was this an evolutionary potentiality?

9. In one sense Judeo-Christian theology evidently offers a firm foundation for the uniqueness of man and for human dignity (for ethical anthropocentrism). But such a theological foundation requires its own justification, with its well-known problems.

10. Cf. Habermas on a possible ethics for non-humans, *Habermas: Critical Debates*, eds. J. B. Thompson and D. Held, London: Macmillan, 1982, pp. 245–250.

11. This is admitted by Apel, cf. his article "The Ecological Crisis as a Problem for Discourse Ethics", in: A. Øfsti (ed.), *Ecology and Ethics*, Trondheim: Tapir, 1992, p. 256 (where he refers to my article in the same book, "'The Beauty and the Beast'. Eco-ethical reflections on the borderline between humankind and beasthood").

12. Habermas, in referring to ecological questions in *Erläuterungen zur Diskursethik* (= *EzD*), Frankfurt a.M.: Suhrkamp, 1991 (pp. 219 ff.), disregards the borderline cases from medical ethics, and hence he does not really face the unpleasant questions of ethical gradualism. The same holds true for Luc Ferry in *Le nouvel ordre écologique* (Paris: Grasset, 1992). This 'speciesist' position, apparently well founded, is an implication of their dichotomic presupposition and their avoidance of a systematic discussion of these borderline cases.

13. From Jeremy Bentham *Introduction to the Principles of Morals and Legislation*, ch. XVII. And in Peter Singer's words: "If equality is to be related to any actual characteristics of humans, these characteristics must be some lowest common denominator, pitched so low that no human

lacks them – but then the philosopher comes up against the catch that any such set of characteristics which covers *all* humans will not be possessed *only by humans.*" From "All Animals are Equal", in: Peter Singer, *Applied Ethics*, Oxford: Oxford University Press, 1986, p. 226.

14. There are special problems concerning the relationship between utilitarianism and discourse ethics. Habermas, a defender of discourse ethics, apparently attempts to integrate utilitarian points in his overall deontological position: he has formulated the so-called 'universalization principle' – (U) – (in "Discourse Ethics", in *Moral Consciousness and Communicative Action*, Cambridge Mass.: MIT Press, 1990, pp. 92–94; German original 1983), stating that a norm is not justified "[u]nless all affected can *freely* accept the consequences and the side effects that the *general* observance of the controversial norm can be expected to have for the satisfaction of the interests of *each individual*". (Also in: "Moral Consciousness and Communicative Action", *ibid.* p. 120: "For a norm to be valid, the consequences and side effects that its *general* observance can be expected to have for the satisfaction of the particular interests of *each* person affected must be such that *all* affected can accept them freely".) As to the critical reactions, cf., e.g., Albrecht Wellmer, *Ethik und Dialog*, Frankfurt a.M.: Suhrkamp, 1986, pp. 81–102 (Engl. transl.: *The Persistence of Modernity*). Also Seyla Benhabib, "In the Shaddow of Aristotle and Hegel: Communicative Ethics and Current Controversies in Practical Philosophy" in: *Hermenuetics and Critical Theory in Ethics and Politics*, ed. M. Kelly, Cambridge, Mass.: MIT Press, 1990, pp. 9–16; and Thomas McCarthy, "Practical Discourse: On the Relation of Morality to Politics", in *Ideals and Illusions*, Cambridge Mass.: MIT Press, 1991, pp. 189–192. Also *The Communicative Ethics Controversy*, eds. S. Benhabib and F. Dallmayr, Cambridge: MIT, 1991; and William Rehg, "Discourse and the Moral Point of View: Deriving a Dialogical Principle of Universalization", *Inquiry*, 34(1991), pp. 27–48. Cf. Habermas's response, e.g. in "Erläuterungen zur Diskursethik", in *EzD*, pp. 119 ff.

In this controversy I join the opponents. To state it bluntly: This principle is at best unclear. The terms "satisfaction" of "interests" and "consequences and side effects" sound utilitarian, though the notion of a "free acceptance by all" can be interpreted as an individual right to use a veto against utilitarian calculations. (This is the Dworkinian point: individual rights play the role of a veto against utilitarian arguments in favor of an overall maximization of utility; rights as "trumps" against utility maximization.) However, since individual interests (and needs) are meant to be discursively "laundered", it all depends on how this discursive laundering is conceived. But at this point I suspect that either this principle is too hypothetical to do the job (as a test), or, when interpreted realistically, the principle is unproductive since it is implausible that everybody concerned should agree on controversial issues (e.g. issues concerning a just distribution of scarce resources). Hence a tension between ideality and reality prevails.

15.   Cf. Habermas on this point in "Erläuterungen zur Diskursethik", *EzD*, p. 223.

16.   Many of these philosophers have contributed greatly to our (re)thinking of the ethical standing of a whole range of different cases, from animals to plants, and even to genes, each having its specific 'striving' or 'interest' in the 'maintenance' of its life (different forms of 'striving' which might transcend not only [self]consciousness and will, but also sentience). Cf. my remarks in "Ethical Gradualism?" in Gunnar Skirbekk, *Manuscripts on Rationality*, Bergen: Ariadne, 1992. Cf. also David G. Porter "Ethical Scores for Animal Experiments", in *Nature*, Vol. 356, 12 March 1992, pp. 101–102.

17.   Cf. Habermas on the interrelation between justice and solidarity, and between individuation and socialization, *EzD*, pp. 9–30, 49–76, and 174–175. Justice embraces not only liberal rights and distributive fairness of scarce resouces, but also mutual recognition to secure our vulnerable social identity (cf. Axel Honneth, *Kampf um Anerkennung*, Frankfurt a.M.: Suhrkamp, 1992; and Seyla Benhabib, *Situating the Self*, Cambridge: Polity Press, 1992, e.g. pp. 189–190).

18.   *Ibid.*

19.   Cf. Karl-Otto Apel: "Kann der postkantische Standpunkt der Moralität noch einmal in substantielle Sittlichkeit 'aufgehoben' werden? Das geschichtsbezogene Anwendungsproblem der Diskursethik zwischen Utopie und Regression", in: *Diskurs und Verantwortung*, Fr.a.M.: Suhrkamp, 1988, pp. 103–153, and Jürgen Habermas: "Justice and Solidarity", in: Michael Kelly, *Hermeneutics and Critical Theory in Ethics and Politics*, Cambridge, Mass.: MIT Press, 1990, pp. 32–52.

20. As part of a thought-experiment we could imagine that there might exist
     intelligent biological beings somewhere else in the universe. Let us call
     them Martians. Let us assume that they were genetically different from
     us. Let us assume that they suddenly showed up on Earth, and that we
     were able to communicate with them. Should we then exclude them
     from the realm of morality, because they belong to another species?
     That would seem counterintuitive – given that they were cute and
     friendly, reasonable and rational, caring and responsible, in short, if they
     possessed those competences and characteristics that we associate with
     mature human beings. So again, a restrictive speciesism would seem
     inadequate.

     But since this is a thought-experiment, let us play with it: if these
     Martians were intelligent and communicative, but were unable to feel
     any pain, would we then be comfortable having them as equal partners
     in ethical discussions? Or would we think that there were quite a few
     moral questions which these Martians were incompetent to deal with?
     In this case I think we would, and should, make a distinction between
     them and us: they would not fulfill all requirements for a participation
     in a practical (moral) discourse.

21. We could say that without participation we do not acquire the notions
     needed for understanding fellow beings, and a bio-bodily existence is
     required for such participation. Concerning act-constitutive notions, cf.
     "Praxeological Reflections" in this collection. Cf. also Hans Skjervheim:
     Objectivism and the Study of Man (1959), and Peter Winch: *The Idea
     of a Social Science* (1958).

22. This creature (or creator) could possibly function as a formalist
     administrator of normative and evaluative questions, but hardly as a
     moral discussant, since the latter presupposes the subtle ability to judge
     in complex moral situations. This does not mean that this creature could
     judge in questions of justice but not in questions of value (according to
     the Habermasian distinction between questions of justice and value
     questions): also the ability to make judgments in cases of justice and
     injustice requires an understanding of what is at stake.

23. These reflections on the status of 'moral subjects' (in relation to 'moral
     agents' and 'moral discussants') can be seen as a contribution to some
     aspects of the current debate on the 'concrete other' (in relation to the
     'generalized other'), cf. e.g. Seyla Benhabib, "The Generalized and the

Concrete Other. The Kohlberg-Gilligan Controversy and Moral Theory", in S. Benhabib, *Situating the Self. Gender, Community and Post-modernism in Contemporary Ethics*, Cambridge: Polity Press, 1992, pp. 148–177. I assume that these reflections add to the point alluded to when (traditional) universalistic moral thinking is criticized for having a rationalistic bias and a body (and gender) blindness. "The moral self is not a moral geometer, but an embodied, finite, suffering, and emotive being" (Seyla Benhabib, "In the Shadow of Aristotle and Hegel: Communicative Ethics and Current Controversies in Practical Philosophy", in: Michael Kelly, *Hermeneutics and Critical Theory in Ethics and Politics*, Cambridge, Mass.: MIT Press, 1990, p. 20; cf. also in S. Benhabib, *Situating the Self*). I interpret this to mean that having a biological body is a condition for being a moral subject, and the qualification of being a moral subject is a precondition for being a moral discussant (but maybe not in the same sense for being a theoretical discussant). (If this is the argument it cannot be turned down as some confusion between the level of justification and the level of application.) But those who speak against gender blindness (*op.cit.* p. 21) might allow themselves to reflect on the possibility that they themselves suffer from species blindness. (However, cf. Benhabib [1992, pp. 58–59] on animals and communication, but not systematically on the issue of ethical gradualism.)

Modernization of the Lifeworld

Universality and Plurality in the Process of Modernization

Prelude

Is there only one societal modernity or are there many? Does the process of modernization lead in one direction or are there different directions, different from that of the West? Or should we say: "from those of the West?", since the major societal institutions and their interrelationships are somewhat different in the United States and in Western Europe, and even within the various parts of Western Europe.[1]

These are overwhelming questions. In this chapter, however, I will focus on philosophical problems related to a notion of lifeworld modernization, that is, related to a notion of modernization in the realm of sociocultural reproduction. My philosophical perspective for approaching sociocultural modernization is that of late Critical Theory, especially as set forth in the works of Jürgen Habermas.[2]

Various questions are raised within this theoretical perspective, questions concerning cultural modernization, for instance: in what sense is there a genuine cultural development, differing from that of technology or economy? In what sense does cultural modernization lead toward universal principles or toward value plurality, or toward both?

Again, these are overwhelming questions, and again I will restrict myself and proceed as follows: I will briefly delineate some major points concerning the terms 'lifeworld' and 'modernization' as they are used in late Critical Theory, and at the same time indicate a few commonplaces that might give intuitive support to some of these points. Then I will discuss a few philosophical problems related to the interconnection of universality and plurality in the process of modernization.

Introductory Remarks

I suppose that in some situations the term *lifeworld* may suggest socio-historical contextuality, whereas the term *modernization* may indicate a process transcending historically given contexts toward universality. If so, in talking about a modernization of the lifeworld, we have already entered the debate on contextuality and universality.

In the theoretical perspective adopted here, modernization is understood as a complex process involving not only technological and scientific development in terms of increased instrumental capacities, but also as a process which involves differentiation of "institutions" (such as economy, politics, and culture) and differentiation of "value spheres" (such as truth, rightness, and aesthetic values), together with interrelated changes within the sphere of socio-cultural reproduction, i.e. within the lifeworld. Modernization of the lifeworld is thus an intricate process leading toward modernity. Modernity is an equally complex notion, including pluralistic differentiations as well as a normative conception of discursive and reflective rationality. Without this *normative notion of rationality*, inherent in modernity, the notion of modernization would lose the character of a *learning process*; it would merely be a notion of change, not one of development in the sense of a possible improvement.

The analysis of modernity and modernization is a hermeneutic task, involving a discursive (and fallible) moving back and forth between a clarification of our preconceptions of modernity and a testing of these conceptions in relation to the historical process (out there, as it were).

The background from which the process of modernization takes off is, to begin with, *tradition*. Later, modernization itself becomes a tradition, in the sense of a relatively permanent and culturally transmitted set of common codes of meaning, common norms, and social identity.

The concepts of modernity, rationality and tradition are thus intertwined at the outset. Within this web we will pay special attention to the notion of the *lifeworld*, and we start with the assumption that the process toward modernity implies not only improved instrumental rationality, but also a significant development of argumentative (or discursive) rationality connected to decisive changes in communicative rationality within the lifeworld (socio-cultural reproduction). In this perspective the notion of the lifeworld can be analyzed by focusing on its ambiguous status: on the one hand, as a background or horizon containing our tacit insight and unthematized outlook on the world and ourselves, and on the other hand, as differentiated forms of life, as contexts and situations for our daily activities and for our inquiries and reflective discourse. This notion of a lifeworld has thus a double status of perspective and context, or of frame and content.

In elaborating his theory of communicative action, Habermas introduces the term "lifeworld" through a discussion of its use by phenomenologists: the lifeworld is "an unproblematically given background".[3] It is "an intersubjectively shared world".[4] It is "total and indeterminate", immunized "against total revision".[5] This is a culturalist concept of the lifeworld, "identifying the lifeworld with culturally transmitted background knowledge".[6] And it is a transcendental concept, conceiving the lifeworld as a collective horizon within which situations and problems occur, whereby the lifeworld remains an unthematized and shared position from which we perceive, act, and interpret.

This phenomenological notion of the lifeworld can itself be elaborated in different ways, either toward a *Fundamentalontologie* as in Heidegger[7] or toward a more descriptive notion of historically constituted horizons (contingent and changeable transcendental horizons, as it were).[8] The latter approach is the one affiliated with *verstehende Soziologie*. The notion of the lifeworld is here conceived from the perspective of participants,[9] and the theoretical task is one of articulating this pretheoretical background. This task can be pursued either (i) narratively (descriptively) or (ii) by investigating the basic functions in linguistically 'mediated' communication for the reproduction of the lifeworld.[10]

Habermas underlines the danger, inherent in interpretative sociology, of a "hermeneutic idealism" when investigating the lifeworld.[11] Within the research programme of the theory of communicative action his main point is thus to elaborate a distinction between social integration and system integration, between "lifeworld" and "system", in order to attain a comprehensive theory of society and its rationalization, avoiding the pitfalls of an "idealistic" (and of a "materialistic") bias.[12] However, in this paper I am not going to look into the concept of system in Habermas's theory of communicative action, neither its own status nor its interrelationship with the lifeworld.[13] My focus is that of lifeworld modernization and of the interplay between rationality and plurality.

To obtain a notion of the lifeworld theoretically fruitful for the theory of communication, Habermas chooses the approach delineated in alternative (ii) above, and he relates this approach to classical theoreticians in sociology (Durkheim, Weber, Parsons, and Mead).[14] For this theoretical purpose, Habermas attempts to distinguish between three reproductive processes and three structural components of the lifeworld; the former are called cultural reproduction, social integration, and socialization, and the latter are called culture, society, and personality.[15] Though each reproductive process is operative for each structural component (giving nine interrelated concepts in a matrix), Habermas emphasizes (a) the cultural reproduction of culture, which results in "interpretive schemes fit for consensus", (b) the social integration of society, resulting in "legitimately ordered interpersonal relations", and (c) the socialization of personality, resulting in "interactive capacities (personal identity)". If such societal processes fail, the result will be (a) "loss of meaning", (b) "anomie", and (c) "psychopathology".[16]

In his universal pragmatics (discussed above, in "Pragmatism and Pragmatics"),[17] Habermas has elaborated a distinction between three "worlds" (discussed in "Madness and Reason" and "The Pragmatic Notion of Nature"), i.e. external nature, society, and internal nature, which again are related to three modes of communication and basic attitudes[18] and to three universal validity claims, i.e. truth, rightness, and truthfulness. By virtue of these distinctions, a "decentered understanding of the world" is made possible, a differentiation which allows for increased rationality. A person who has acquired the ability to relate himself reflectively and adequately to these world perspectives with their validity claims and to the three different speech perspectives (in first, second, and third person) has acquired an ability to communicate with reflexivity and reciprocity.

In order to get a promising theoretical perspective for elaborating a developmental notion of lifeworld rationalization, which is different from rationalization in terms of improved instrumental and strategic rationality, Habermas attempts to bring the differentiated reproductive processes and structural components of the lifeworld together with the differentiated perspectives of speakers and of pragmatically rooted worlds and basic validity claims. His intention is to achieve a developmental-logical justification for a theory of lifeworld rationalization through an elaboration of discursive and reflective rationality and differentiation. The Hegelian flavor of the project stems from this attempt at a 'mediation' between a theory of modernization (and socialization) and a theory of speech act inherent in normative rationality.

This, we could say, is partly a philosophical task, partly a historical or empirical one, or simultaneously both.[19] It implies investigations of the extent to which there have been such structural differentiations of the lifeworld,[20] including "separation of form and content" (making discursive solutions possible) and "growing reflexivity of symbolic reproduction".

This is also the point where Habermas adopts a reinterpreted version of the Kohlbergian theories of maturation and of moral development.[21] Habermas attempts to adopt a version of the Kohlbergian scheme as an argument in favor of a general development of the idea of justice, leading up to a stage of discursive rationality. If successful, this attempt is supposed to represent an argument in favor of the idea of a genuine rationalization process of the lifeworld, logically different from that of the growth of instrumental knowledge and control.

The Habermasian project of lifeworld modernization is characterized by many perspectives and levels, at the same time as each element, as well as the interrelationships between elements, is fallible and open to challenge. It represents an ongoing research programme, not the final word. In each case we could ask whether the schemes distort the material, or whether they are sufficiently "hermeneutically sensitive" to the complexity of the subject matter. There is, for the most part, no simple answer to these questions. In each case we have to rely on careful discursive analyses; it is primarily a question of a "balance of plausibility".[22]

This is the point at which reconstructive demands of superiority in terms of comprehensivity, consistency, and reflexivity merge with self-referential demands of theoretical inescapability (and thus of "alternativelessness").[23]

We shall return to some of these problems. At this point I will close my preliminary remarks with a quotation from Habermas.[24]

"I can introduce here the concept of the Lebenswelt or lifeworld, to begin with as the correlate of processes of reaching understanding. Subjects acting communicatively always come to an understanding in the horizon of a lifeworld. Their lifeworld is formed from more or less diffuse, always unproblematic, background convictions. This lifeworld background serves as a source of situation definitions that are presupposed by participants as unproblematic. In their interpretive accomplishments the members of a communication community demarcate the one objective world and their intersubjectively shared social world from the subjective worlds of individuals and (other) collectives. The world-concepts and the corresponding validity claims provide the formal scaffolding with which those acting communicatively order problematic contexts of situations, that is, those requiring agreement, in their lifeworld, which is presupposed as unproblematic.

The lifeworld also stores the interpretive work of preceding generations. It is the conservative counterweight to the risk of disagreement that arises with every actual process of reaching understanding; for communicative actors can achieve an understanding only by way of taking yes/no positions on criticizable validity claims. The relation between these weights changes with the decentration of worldviews. The more the worldview that furnishes the cultural stock of knowledge is decentered, the less the need for understanding is covered in advance by an interpreted lifeworld immune from critique, and the more this need has to be met by the interpretive accomplishment of the participants themselves, that is, by way of risky (because rationally motivated) agreement, the more frequently we can expect rational action orientations. Thus for the time being we can characterize the rationalization of the lifeworld in the dimension "normatively ascribed agreement" versus "communicatively achieved understanding". The more cultural traditions predecide which validity claims, when, where, for what, from whom, and to whom must be accepted, the less the participants themselves have the possibility of making explicit and examining the potential grounds on which their yes/no positions are based."

What determines the process of modernization is this dynamic transition between the lifeworld as an unthematized, traditionally 'mediated' horizon (and resource), and the lifeworld as a historically constituted competence of discursivity and reflexivity, of reciprocal perspective-taking and trans-contextual universality.

A Reminder from Political Theory

I would like to briefly recall the antagonism in political history between a *contextualist and historicist notion of tradition* and a *universalistic notion of argumentative rationality*, the former being related to classical conservatism and the latter to radicalism in the sense of the Enlightenment.

The conservative position, from Burke to Gadamer, emphasizes *the wisdom of tradition*.[25] Individuals and groups are regarded as fallible. Correction is only possible through listening to the wisdom of history; within the historical process things are tried out and finally settled by experience, not decided by airy ideas and by speculative plans for revolutionary change! Not only does tradition have the upper hand, intellectually and morally, compared with individuals and groups, but since man is constituted by tradition – for his identity, preferences and worldview – tradition also has a practical or political primacy over the individual. Stated briefly and crudely: tradition, not the individual, is the moral and cognitive subject; and tradition, not the individual, is the final agent of politics.

Standard counterpositions to this form of communitarian traditionalism are found in various forms of individualism and rationalism, be they utilitarian, contractarian or libertarian. They are represented within and promoted by the broad movement of the Enlightenment, which underlines both (i) the value of *universal and critical rationality* embedded in emancipated individuals and (ii) the importance of *instrumental and moral rationalization* inspired by scientific progress.

According to these traditionalists, man can never really transcend his historical and cultural situatedness; man can only reflect upon one part of it at a time and improve it tentatively and piecemeal. Any attempt at total criticism and total change is doomed to failure. Such attempts are immature deeds and dreams, since man as a social being is essentially formed by history and culture. Tradition is therefore not just a collection of inherited attitudes and social patterns which in principle could be removed. On the contrary, within any tradition there are some deeply embedded preconditions – common norms and notions and common codes of meaning – which inevitably structure our human identity and the world as it appears to us from within that tradition. Therefore, tradition in this sense cannot be made an object for complete elucidation, nor for complete change; it can only be thematized and discussed partially and step by step, never as a whole; it can only be perspectivized from one position at a time, from one position available within a given tradition.

Thus, tradition can be talked about and evaluated, and possibly changed and improved; but no radical criticism is possible.

The main counterposition to this traditionalism, that of the Enlightenment, argues in favor of the possibility of an ongoing rational criticism directed against any given tradition, be it religious doctrine or daily life. It argues that such a criticism is possible, and necessary. As a permanent endeavor, this criticism opens the way to cultural improvement and political progress; it represents a transcending process, leading away from traditional situatedness toward more universal and valid views.

This counterposition holds that *rationality*, *qua* such an open criticism, is both possible and required; it holds that *rationalization*, *qua* a rational improvement of tradition, is equally possible and required, namely in terms of a continuous process; and within this process of improvement attention is primarily to be given to the elimination of those aspects of a tradition which are found cognitively untenable or morally unacceptable. In acting against what is worse, this process of rationalization promotes what is better, or at least, what is less bad. In trying to eliminate that which in this sense is 'negative', this rationalization promotes what is 'positive'. In this sense the Enlightenment project represents an attempt at promoting progress.

Talking in terms of the Enlightenment tradition – an anti-tradition which itself has become a main tradition within the multiple process of modernization – it is worthwhile recalling that this joint attempt at promoting epistemic universalization and instrumental rationalization only becomes a real possibility, as well as a rational requirement, once man has reached the stage of maturity typical of modernity. At earlier stages, universal rationality was a mere possibility.

We may sum up this brief reminder from the realm of political philosophy in the following statement. These two ideal-type positions from political and intellectual theory, traditionalism and radicalism, or contextualism and universalism, have their equivalents in the philosophy of scientific research, viz. in terms of a historicist position on the one hand and a rationalist position on the other – each of them having its strong and its weak points; if the historicist position is stated radically, claiming the historical relativism of any intellectual position, it ends up in self-referential inconsistency, entailing its own historical relativism; if the rationalist position is stated radically, claiming the correctness of its own notion of rationality quite independently of any historically given version of scientific work, this implies the irrelevance of any historical experience from earlier scientific work for the question of what is scientifically rational and what is not.[26]

This sketchy reminder of the well-known intellectual scenario, that between traditionalism and rationalism, serves to indicate the intuitive plausibility of the claim that there ought to be some middle way, some Hegelian *mediation*, between the two extremes.[27] It ought to be possible to state a position according to which the core of the rationalist view of the Enlightenment is taken care of, at the same time accommodating the skeptical counter-arguments from the historicist perspective.

Cases of Lifeworld Modernization

From this point of view I will approach the notion of a modernization of the lifeworld by presenting a few cases which, in my view, are intuitively reasonable. I assume that a 'mediation' between theoretical and culturally embedded notions represents more than a pedagogical activity. To the extent that our theoretical concepts depart from and interrelate with our everyday form of life, it could be useful to confront theoretical concepts with lifeworld conceptions (as it could be useful to confront lifeworld conceptions with theoretically elaborated concepts).[28]

(a) A distinction between Man and Nature

The first case is a classical case, indeed a paradigmatic one: a differentiation between phenomena that can be talked to and influenced by being talked to, and phenomena that cannot be influenced by being talked to – in short, a differentiation between what we are accustomed to calling subjects and objects. The latter can only be influenced by appropriate physical intervention, whereas the former can be influenced by words alone, to the extent that the words uttered are understood and that some communication is thus already established.

There are various ways of accommodating this differentiation, ontologically and methodologically, and there are different problems related to possible borderline cases, including mental disease or intoxication or the status of higher animals: are the humans and animals in question to be seen as 'objects' or 'subjects', as determined only by causes or also by reasons?[29] But despite such controversies and refinements, the paradigmatic distinction between phenomena that are open for verbal communication and those that are not seems well entrenched and hard to escape once it is in place.[30]

This differentiation makes possible, on the one hand, rationalization in terms of causal explanations and technical interventions and, on the other, refined communication and argumentation.[31] Through this basic differentiation, and through these elaborations in terms of possible instrumental intervention and of communicative and argumentative interaction, we have a classical case of modernization: a formerly undifferentiated form of life is differentiated in relation to phenomena with different characteristics (Man and Nature). This makes possible two paradigmatically different ways of thinking and acting, and two learning processes and ways of rationalizing. Through this differentiation and its inherent potential for rationalization, the lifeworld itself is led into a process of change and modernization.

To the extent that this differentiation enables man to improve his secular control of vital conditions, this case of a modernization represents at the same time an instance of a secularization and desacralization of the lifeworld. Events and actions are increasingly understood in terms of natural causes or good reasons. A disenchantment of the world (lifeworld) is under way.

A similar possibility is opened up by a cultivation of verbal interaction. Through verbal interaction, participants tend to appear as equals, different from gods and from beasts. Through persistent questioning and discussion we have a mutual recognition of co-discussants as being both reasonable and fallible.

This differentiation of rationality into instrumental rationality toward nature and communicative rationality between humans, makes it possible to question magic and myths and to thematize traditions and taboos. Through a linguistification of the sacred, lifeworld and nature alike are made accessible to secular understanding and explanation.

In presenting this case of a distinction between Nature and Man as one that is intuitively plausible in the perspective of lifeworld modernization, I do not want to overlook its many puzzles and intricacies, e.g. those related to borderline cases.[32] Nor do I want to question the possibility of cultural loss owing to this disenchantment of the world.[33] I merely want to emphasize the persistence of this differentiation and its importance for an ongoing rationalization along different lines (leading up to scientization and professionalization, through the natural sciences as well as through the sciences of man and of society).

(b) Institutional differentiations

Whereas the former case (in § [a]) is primarily related to modernization in the sense of rationalizability, that is, of differentiations leading to learning processes, this second case is primarily related to modernization in the sense of institutional differentiations, for instance, in terms of the building of states and the division of labor. I assume that at the outset these differentiations are commonly accepted as cases of lifeworld modernization, indeed that they are so well known that this reference itself suffices for making the point. But I want to add a few remarks to further implications at different levels.

The differentiation of a state at the institutional level implies sociopolitical differences which again require a normatively acceptable legitimation; differences in power (and wealth) require a justification. The attempts at legitimating state power (and differences in wealth and in duties) tend to change in accordance with the general process of rationalization, ranging from justifications based on mythical and religious narratives to theological and metaphysical theories, and to utilitarian-functional and contractarian-discursive arguments. The need for regulations between states and global institutions, and for their normative legitimation, represents a subsequent step within this process of modernization.

At a lower level there is a complementary movement in terms of various role specializations, from an increasing division of labor and political stratifications to multiple recreational roles. Along these lines we get modern societies with a high degree of specialized activities and roles, and with a flexible social identity allowing one and the same person to move in and out of a plurality of roles and situations. Instead of having a lifetime identity, given by one's fixed social position, each person can change and form his or her identity throughout life, by experience and cultivation. Each person is entitled to universal rights and capacities as well as to private characteristics and affiliations.

These are deep changes of man and his world, that is, changes of the lifeworld related to the process of modernization, both at the level of institutional differentiation, at the level of rationalized justification, and at the level of social identity.

(c) Cultural plurality and self-referential skepticism

Whereas the first case (in § [a], i.e. the Man-Nature distinction) has roots back in the origins of the process of modernization, to the ancient quarrel around the complex transition from mythos to logos, and whereas the second case (in § [b], i.e. that of institutional specializations) is fairly old, our third case is primarily situated within modern times, the case being that of cultural plurality, within a common legal-political frame challenged by skepticism.

The experience of cultural difference is certainly an old one. What I am referring to here is the experience of cultural differences within one's own culture or lifeworld. I do not primarily have social differences in mind, nor individual differences, but cultural ones such as those stemming from different religions or metaphysical beliefs. In short, I am thinking of the classical theme of an increasing cultural plurality in Western societies, a plurality which has developed from the erosion of a common religious and metaphysical rock bottom toward a cultural manifoldness and even an intellectual skepticism.

Cultural manifoldness can prevail within a common cultural frame. The manifoldness is then 'mediated' by cultural homogeneity at a higher level. This would be a pre-modern solution of tensions created by cultural plurality. In modern societies, cultural manifoldness can to a large extent exist within a formal, apparently neutral, frame of law and order, that is, within a differentiated legal and political institution with legitimacy across the cultural and religious boundaries. This is the modern solution (we could say, the lesson learned during the wars of religion in the seventeenth century[34]). It implies a differentiation between culture in the sense of religious belief and confession and the realm of law and political power. Tolerance and equality within society are here rendered possible by a commonly accepted and actually functioning realm of political principles and procedures.

The occurrence of this solution to cultural and religious plurality represents a change within the realm of the lifeworld; it restructures the lifeworld inherently. At the same time it changes the lifeworld by differentiating, out of the lifeworld, a relatively independent institution of law and politics. Since religion primarily remains within the realm of the lifeworld, the differentiated institution of law and politics can now undergo an autonomous development in terms of secular rationalization and desacralized legitimation.

Two points should be made.

(i) The ongoing process of rationalization did not stop at a criticism of religious doctrines, but went on to question any claim of metaphysical truth. This implies that not only do modern societies embrace cultural plurality right down to basic religious and metaphysical beliefs and principles, these beliefs and principles are themselves attacked and undermined by skeptical questions and attitudes. Any claim for a religious or metaphysical foundation asks for a justification, in the final instance, a rational justification. Such a rational justification can in the end only be given by free and enlightened argumentation. The final ground is no longer to be found in substantial religious or metaphysical theses, but is itself this self-critical argumentative rationality.

This represents a rationalization of the lifeworld, of its codes of meaning, its sense of acceptable norms, and its version of self-understanding. This also implies that fundamentalist beliefs are weakened, and that coexistence between believers of different religions could be stabilized on a higher level.

But this criticism and skepticism, inherent in the notion of argumentative rationality, does not leave the differentiated institutions of law and politics untouched. Their claim to provide a foundation and justification is also questioned. This process results not only in cultural plurality, and a skeptical questioning of any religious or metaphysical belief, but we also have a skeptical questioning of any normative foundation, be it cultural, legal or political. Not merely cultural plurality, but also intellectual plurality and total skepticism are modern predicaments.

(ii) The second point is that of a certain erosion or shrinking of the lifeworld. Not only is a realm of law and politics gradually lifted out of the lifeworld, but also an institution of economy. Production and distribution are widely separated from the realm of sociocultural reproduction and interaction, separated partly in time and space and partly by their internal logic. The latter point entails a change toward increasingly strategic actions in terms of exchange in a market by the use of money (as a standard for exchange value) and toward increasingly instrumental actions in the productive relation to nature.

After these gradual separatings of an institution for law and politics and of an institution for work and exchange out of the lifeworld, the expansion and rationalization of these very institutions tended to influence the lifeworld, both by draining it of many of its traditional activities and by invading it with their own special forms of functioning. In short, money and law tend to 'colonize' a culturally pluralistic and potentially (self-)skeptical lifeworld.[35]

Hence we may ask: what are the possible and desirable forms of organizing these differentiated institutions and their interrelationships, and what are the most convincing visions of our self-critical rationality and of a global ethics?

These are open questions, constantly discussed and investigated. Modern plurality and rationality remain the horizon within which these questions are raised and possibly settled. Skepticism and discursive (argumentative) rationality thus represent a predicament for culturally modernized societies.

(d) Rationality attacked and defended

After this brief reminder of three intuitively plausible cases of modernization of the lifeworld – viz. (a) that of a differentiation between Man and Nature and the subsequent possibility for explanatory and hermeneutic rationalizations, (b) that of a differentiation of state building and of sociopolitical specializations, and (c) that of cultural plurality and universal legality in need of rational justification, leading up to the modern debate around skepticism and rationality – after this reminder, I would like to make some further comments on the debate on rationality and skepticism.

The awareness of irrationality in modern societies, from destructive technological potentials to institutional shortcomings, lends an ironical ring to the unreserved characterizing of modernity by rationality ("modernization through rationalization"). In virtue of this rationality and this progress, mankind today faces deep crises, reaching from ecology to organizational and socio-cultural problems. A criticism of modernity and its fatal rationality is therefore reasonable and just.[36]

Nevertheless, there is no way of returning to pre-modernity.[37] On the material level, any such return would imply such a tremendous change, for instance in demographic figures, that the idea is practically impossible as a plan for action. And at the intellectual level, it is close to impossible just to think that we could undo all the learning, all the distinctions, and all the reflective capacities that we have acquired.

This latter point can also be stated in terms of self-referential arguments: in order to criticize the present situation we have to possess rational arguments and a competence in using them. It is only by applying such a self-critical rationality that we can point out what is wrong in the modern world.

This is the formal version of the argument. It reminds us that we need rationality, in its various forms, in order to establish a new and better society, just as we need this rationality, in its various scientific, technical, and scholarly forms, in order to know that our criticism of failures and shortcomings really is what it claims to be, namely, a critical indication of real failures and shortcomings.[38]

So evidently there is no way back to an undifferentiated position, away from the multidisciplinary and reflective-discursive rationality which in its fallibility is our only intellectual assistance.

This does not mean that scientific or argumentative activities are the most enjoyable and valuable of human endeavors and that we should be committed to and occupied with these activities as often as possible. Life is certainly more than rationality and discourse.[39]

Nor does it mean that the different scientific and scholarly disciplines possess the only forms of language that are communicatively meaningful. Language, as we know, is a subtle thing. Even in an utterance about a given state of affairs, more is at stake than what is explicitly stated. Such an utterance also communicates something about the personal and socio-historical situatedness of the utterer, both through the conceptual perspective chosen (and not chosen), through the collective experience and meaning that is embedded in the language used (as part of the "objective spirit" or the historically transmitted intersubjectivity), and, maybe, through something that is creatively and actively adduced by the utterer (to the extent that the utterer takes on the role of a creative user of language, for instance, that of a poet).

Here we touch upon a level of tacit knowledge (Polanyi), either 'mediated' by tradition or created consciously or unconsciously. These are aspects of communication and insight that can be mentioned and talked about only indirectly. Practices like *showing*, either by case studies or by poetic expressions, or maybe by new training and personal experiences, might be required here. These are the complementary aspects of modern rationality, the 'night aspects' of its multidisciplinary differentiations and of its fallible though unavoidable reflective-discursive procedures.

More examples of lifeworld modernization might be mentioned, for instance the differentiation between norms and facts. However, this brief survey is not meant to be exhaustive. For one thing, I have not looked into the classical differentiations between the institutions of science, jurisprudence, and art, and the value spheres of truth, rightness, and taste (reminiscent of Kant).

Having recalled these cases of lifeworld modernization, I now proceed to the philosophical discussion of rationality and plurality in modern societies.

Universality and Plurality: the Principle of Justice and its Application

Moral maturation could be conceived as a learning process leading toward higher stages of role taking and reflexivity, i.e. as the acquisition of the ability to judge universalistically. Accordingly, moral maturity consists of the acquisition of universalizability as the highest principle of justice. In what sense does this notion of moral maturation imply an ability to apply this principle of justice in a plurality of contexts? We will take a brief look into the problem of justice as universalizability and the problem of the application of this principle in a pluralistic world.

By reinterpreting the Kohlbergian scheme of moral development[40] in terms of his notion of a 'decentering' of 'world understanding', by persons capable of flexibly applying 'world perspectives' and 'speaker perspectives', Habermas conceives the transition toward higher levels as a learning process, leading toward increased reflexivity and reciprocity.[41] The process is conceived of as progress in the sense that the agent is supposed to be able to reconstruct a lower stage in terms of a higher stage. The highest stage represents complete reciprocity in terms of universalized role taking. This is achieved through real discourse. Hypothetical or monological discourses would not do. They would not represent a learning process through reciprocal role taking. At the final stage we have both a moral maturity (reciprocity and reflexivity) among the participants and a discursive justification in terms of universalizability concerning interpretations of interests (or needs).

Habermas has continued his elaboration of the various aspects of this conception of moral development.[42] Here I will briefly indicate some critical questions related to the Habermasian elaborations of the notion of moral maturation. A few comments will be made on epistemic status (i), on the status of normative justification (ii), on the general interpretative adaptation into the theory of communicative action (iii), and on the question of contextual application (iv).

(i) The relation between a normative theory of moral development and its empirical basis is a tricky one.[43] Habermas sees his project as reconstructive; it is not merely empirical, nor purely philosophical. As reconstructive it is understood as being hypothetical and fallible.[44] And as reconstructive it is meant to have a critical force. How is such a project to be validated?

(a) There is, in such a project, a claim of *conceptual consistency* or *coherence*: the various elements of the theory have to be mutually supportive, or at least not mutually inconsistent or incompatible. There should be conceptual coherence with related theories or conceptual frames regarded as representative and well established. This is what Habermas tries to provide, with regard to an amazing amount of theories and interpretations: a comprehensive hermeneutics, justified by conceptual coherence.

(b) But there is also some claim as to an *empirical fit*, as it were. This goes for empirically related elements that are incorporated into this reconstructive theory (as in the empirical foundation of those elements in the Kohlbergian scheme that are adapted by Habermas), and it goes for empirical implications of the theory (as, for instance, the claim that the lifeworld is being colonized).[45]

(c) Reconstructive theories have to meet a *demand for recognizability by the actors*. As participants of a reconstructed activity (or development), the agents should be able to recognize their own activity (development) through this reconstruction. A valid reconstruction should be *nachvollziehbar*, that is, internally recognizable and discursively acceptable as valid by the participants themselves.

(d) The *normative* element is supposed to be recapitulated (*nachvollzogen*) by participants and to be *justified as normatively valid* in terms of the stage of discursive rationality from which the reconstruction is conceived. Finally, the whole conception of moral development should be tried out discursively; that is, there is no one-man-hermeneutics. But this need for full argumentative redemption is especially acute when it comes to the final normative foundation (of the highest stage). This is a question to which we will return in discussing the *Auseinandersetzung* between Habermas and Apel (in the next chapter).

(e) The ambiguity of the term 'truth claim in theoretical discourse' invites a few reflections. It is underdetermined with respect to its empirical content.[46] I, for one, would prefer to talk about 'truth claims' in connection with validity claims in empirical theories, *as well as* in connection with various kinds of experiences, and I find it useful to *distinguish* between these validity claims ('theoretical truth claims' and 'empirical truth claims') and claims in favor of conceptual adequacy. The latter claims I could call *adequacy claims* or *claims of conceptual adequacy*.[47] In these cases we do not claim that something is the case, but that a certain concept is appropriate to some phenomenon.[48] Here we find ourselves within the well-known spiral between preconceptions and subject matter, a spiral which can be elaborated hermeneutically and discursively (critically): we try out our preconceptions in relation to the paradigm case and its context; and we try to find the borderlines for the application of these conceptions.

(f) The question of conceptual adequacy is decisive in both theoretical and normative validity claims: in making theoretical (empirical) statements and in raising normative validity claims we presuppose the adequacy of our concepts.[49] Furthermore, when we investigate competences and preconditions we do not claim that something is the case on the level of what is experienced, nor that something can be explained causally or hermeneutically in a certain way, but that some competence or precondition is constitutive, and perhaps, *unavoidably constitutive* in some sense. These claims we might call *precondition claims*, or *unavoidability claims*. In talking in terms of such modalities, we may well use arguments from absurdity, trying to show how the preconditions under investigation can be said to be constitutive for intelligibility (or how the competence under investigation can be said to be enabling for some performance).[50] Thereby we approach the question of transcendental arguments, that is, of self-referential arguments from undeniability.

The distinctions between *adequacy claims* and *unavoidability claims* could be thought of as a gradual one, at the same time as there are gradual transitions from these two claims to the claims of *truth* and of *rightness*.[51] But such gradual transitions do not undermine the point of making these distinctions.

(ii) There are at least two fundamental normative questions. One is the question of the *justification* of the highest principles.[52] The other, closely connected to the first, is that of justifying the idea that moral thinking in terms of principles (stage six) represents a *higher stage* than moral thinking in terms of contract or of utility (stage five).

Habermas reinterprets the normative foundation of the Kohlbergian scheme from the perspective of discourse ethics. This means that he reinterprets the sixth stage, or introduces a seventh stage, that of *discourse ethics*. To the extent that discourse ethics does indeed make good its claim to give an ultimate normative justification, the question of the normative foundation for this developmental scheme is thereby settled – not through precritical fundamentalism, but through a procedural self-referential ethics.[53]

If moral thinking in terms of principles (stage six, e.g. as in Kant) is said to represent a higher moral stage than thinking in terms of contract or of utility (stage five, e.g. as in Hobbes or Mill) then this certainly cannot be justified by *empirical* research. Only normative argumentation can justify such a claim: in normative argumentation there is an equality between the participants, not an asymmetry between investigator and investigated. Even though the empirical foundation also for the first four stages can be challenged, both as to the narrowness of the data and as to the bias of the concepts, the claim of moral progress or maturity at these first stages can nevertheless be viewed as being basically empirical, in a sense in which the claim of moral progress leading from stage five to stage six cannot. By reinterpreting this developmental scheme in the perspective of discourse ethics, Habermas transfers the burden of proof to where it belongs, to *philosophical* discourse.

Another aspect of Habermas's moral-philosophical intervention into the Kohlbergian scheme is his indication of the philosophical reason for talking of a *stage 'four-and-a-half'*, that is, of a stage of philosophical skepticism concerning the possibility of reaching a rational answer to basic normative questions. This position, held by philosophers from Nietzsche to Popper, represents a theoretically 'stable stage', as it were, and it should thus be considered in a scheme of moral development.[54]

Habermas indicates how the transition from the conventional to the postconventional level (from stage four to five in the Kohlbergian scheme) represents a dramatic change, since the normative and social order is thereby questioned. This is a dramatic change in the life of an individual, and it is a dramatic change in history (the transition to modernity with its deep doubts and all-embracing questions). For the theory of lifeworld modernization, the transition from conventional to postconventional morality is of major importance.

(iii) Having indicated how Habermas reinterprets the normative problems of the Kohlbergian scheme from the perspective of discourse ethics, I will briefly recall how he attempts to integrate this scheme into his theory of communicative action.

We have already indicated how discourse ethics is related to *universal pragmatics*, which again is related to *lifeworld modernization*. We have, in particular, the pragmatically grounded ability to differentiate between three perspectives of speakers and between three perspectives of worlds and their correlated universal validity claims, as well as the ability to justify discursively the claims of truth and rightness. There are various important capacities in this respect, which are acquired, ontogenetically and phylogenetically, through a process of learning and socialization (this process represents a genuine rationalization of the lifeworld, and hence a lifeworld modernization). From the perspective of the Habermasian theory of communicative action (discourse ethics and universal pragmatics included), the Kohlbergian scheme of moral development is thus critically reconsidered and adapted in order to fit an overall model of rationalization and modernization.

Habermas thus adopts Kohlberg, seeking support for his own theory of universal development of moral capabilities. But as indicated, this is an adoption by way of thorough reinterpretation. In adapting the Kohlbergian scheme for his theory of sociohistorical development, Habermas elaborates a model (of seven or six stages) of moral learning and moral maturation. Each stage represents a self-contained horizon for normative reactions and conflict solving. One stage is higher than another when the former allows for problem solving which the latter does not, and when a person involved can successfully reconstruct a lower stage from a higher one. Conceptual enrichment tied to a process of expanding role taking and reflection is thus decisive for the development of morality.

(iv) Also in Habermas's design, this model – in its attempt at pinpointing the essence of a development of moral competence leading to modernity – can be interpreted as presenting modernization as a *unilinear process*, i.e. the acquisition of the principle of justice as universalizability is basically conceived of as a unilinear process. But what about the ability to apply moral norms adequately? In a modern society the ability to master a *plurality* of moral contexts, perspectives, and levels is a necessary component of *moral maturity*. Universalistic justice and contextualistic application have to be combined.[55] Against the tendency of a unilinear Hegelianism, which conceives of moral maturation primarily (or uniquely) as an irreversible and invariant 'sublation' toward higher stages in terms of normative justification, it is argued that a theory of moral maturation has to incorporate a competence in mastering plurality, especially when we intend to do justice to a modern differentiated world. To be sure, the Habermasian conception of modernization through differentiation contains a notion of context plurality in modern societies, inter alia in terms of specialized institutions. This perspective makes possible one way of elaborating the question of the contextual application (of moral principles).[56]

A counterargument against such an attempt at a 'mediation' between universalistic justification and contextualist application could consist of an emphasis on the distinction between the *acquisition* of a moral principle and its *application* in various contexts. The process of acquiring moral competence is understood in *unilinear* terms. Simultaneously one must learn how to *apply* this moral competence in a *plurality of contexts*. And acquisition and application are conceptually of different natures, even though they are empirically correlated.[57]

This counterargument makes some sense when acquisition is seen as discursive acquisition, as discursively justified acquisition. Then one could argue that the justification of a norm is logically distinct from its application. However, one has to look into the intricacies of this distinction between justification and application. What about the language used in describing the norm that is under discursive justification? In what sense can this language possibly be said to be context-independent?[58]

I assume that the answer to this question depends among other things on the level at which the norm under discussion is located. When the norm under discussion belongs to the norms that are *constitutive* for discursive activities, we can more easily argue in favor of its context-independence than when the norm is one regulating non-discursive activities. One of the meta-norms of practical discourse is the requirement of the mutual recognition among discussants of being sufficiently rational and fallible to pursue an argumentation. Such 'norms of the frame' do allow for a distinction between context-independence and contextdependence: the language appropriate for describing these discourse constitutive norms, and for reflecting on them, is context-independent in a particular sense.

But this is hardly the case that matters, since these meta-norms are not to be applied in various contexts in the same sense as moral norms.[59] These latter norms, which, when questioned, represent *the regular contents of practical discourses* questioning their justification, are prone to a dependence on the language within which they are articulated: the conceptual perspective embodied in the language applied in identifying and then discussing these norms is hardly context-independent in the same sense as the norms constitutive of discourse.[60]

Because of the constitutive role of the language chosen for any of these 'material' moral norms (in contract to the discourse-constitutive ones), it is far from clear that there is a sharp distinction between a putative context-independent justification of such moral norms and their contextual application.

At the same time as there are reasons for talking in terms of a learning process through an 'overcoming' of relatively undifferentiated stages toward more differentiated ones, and thus for talking in terms of progress – of a development leading *away from* recognized shortcomings and in that sense *toward* something better or higher – it can also be argued that modernity, through its various differentiations, is characterized by *plurality* and *uncertainty*. Moral maturity, in a modern society, implies an ability to switch flexibly and adequately between different spheres and different roles, an ability to see when and where it is appropriate to reason in terms of cost-benefit and when and where it is appropriate to reason in terms of principles (à la Kant), for instance, in moving between business and jurisprudence or between different cases in medical ethics. To know one's way around, in an ambiguous and restless world, is part of the practical competence needed in a modern society.[61]

This developmental scheme represents a notion of linear moral progress, but it does not thereby entail a denial of the possibility of a flexible application of moral concepts and norms according to the nature of the various institutions or contexts. Even though development is conceived as linear, this does not imply that a person who has reached the highest stage cannot, or should not, apply principles from lower stages (stage five) within special contexts; the market does not function normatively like a court, nor like a moral discussion, though there are legal preconditions, and moral preconditions, also for market behavior.[62] Hence, Habermas's conception of lifeworld modernization does not exclude pluralism and uncertainty, in this sense.[63]

I will not go further into this elaborate scheme of moral development, and the different versions of it found throughout Habermas's work. Having indicated some general points of interest for the question of lifeworld modernization, I will just emphasize that this comprehensive project of a theory of communicative action is explicitly presented as a fallible one, open to various arguments for and against. I will, in the next chapter ("Rationality and Contextuality"), discuss philosophical problems related to the interconnection of rationality and contextuality in modern societies.

NOTES

1. Is there a Japanese way to modernity, with specific interrelations between tradition and politics, and between politics and economy – maybe less individualistic, and less universalistic? (Cf., e.g., Johann Arnason: "The Modern Constellation and the Japanese Enigma," part 1 in: *Thesis Eleven*, No. 17, part 2 in: *ibid.* No. 18/19.) And what about a specific Muslim way to modernity, under the impact of modern technology and weaponry, modern science and intellectual critique, of market exchange and media, legal institutions and social mobility? Or is populistic traditionalism incompatible with modernity: are fundamentalism and critical reflection mutually exclusive? What is feasible and desirable – e.g. Islamic and Jewish states, or sobering differentiations between politics and religion? (Cf., e.g., William Montgomery Watt: *Islamic Fundamentalism and Modernity*, London: Routledge, 1989.)

2. Cf. e.g. *Communication and the Evolution of Society* (= *CES*), Boston: Beacon Press, 1979 (German original 1976); *The Theory of Communicative Action* (= *TCA*), Boston: Beacon Press, Vol. I, 1984, Vol. II, 1987 (German original 1981); *Moral Consciousness and Communicative Action* (= *MCCA*), Cambridge, Mass.: MIT Press, 1990 (German original 1983). Classical anthologies on this debate are *Habermas: Critical Debates* (= *HCD*), eds. J. B. Thompson and D. Held, London: Macmillan, 1982, and *Habermas and Modernity* (= *HaM*), ed. Richard Bernstein, Cambridge Mass.: MIT Press, 1985. Cf. also S. K. White: *Jürgen Habermas, Reason, Justice and Modernity*, Cambridge: Cambridge University Press, 1988, which gives a fair presentation of the structure in Habermas's recent work, including his theory of lifeworld modernization. (The book is less elaborate as to the philosophical debates on justification and universality, cf. the debate between Apel and Habermas.) See also T. McCarthy, *Ideals and Illusions* (= *IaI*), Cambridge, Mass.: MIT Press, 1991; R. Bernstein, *The New Constellation*, Cambridge: Polity Press, 1991; and S. Benhabib, *Situating the Self* (= *StS*), Cambridge: Polity Press, 1992. Cf. also Habermas's recent publications: *Erläuterungen zur Diskursethik* (= *EzD*), Frankfurt a.M.: Suhrkamp, 1991, and *Faktiziät und Geltung* (= *FG*), Frankfurt a.M.: Suhrkamp, 1992.

3. *TCA* II, p. 130. "...the unquestioned ground of everything given in my experience, and the unquestionable frame in which all the problems I have to deal with are located." Quotations p. 131 (from A. Schutz and T. Luckmann: *Structure of the Lifeworld*). Cf. also Habermas's discussion of the notion of the lifeworld in Husserl in: "Edmund Husserl über Lebenswelt, Philosophie und Wissenschaft," in: *Texte und Kontexte* (= *TuK*), Frankfurt a.M.: Suhrkamp, 1991, pp. 34–48.

4. Habermas, *TCA* II, p. 130. Also "...my lifeworld is not my private world but, rather, is intersubjective;..." from Schutz and Luckmann, *ibid.*

5. *TCA* II, pp. 130 and 132. Also "...situations change, but the limits of the lifeworld cannot be transcended".

6. *TCA* II, p. 134.

7. For critical remarks on the notion of the lifeworld in Habermas, from the point of view of philosophical phenomenology, see F. Olafson: "Habermas as a Philosopher," *Ethics*, Vol. 100, No. 3, 1990, pp. 641–657.

8. Cf. e.g. Fred Dallmayr on a weak and a strong notion of the lifeworld (Schutz and Gadamer/Heidegger, resp.) in: *Polis and Praxis*, Cambridge, Mass.: MIT Press, 1984, pp. 243-244.

9. *TCA* II, p. 137. Cf. e.g. Skjervheim and Winch.

10. *TCA* II, p. 137. In the latter case (the analysis of preconditions) we approach a "strong" notion of lifeworld – though there is a difference between investigating a-historical conditions for Man and the lifeworld (as in the analysis of "Dasein") and investigating conditions for historical formation (which is at stake in the analysis of lifeworld modernization).

11. *TCA* II, p. 148.

12. *TCA* II, pp. 150 ff. Cf. the very title of *TCA* II: "Lifeworld and System. A Critique of Functionalist Reason." Still the problem remains as to the epistemological status of 'lifeworld' and 'system': are they to be conceived as two conceptual perspectives or as two spheres of reality? See next note.

13. I am neither going to look into the question of the 'uncoupling' of the system and the lifeworld, nor into the question of the 'colonization' of the lifeworld by the system. I will restrict myself to the following remarks.
    An important discussion has been whether the *distinction between lifeworld and system* should primarily be understood as an *ontological* distinction (*in re*) or as a *methodological* distinction (*in dicto*). (This is an ambiguity similar to the one discussed in connection with the notion of nature in Habermas, cf. "The Pragmatic Notion of Nature" in this collection.) Habermas talks on the one hand as if the distinction is one of performative perspectives (either actions are seen in a participatory perspective, as normatively integrated, or actions are seen in an objectivating perspective, through system integration). On the other hand he talks of a colonization of the lifeworld by the system, a way of talking which suggests an ontological interpretation of the distinction. For critical remarks cf. e.g. Thomas McCarthy: "Complexity and Democracy, or The Seducements of Systems Theory," *New German Critique*, No. 35, 1985, pp. 27–53, also in: *Ideals and Illusions* (= *IaI*), Cambridge Mass.: MIT Press, 1991, pp. 152–180; also Axel Honneth: *Kritik der Macht*, Frankfurt a.M: Suhrkamp, 1985, ch. 9.
    Habermas has elaborated this distinction partly from one between

material reproduction and symbolic reproduction (e.g. *TCA* II pp. 348–349) and partly from a distinction between actions that are 'system integrated' and actions that are 'socially integrated' (e.g., *TCA* I, pp. 87–88, 357–360). If these distinctions are not merely conceived as analytic definitions, but as distinctions with a claim to conceptual adequacy, it is hard to see how some overlap can be avoided: in material reproduction (paradigmatically, economic life) the use of symbols is involved, in symbolic reproduction (paradigmatically, rearing children) material reproduction is involved. For a discussion of these questions, cf. Nancy Fraser in *New German Critique*, No. 35, 1985, e.g. p. 103. For a lucid discussion of the implications of the Habermasian tendency to conceive economy and politics in system-theoretical terms, and the view that Habermas has been inspired and seduced by Niklas Luhmann, cf. Thomas McCarthy in: *Ia*l, pp. 160 ff.

However, Habermas accepts that at this point he is guilty of unclarity and inconsistency (he talks about "Unklarheiten und widersprüchliche Formulierungen", viz. in "Entgegnung," in *Kommunikatives Handeln*, eds. A. Honneth and H. Joas, Frankfurt a.M.: Suhrkamp, 1986, pp. 377–405, quotation pp. 377–378). He says: "Ich habe Sozial- und Systemintegration zunächst als zwei *analytisch* zu trennende *Aspekte* der gesellschaftlichen Integration eingeführt. Unter diesen Aspekten lassen sich Ordnungsbegriffe einführen, die in der vorläufigen Definition der Gesellschaft als "systemisch stabilisierter Handlungszusammenhänge sozial integrierter Gruppen" ebenfalls nur analytisch zu trennende Aspekte desselben Gegenstandes anzeigen." (Habermas, *op.cit.* p. 379.) Habermas adds the follow remarks: "Allerdings verändert sich dieses relativ klare Bild, wenn man jenen evolutionären Trend berücksichtigt, den ich als "Entkoppelung" von System und Lebenswelt beschrieben habe. McCarthy hat meine These erläutert, daß die beiden Aspekte der Gesellschaft, die zunächst nur als verschiedene Perspektiven der Betrachtung derselben Phänomene eingeführt werden, für moderne Gesellschaften auch eine essentialistische Konnotation gewinnen und den Blick auf verschieden strukturierte Bereiche der gesellschaftlichen Realität selber freigeben." (*Op.cit.* p. 383.)

At this point we could add a critical remark: Concepts disclose reality, but in highlighting certain aspects they leave something else in the dark. To the extent that the conceptual distinction between 'lifeworld' and 'system' is used in analyzing modern societies *politically*, there is a danger of overlooking the constitutive function of norms, in law and morality, for both market economy and bureaucratic politics; and there is also a danger of overlooking the political difference between these two paradigmatic cases of the 'system' (state and market): politics is not merely a play of power, but also (partly) a matter of public discussion and *Bildung*, and the implementation of discursively established conclusions is often a matter of political actions through administrative institutions. A political *Gleichschaltung* of market economy and of administrative politics (both defined as 'system') is therefore politically suspicious; in practical terms it implies a depolitization in the sense that it blurs the 'political primacy' of the state versus the market. It is vital to defend lifeworld and discourse, but it is politically fatal to attack the state (the legal and political institutions) in the same way as one attacks the market. Habermas (like the other Frankfurt philosophers) has relatively little to say about the internal dynamics of market economy. Until recently, even the realm of politics was less thoroughly elaborated than that of the lifeworld. In his latest book, however, the realm of politics is extensively discussed, cf. *Faktiziät und Geltung. Beiträge zur Diskurstheorie des Rechts und des demokratischen Rechtsstaats*, (= *FG*), Frankfurt a.M.: Suhrkamp, 1992.

14. *TCA* II, pp. 139–140. For a recent discussion of the notion of a lifeworld, see *Nachmetaphysisches Denken*, Frankfurt a.M.: Suhrkamp, 1988, pp. 82–104.

15. *TCA* II, p. 142, figure 21.

16. The dimensions of evaluation for these reproductive processes are rationality of knowledge, solidarity of members and personal responsibility. Habermas, *TCA* II, pp. 142–143, figures 21 and 22.

17. "What is Universal Pragmatics?" in: *CES*, p. 68. Elaborated anew in "Intermediate Reflections" in: *TCA* I.

18. These modes of communication and attitudes are (i) a cognitive mode of communication and an objectivating attitude; (ii) an interactive mode of communication and a conformative attitude; and (iii) an expressive mode of communication and an expressive attitude. Cf. "What is Universal Pragmatics," in: *CES*, pp. 1–68 (scheme p. 68). Further elaboration, *TCA* I, pp. 273–337 (e.g. figure 16, p. 327).

19. As Habermas points out, methodologically the problem is (for one thing) how to investigate competences and conditions empirically through their performances or instances. (Cf. e.g. *MCCA* p. 187.) This indicates a difficult field between philosophy and empirical research. (Cf. my point in favor of arguments from absurdity in investigating conditions and competences: "Arguments from Absurdity." There I also indicate reasons for holding a gradualist view on the relationship between philosophical and empirical research.)

20. *TCA* II, pp. 145–146.

21. I will refer to these theories later, cf. e.g. Lawrence Kohlberg: *Moral Stages and the Idea of Justice*.

22. Cf. my criticism of a schematic use of a distinction between external nature and society, in "The Pragmatic Notion of Nature". A related theoretical problem is that of the status of the basic conceptual perspectives. To what extent are the basic conceptual schemes, such as the division into three basic validity claims, a matter of mere decision, or (as for the related division into science, justice, and art) a matter of an ethnocentric bias? (As to the discussion of a possible 'eurocentrism', cf. T. McCarthy in: *IaI*, p. 134.) Could the basic conceptual schemes be justified theoretically, without the pitfalls of traditional fundamentalism? Cf. the trilemma of metaphysical attempts at ultimate grounding, e.g. in the debate between Karl-Otto Apel: *Transformation der Philosophie* and Hans Albert: *Transzendentale Träumereien*. Or could the basic conceptual schemes be justified hermeneutically, without the pitfall of historicist relativism?

23. Cf. Thomas McCarthy's discussion: "Rationality and Relativism: Habermas's 'Overcoming' of Hermeneutics," in: *Habermas, Critical Debates* (= *HCB*), eds. J. B. Thompson and D. Held, London: Macmillan, 1982, pp. 57–78. Cf. Habermas on "inescapability", in: *MCCA*, p. 130.

24. *TCA* I, pp. 70–71.

25. I am speaking here in European terms when distinguishing between *conservatism* (as in Burke) and *liberalism* (Bentham, Smith, etc.). (I do not apply the North American terminology according to which liberalists are called conservatives, and social democrats are called liberals.)

26. Cf. Habermas in: *HCD*, p. 245, where he refers to the need to elaborate our notion of scientific rationality from historically given cases of scientific rationality: "...the theory of knowledge, which has to orientate itself to *successful* examples of theory formation,...".

27. On the controversy between liberals and communitarians, and the attempt at a communicative synthesis (mediation), cf. e.g. Kenneth Baynes, "The Liberal-Communitarian Controversy and Communicative Ethics", *Philosophy and Social Criticism*, 14(1988), pp. 293–315; Charles Taylor, "Cross-Purposes: The Liberal-Communitarian Debate", in *Liberalism and the Moral Life*, ed. N. Rosenblum, Cambridge, Mass.: Harvard University Press, 1989, pp. 159–183; Michael Walzer, "The Communitarian Critique of Liberalism", *Political Theory*, 18(1990), pp. 6–23; Seyla Benhabib, *Situating the Self*, Cambridge: Polity Press, 1992.

28. Cf. "Praxeological Reflections" in this collection.

29. Consider borderline cases between man and mammals, discussed in "Ethical Gradualism and Discourse Ethics". As to the criticism of schematic distinctions between Nature and Man (Society), cf. "The Pragmatic Notion of Nature".

30. Once realized, this distinction can be critically discussed or refined, but not really done away with. Its realization is part of a learning process that gives us a better grasp of our lifeworld realities, in the sense that these realities are now transformed in a way that opens the way to a technical and scientific explanation and domination in the case of objects (Nature), and for communicative and argumentative interaction in the case of subjects (Man), i.e. they open the way to rationalization of the world, and this rationalization apparently represents some kind of an irreversible transition.

31. Also in cases where there are reasons, we can legitimately ask for causes (even for different kinds of causes). But I will not here go into the well-known discussion on the interrelation between causes and reasons.

32. One such case is the status of animals. Cf. again the question of borderline cases between humans and non-humans, in "Ethical Gradualism and Discourse Ethics".

33. Cf. Jürgen Habermas: *HCB*, p. 228: "If the balance of happiness (which is difficult to weigh) shifts at all, it certainly does not do so in dependence on rationalisation of the life-world".

34. And forgotten in the 1990s? (Cf. e.g. the Yugoslav tragedy.)

35. *TCA* II, pp. 318 ff.

36. Cf. the post-modernist criticism, from Nietzsche and Heidegger to Foucault and Derrida. Among the subtle cases of critical *Auseinandersetzungen*, cf. Dominique Janicaud, *Les Pouvoirs de la Science*, Paris: Vrin, 1987.

37. Cf. G. Skirbekk, "La rationalité scientifique comme destin", in: G. Skirbekk, *Rationalité et Modernité*, Paris: L'Harmattan, 1993.

38. There are many cases for which this self-referential argument could and should be applied, by letting it work from within, as it were. Cf. "Ecological Crisis and Technological Expertise", in Gunnar Skirbekk, *Eco-Philosophical Manuscripts*, Bergen: Ariadne, 1992.

39. Cf. Habermas in: *HCD*, p. 235: "Nothing makes me more nervous than the imputation – repeated in a number of different versions and in the most peculiar contexts – that because the theory of communicative action focuses attention on the social facticity of recognised validity-claims, it proposes, or at least suggests, a rationalistic utopian society."

40. The psychologist Lawrence Kohlberg, who was inspired by Piaget and Kant, argues for the thesis that all children pass through the *same* stages in developing their capacity for moral judgment in the sense of judgment concerning justice. (E.g. Lawrence Kohlberg: *Essays in Moral Development*, San Francisco, 1981.) Moral maturation is seen as a development in six stages, a development which involves an increasing capability to 'differentiate' (between a notion of duty based on moral autonomy and notions of duty based on practical considerations) and to 'integrate' (by interpreting moral judgments as to their universalizability by taking into account the claims and perspectives of other persons), leading toward improved reciprocity and increasing universality. He claims that there is an isomorphism between the development of social concepts and the development of the ability to make universalistic moral judgments.

His empirical basis consists of answers from a selected number of children, of different ages and from different countries, to some standard stories told to them. The stories told involve moral conflicts and the children are supposed to reveal their moral maturity by the way they express what they would do to solve the problems involved.

Kohlberg's conclusion is one in favor of a moral universality as to the development of the idea of justice in children. The six stages (and three levels) of moral development are by Kohlberg characterized in these terms:

Preconventional level
(Stage 1) *Punishment and obedience*
(Stage 2) *Individual instrumental purpose and exchange*
Conventional level
(Stage 3) *Mutual interpersonal expectations, relationships, and conformity*
(Stage 4) *Social system and conscience maintenance*
Postconventional level
(Stage 5) *Prior rights and social contract or utility*
(Stage 6) *Universal ethical principles*

See also Kohlberg's summary, *ibid.*, 1981, pp. 409 ff.

Kohlberg sees moral maturation as a learning process in which socio-cognitive learning enables socio-moral learning. He conceives of each stage as a structured whole. The sequence from stage to stage is invariant and irreversible. The stages of moral development thus represent a hierarchy in which lower stages are overcome (*aufgehoben*) in the higher ones. We could thus characterize his conception of moral development as 'unilinear Hegelianism'.

Kohlberg's project is open to various objections, e.g. questions of its empirical foundation (as in § (i) below), questions of its normative foundation (ii), questions of the conceptual set-up, for instance as to the link between socio-cognitive development and moral development and as to the plausibility of the transition from stage to stage (iii), and questions concerning the relationship between universalistic justification and contextual application (iv).

(i) Kohlberg's thesis is open to support and to resistance from empirical data from different disciplines, such as social psychology, comparative anthropology, and sociology. In general terms it is fair to say that this empirical work is not completed and that what has been done so far is not uniquely supportive. For one thing, Kohlberg's own empirical testing is rather narrow: his empirical data stem from verbal reactions from children of different ages from different countries to stories presented to them. Not only is the number of children fairly small, and not only is it questionable whether his questions and cases are sufficiently impartial with respect to cultural differences, but by choosing verbal reactions to prearranged stories instead of observing their moral behavior in real situations, Kohlberg cuts himself off from what could have been his own learning process in trying to figure out what is really going on "out there".

A similar point has recently been made by anthropologists, as a warning against an uncritical use of earlier research results. The answers given by earlier informants have been questioned, since there are now reasons to think that these informants have time and again given the answers which the informants thought would please the field-worker. For instance, myths and rites could have been (unconsciously or consciously) emphasized and dramatized or otherwise biased in order to meet what was conceived of as the inquirer's expectations. The special position of the informants within a given society might also have been underestimated. In such cases, the empirical data, based on verbal reactions from these informants and not on participant observation, could prove to be unreliable.

We also have the following problem, concerning the interrelationship between the empirical and the theoretical perspective: *empirically*, moral development appears as a *gradual* process; *retrospectively*, however, this process is reconstructible in terms of *paradigmatic stages*.

All in all, the empirical basis is thus rather weak both quantitatively and qualitatively. (Cf., e.g., T. McCarthy, *Ia1*, pp. 136–151; Habermas's response, *HCD*, pp. 258–261.)

(ii) Kohlberg explicitly attempts to 'mediate' between psychological research and philosophical argumentation. The question of the normative foundation of his project is to be seen in this perspective; he is aware of the danger of a naturalistic fallacy. (Cf. his essay "From Is to Ought: How to commit the Naturalistic Fallacy and Get Away with It in the Study of Moral Development," in T. Mischel, ed., *Cognitive Development and Epistemology*, New York: Academic Press, 1971, pp. 151–235.) Even so, and even though he talks in terms of ideal role taking and universalizability as the highest moral point of reference, he does not elaborate a self-referential discourse ethics which (in my view) could purge him from the sneaking suspicion of untenable naturalistic or metaphysical assumptions. Concerning the debate about the highest stage, cf. e.g. L. Kohlberg, "The Claim to Moral Adequacy of a Highest Stage of Moral Judgment", *Journal of Philosophy*, 70(1973), pp. 630–646; J. Habermas "Justice and Solidarity: On the Discussion concerning 'Stage 6'", in: *Hermeneutics and Critical Theory in Ethics and Politics*, ed. M. Kelly, Cambridge, Mass.: MIT Press, 1990, pp. 32–52 (German original, 1986; also *EzD*, pp. 49–76); K.-O. Apel, "Die transzendentalpragmatische Begründung der Kommunikationsethik und das Problem der höchsten Stufe einer Entwicklungslogik des moralischen Bewußtseins", in: *Diskurs und Verantwortung. Das Problem des Übergangs zur postkonventionellen Moral*, Frankfurt a.M.: Suhrkamp, 1988, pp. 306–369; also T. McCarthy, *IaI* (see above).

(iii) There is a web of conceptual and empirical themes related to the interconnection between socio-cognitive and moral development, as well as to the transition from one stage to the next. This is where Habermas attempts to improve the Kohlbergian conception of moral development by reinterpreting it within the perspective of communicative action. Habermas aims at a developmental justification of Kohlberg's stages and transitions by interpreting them through the conceptual framework of the three speaker perspectives, the three worlds and validity claims of universal pragmatics, and the three reproductive processes and structural components. He thereby hopes to make the Kohlbergian project fruitful for his own theory of modernization and rationalization. We shall look into some of Habermas's proposals. (Cf. T. McCarthy, *ibid.*)

(iv) For the discussion of application and contextuality, cf., e.g., J. M. Murphy and C. Gilligan "Moral Development in Late Adolescence and Adulthood: a Critique and Reconstruction of Kohlberg's Theory," in: *Human Development*, 23(1980) pp. 77–104; L. Kohlberg: "A Reply to Owen Flanagan," *Ethics*, 92 (April 1982), p. 53; Owen Flanagan and Kathryn Jackson, "Justice, Care, and Gender: The Kohlberg-Gilligan Debate Revisited", *Ethics*, 98(1988) pp.622–637; K. Günther, *Der Sinn für Angemessenheit. Anwendungsdiskurse in Moral und Recht*, Frankfurt a.M: Suhrkamp, 1988, pp. 176–197; and Seyla Benhabib, *Situating the Self*, Oxford: Polity, 1992. Also Habermas in *MCCA*, pp. 172–175, and *EzD*, e.g. pp. 137–142. (I will pursue some aspects of this problem also in the next chapter: "Rationality and Contextuality").

41. Cf. Habermas's *Moralbewußtsein und kommunikatives Handeln*, 1983. English translation *Moral Consciousness and Communicative Action* (= *MCCA*), Cambridge, Mass.: MIT Press, 1990, especially "Reconstruction and Interpretation in the Social Sciences" (pp. 21–42) and "Moral Consciousness and Communicative Action" (pp. 116–194). Also *The Theory of Communicative Action* (=*TCA*), German original 1981; and *Erläuterungen zur Diskursethik* (= *EzD*), 1991. Relating to the current discussion, cf. Jürgen Habermas "Justice and Solidarity: On the Discussion concerning 'Stage 6'", in: *Hermeneutics and Critical Theory in Ethics and Politics*, Michael Kelly (ed.), Cambridge, Mass.: MIT Press, 1990, pp. 32–52. (Also in *EzD*, pp. 49–76.) Carol Gilligan (*In a Different Voice*, Cambridge, Mass.: Harvard University Press, 1982) argues in favor of a seventh stage, reintegrating context dependency. Habermas replies (in *MCCA*, pp. 175–184) that there is no need for a postconventional contextualist stage, but that universalization and contextualization could be mediated by properly differentiating and integrating justification and application (and motivation). Cf. also Seyla Benhabib, *Situating the Self*, Cambridge: Polity Press, 1992.

42. At this point we should recall two versions of his developmental scheme. A revised version from the perspective of development of ego identity and of morality may be found in "Moral Development and Ego Identity," *CES*, p. 89 (schema 4). From the perspective of moral consciousness and communicative action, a revised version is presented in *MCCA*, Table 4, pp. 166–167, in "Moral Consciousness and Communicative Action," pp. 116–194. In the former case, Habermas operates with seven stages, in the latter (and later) with six. (Cf. his arguments [*ibid.* pp. 175–184] against Carol Gilligan suggesting a seventh stage of "field dependency" [*In a Different Voice*, Cambridge, Mass.: Harvard University Press, 1982]: with a proper differentiation and reintegration of problems of justification and application, a "postconventional contextualist stage" is not needed).

43. Cf., e.g., Habermas: *HCB*, p. 259.

44. Cf. Jürgen Habermas: "Interpretive Social Science vs. Hermeneuticism," in: *Social Science as Moral Inquiry*, eds. N. Haan *et al.*, New York: Columbia University Press, p. 261: "It is important to see that rational reconstructions, like all other types of knowledge, have only a hypothetical status. They may very well start from a false sample of intuitions; they may obscure and distort the right intuitions; and they may, even more

often, overgeneralize particular cases. They are in need of further corroboration. What I accept as an antifoundationalist criticism of all strong a priori and transcendentalist claims does not, however, block attempts to put rational reconstructions of supposedly basic competences on trial and to test them indirectly by employing them as input in empirical theories."

45. The latter claims, regarded as empirical claims, are subtle ones, since they are conceptually constituted (and concepts alone do not make empirical claims) and partly concern idealizations and preconditions which can only be indirectly tested against empirical reality.

46. Cf. my critical comments in: "Pragmatism and Pragmatics" in this collection.

47. To the extent that the validity claim of "intelligibility" (in Habermas's *Wahrheitstheorien*) is presented as a precondition of discourse, and therefore not as a discursive validity claim at the level of practical and theoretical validity claims, we should nevertheless understand this validity claim of intelligibility as being part of what is discussed in these two latter cases (truth and rightness). This is also what Habermas implies (*ibid.*) by emphasizing the importance of a reflective discourse on linguistic schemes as to their adequacy. And this is the reason why the reflective discussion of 'linguistic schemes' is required in any practical or theoretical discourse.

48. The notion of truth as correspondence and that of conceptual adequacy have been under attack from various positions (cf. e.g. G. Skirbekk ed., *Wahrheitstheorien*, Frankfurt a.M.: Suhrkamp, 1977), recently also from post-modernists (such as Derrida) and post-empiricists (such as Rorty). They argue (or 'talk') in favor of a way of talking according to which language is seen as contingent: "... the world does not provide us with any criterion of choice between alternative metaphors,..." (Richard Rorty, *Contingency, Irony and Solidarity*, Cambridge, Cambridge University Press, 1991, p. 20, first ed. 1989). Rorty (referring to D. Davidson) talks about (and in favor of) a "treatment of language which breaks *completely* with the notion of language as something which can be adequate or inadequate to the world or to the self."

Two critical remarks: (i) Rorty will redescribe, not argue, in order to avoid charges of self-referential inconsistency (to which Derrida is liable, according to Rorty, cf. *ibid.* pp. 8–9). But still he makes "claims" (also explicitly, *ibid.* e.g. pp. 9 and 20), and hence the question of self-referential inconsistency reappears. (See Richard Bernsteins, *The New Constellation*, Cambridge: Polity Press, 1991, pp. 258–292, esp. pp. 278 ff. on universality.) (ii) In a praxeological perspective the Wittgensteinian aspect of Rorty's criticism of metaphysics is easy to buy. But from a praxeological perspective, Rorty talks in holistic and general terms (both in his criticism of traditional philosophy and in his own contributions within the literary conversation about the Western tradition) instead of critically elaborating human activities and their 'contingent necessities'.

Be this as it may. I will just make these claims: Historically created institutions allow for a notion of relative adequacy (and inadequacy) as to our conceptual grasp. In these cases, it is not a question of language as such or of reality as such, but of situated activities and their inherent concepts. (Cf. "Praxeological Reflections" but also "Arguments from Absurdity" and "Pragmatism and Pragmatics"). In many activities there are deep ambiguities, but some are conceptually clear-cut (such as modern specialized institutions, e.g. legal procedures – this, I think, is the sound point in Klaus Günther's work on 'application discourses' in favor of *Angemessenheit*, adequacy). Among the interesting cases, in my view, are large scale projects with an inherent need for interdisciplinarity. Cf. "Science and Ethics" and "Ecological Crisis and Technological Expertise" (in G. Skirbekk, *Eco-Philosophical Manuscripts*, Bergen: Ariadne, 1992) where I try to show the possibility and importance of a notion of 'relative adequacy', underlining the primacy of *in*adequacy and its melioristic 'overcoming'. My praxeologically inspired 'gradualist meliorism' is an attempt to avoid both the idea of holistic, 'positive adequacy' and that of holistic contingency (as in Rorty).

49. Conceptual adequacy claims do not "generalize particular cases" in the sense that they make statements that are 'too general', for they do not make statements. But they may very well be inadequate when used for the wrong cases or at the wrong places. To situate them correctly is essential, that is, their contextualization and application are essential for their validity.

50. Cf. again "Arguments from Absurdity".

51. There are empirical validity claims that are tested 'directly', without discourse; cf. the color test in "Pragmatism and Pragmatics" in this collection.

Regarding the Habermasian conception of lifeworld modernization, it is worth pointing out that this 'theory' primarily represents an elaborated conceptual framework, implying validity claims of conceptual adequacy; it is not primarily an 'explaining' theory, though it does entail various empirical validity claims, more or less indirectly. And it does entail claims about competences and about preconditions, some of these being norms constitutive for discourse and for communicative actions.

Habermas's conception of system integration and social integration (system and lifeworld) does have a *methodological* implication, something like: "be aware of possible conflicts along this line!" Habermas thus provides social researchers with good reason to expect to find promising projects in this area. For politically committed persons, it gives a clue as to what kind of conflict we can expect. For both perspectives (research and politics), the Habermasian 'theory' presents powerful *conceptual tools* for grasping what is going on. But in neither case does this theory tell us, or predict for us, what (concretely) is going to happen. It does not make that kind of empirical validity claim. In this sense, the theory is not empirically falsifiable. But it does claim conceptual adequacy and relevance, and it is clearly possible to discuss the validity of these claims. And in making such conceptual adequacy claims it implies or supposes that various things do exist, things about which we could explicitly make empirical (or theoretical) validity claims. In this sense there is no clear-cut distinction between conceptual and theoretical (empirical) validity claims.

Finally, in negative terms, this theory implies a critique of conceptual perspectives that for one reason or another are less comprehensive or less reflective, such as that of rational choice. The Habermasian conception represents a critique in the sense that it demonstrates a superior conceptual adequacy. This does not mean that other conceptual perspectives are simply inadequate, but that their relative shortcomings (as to their adequacy claims) should be kept in mind, and that the question should be raised as to what kind of context they fit best. (However, a social theory like that of rational choice does not only represent a conceptual perspective, but is also a quite powerful theory for explanation.)

52. Cf. Thomas McCarthy's comment on these problems: "Rationality and Relativism: Habermas's 'Overcoming' of Hermeneutics," in: *Habermas. Critical Debates* (= *HCD*), eds. J. B. Thompson and D. Held, London:

Macmillan, 1982, pp. 57–78, also revised in: *Ial*, pp. 127–151. For the discussion concerning the highest level, cf. Lawrence Kohlberg, Dwight Boyd, and Charles Levine: "Stage 6 Revisited," and Bill Puka: "The Majesty and Mystery of Stage 6" published in: *The Moral Domain*, Cambridge, Mass.: MIT Press (in German, in *Zur Bestimmung der Moral* [= *ZBM*], eds. W. Edelstein and G. Nunner-Winkler, Frankfurt a.M.: Suhrkamp, 1986); and Jürgen Habermas: "Justice and Solidarity: On the Discussion concerning 'Stage 6'," in: Michael Kelly, *Hermeneutics and Critical Theory in Ethics and Politics*, Cambridge, Mass.: MIT Press, 1990, pp. 32–52 (in *ZBM* 1986); K.-O. Apel, "Die transzendental-pragmatische Begründung der Kommunikationsethik und das Problem der höchsten Stufe einer Entwicklungslogik des moralischen Bewußtseins", in *Diskurs und Verantwortung. Das Problem des Übergangs zur postkonventionellen Moral*, Frankfurt a.M.: Suhrkamp, 1988, pp. 306–369

53. Cf. note 40 above. As to the discussion of discourse theory itself, see e.g. "Pragmatism and Pragmatics" and "Contextual and Universal Pragmatics".

54. But why should this be the *lowest* among the stages of explicit moral reasoning? Why should not this stage stand higher than that of contractarians and of utilitarians? These are not merely empirical questions, to be answered by questionnaires or by participant observation. Only philo-sophical argumentation will do.

   By locating ethical skepticism at the entrance to the postconventional world, Habermas indicates how he conceives of this transition as a dramatic one. But even so, what are the convincing arguments which show that ethical skepticism is less mature or less rational than utilitarianism? (In some cases, I assume, it might be the other way around. Cf. G. Skirbekk, *Nihilisme?*, Oslo: Tanum, 1958, Engl. tr. 1973.)

55. In *Essays in Moral Development*, II, San Francisco, 1984, pp. 149, Lawrence Kohlberg refers to a double aspect of maturation, the reflective mastering of general principles and a reflective mastering of concrete situations: "The developing human being and the moral philosopher are engaged in fundamentally the same moral task. .... The task is arriving at moral judgments in reflective equilibrium – between espoused general principles and particular judgments about situations."

56. Cf. K. Günther's elaboration of a notion of discursive application (*Anwendungsdiskurs*) in *Der Sinn für Angemessenheit. Anwendungsdiskurse in Moral und Recht* (= *SfA*), Frankfurt a.M.: Suhrkamp, 1988.

57. Cf. these questions discussed in the 'Gilligan debate', see e.g. S. Benhabib, *Situating the Self*, Cambridge: Polity Press, 1992, chapters 5 and 6 (pp. 148–202).

58. Cf. K.-O. Apel's distinction between pure normative justification (reflective *Letztbegründung*) and hermeneutic application (often referred to as part A_1 and A_2 of discourse ethics), and also practical application in (potentially) strategic contexts (often referred to as part B), e.g. in "Kann der postkantische Standpunkt der Moralität noch einmal in substantielle Sittlichkeit 'aufgehoben' werden? Das geschichtsbezogene Anwendungsproblem der Diskursethik zwischen Utopie und Regression," in: *Diskurs und Verantwortung*, Frankfurt a.M.: Suhrkamp, 1988, pp. 103–153. (Cf. Habermas's criticism of these Apelian distinctions, *EzD*, especially pp. 197–198.)

Cf. Albrecht Wellmer on the relation between consensus and argument, in: *Ethik und Dialog*, Frankfurt a.M.: Suhrkamp, 1986, pp. 82–112. See also "Pragmatism and Pragmatics".

59. A crucial point in discourse ethics is the link between 'precondition' ('frame') and 'content', implying that any moral inequality, on the level of 'content norms', which contradicts the equality of the procedural norms of the 'frame', is ruled out. This is how ethnocentric positions, such as fascism, are excluded. However, in real life there might be cases where repressed groups might agree to discriminatory treatment of themselves. This raises the question of the competence required of the participants (and the need for advocatory representation). (Such cases are to be distinguished from cases of rationally grounded, voluntary self-sacrifice.)

On the analysis of 'constitutive' and 'regulative' norms inherent in scientific inquiry, cf. K. E. Tranøy's case oriented 'arguments from absurdity', referred to in the section 'Critical Aftermath' in "Pragmatism and Pragmatics".

60. However, we could reason here in terms of specialized institutions: in modern societies the various contexts are largely clear-cut institutions (such as legal procedures), for which the question of the conceptual (linguistic) adequacy is in principle answerable. (Cf. the Habermasian

conception of modernization in terms of a specialization of institutions.)
From this premise we could reason in terms of an 'application discourse',
concerning the conceptual adequacy question in the various modern, 'pre-
cut' contexts. (Cf. the pro-Habermasian elaboration of this conception in
Klaus Günther, *Der Sinn für Angemessenheit. Anwendungsdiskurse in
Moral und Recht.*)

This attempt at an adequate conceptional application (at an adequate
conceptual contextualization by means of 'application discourses')
represents a fallible task: it is loaded with similar problems as the ones we
encounter in 'validation discourses' oriented toward an idea of a perfect
consensus, in which all possible perspectives (also future ones!) are
realized and harmonized. (Cf. the idea of an ideal speech situation in
which all possible hindrances are known, and eliminated. This point is
discussed and criticized in "Pragmatism and Pragmatics": I have argued
that we can only obtain a 'directional' idea of such an ideal; operationally
what we have are ideals of improvement, of 'overcoming' what is seen to
be relatively *less* acceptable than it could have been. Catchwords are
meliorism and gradualism.)

Since I do not accept the assumption of an (operational) idea of a
perfect consensus (nor of a perfect ideal speech situation), it follows that
in my view no justified consent (nor any high-stage discursive situation)
is ever totally free from contextuality in the sense that a *special* set of
conceptual perspectives is implied. The possibility of harmonizing all
possible conceptual perspectives (including *future* ones), and of knowing
it, is not a possibility available for our 'adequacy discourse'. (This is my
answer to Habermas concerning the possibility of 'universally accepted
interpretations of needs', cf. *EzD*, pp. 201–203.) However, being a
fallibilist in this sense, I am also a meliorist, accepting the idea of the
possibility of improving any conceptual (linguistic) grasp discursively.
Furthermore, in *reflective discourses*, when we discuss the meta-norms of
discourse, the situation is another, for self-referential reasons; stuck in our
self-reflective language, we are free from the problems of contextuality
referred to above.

61. Cf. my argument in favor of a practical symbiosis of discourse ethics and
the ability to master a multidimensional and partly ambiguous world, in:
"The World Reconsidered" in: *Thesis Eleven*, 30(1991), pp. 17–32. (Also
"Political Culture", in G. Skirbekk, *Eco-Philosophical Manuscripts*,
Bergen: Ariadne, 1992.)

62. Cf., e.g., Martin Hollis: *The Cunning of Reason*, Cambridge: Cambridge University Press, 1987; and R. E. Goodin, in: *Responsibility, Rights & Welfare*, ed. J. D. Moon, Boulder: Westview, 1988. Also Habermas, *FG*.

63. We may well argue that the competence to think and act at the highest stage is characteristic of modernity. Then the question of a distinction between stage six and stage seven becomes crucial: in the perspective of discourse ethics, a stage seven can be interpreted to mean that a person is enabled to discuss *when necessary*. That does not imply that this person in each and every situation should adopt Kantian principles (stage six) rather than utilitarian ones (stage five) – that question has to be judged in each case, according to the situation and institution within which the person (and his moral problem) is located. There are institutionally constituted cases in which utilitarian reasoning is required, even for a person who has acquired the highest stage of moral maturity and reflection. If, contrary to this, only a strictly Kantian perspective had to be applied for anyone who had reached the highest stage, regardless of the situation, this would imply a severe lack of contextual flexibility, and in that sense, of moral maturity.

The claim that modernity requires the highest stage of moral reasoning is thus an ambiguous one, in need of clarification. In the modern world, what is morally required is an ability to recognize principles of reciprocity and to apply them in a differentiated and ambiguous reality. Moral maturity in a modern world also implies an ability to apply *different forms* of normative reasoning in different situations. This point indicates why a capacity for pluralistic contextualization has to be integrated into the overall picture: the scheme cannot represent merely a one-way move upward, but must rather be seen as representing a landscape within which a mature person is able to move skillfully around.

Rationality and Contextuality

A Modern Predicament

In light of the views expressed in the preceding chapter on universality and plurality in the process of modernization ("Modernization of the Lifeworld"), I will discuss some important issues related to rationality and contextuality in modern societies. From a pragmatic perspective I will pay special attention to the question of whether a normative foundation should (and could) primarily be given in terms of discursive and reflective rationality (Apel) or in terms of the moral implications of a modernized lifeworld (Habermas). As a kind of 'post-skeptical rationalist', I will argue in favor of contextuality and plurality, both in relation to the Habermasian notion of rationality and justice inherent in the modern lifeworld, and in relation to the Apelian notion of rationality, including normative rationality, founded in self-referential arguments. In this sense I will argue in favor of a third approach, reinterpreting and mediating Habermasian and Apelian conceptions.

Rationality and Lifeworld

Does modernity mainly consist of conceptual and social fragmentation, with merely contextual rationality and normativity, or is it also at some level integrated with and constituted by a universal rationality which even embraces a normative foundation? We have followed a few lines of argument in favor of a notion of moral maturation in terms of an acquisition of principles of universalization. These lines of argument have basically been of a Habermasian provenance. The Habermasian project, within which the notion of lifeworld modernization was discussed, is both comprehensive and complex. It relates itself to theoretical perspectives from different disciplines, and there is a web of claims and hypotheses, supported or challenged in various ways at different levels. With its comprehensive and explicitly fallible nature, trading various kinds of conceptually transformed support or resistance, it represents a paradigm case of a multi-perspective research project, oriented toward inherent coherence.[1] In one sense it is pluralistic and fallibilistic, to the postmodernist's delight. In another sense, its components are conceptually interrelated to a degree that keeps it at some distance from a bewildering reality.

We have looked into some of the ties and knots that hold together this conceptual network of lifeworld modernization. A key notion has been development in terms of differentiation and rationalization. At this point more should be said about the notion of *rationality* involved. I begin by recalling some main aspects of the pragmatic conception of rationality as it is elaborated in universal pragmatics and in discourse theory (and discussed in previous chapters, e.g. in "Pragmatism and Pragmatics").

A crucial point in *universal pragmatics* is the claim that normative rationality is inherently embedded in our speech acts. Rationality, also normative rationality, is embedded in social reality, as it were.[2] This is the point which allows for communicative actions based on mutually acceptable norms, which in cases of doubt or dissent can in principle be settled through rational procedures. (It does not allow merely for purposive actions guided by preferences and interests beyond rational consent.) This rational core inherent in our speech acts makes possible a rational intersubjective justification (redemption) of basic normative questions, as distinct from the use of power or pressure, of voting or compromise. It thereby also makes possible a rationalization of the lifeworld different from that of technological and economic development.

As we know, Habermas has argued that there are four universal validity claims inherent in any speech act, namely a claim of truth, a claim of rightness, a claim of intelligibility, and a claim of authenticity.[3] In actual speech acts these claims are more or less implicit, but they are always present in some form or another. They represent deep pragmatic competences in sane adults: a speaker claims or presupposes that something is the case, and that he, if questioned, would be able to give sufficiently good reasons to justify (or redeem) this claim. If he does not, he is not really making that claim (or presupposition). The listener is implicitly invited to trust him, but also to ask for reasons in cases of doubt or disagreement. This makes discursive solutions possible, by means of an argumentation without restraints other than those of the better argument. Likewise a speaker makes normative claims, at least implicitly, to the extent that the speaker assumes that the speech act is correctly presented in the given situation, and thus that he, if questioned, should be able to give sufficiently good reasons to show that this is the case. This again can lead to a discursive justification (redemption) of this normative validity claim. In this sense there are two discursively justifiable (redeemable) validity claims inherent in any speech act, at least in some implicit form, namely a claim of truth and a claim of rightness. This, to be sure, is not to say that all such validity claims are valid. Nor does it mean that all validity claims are 'redeemable' in the sense that they would lead to *one* answer, for which there is consensus.[4] There are certainly many normative questions that through discourse will reveal their 'adiaphorous' nature, in the sense that different answers turn out to be equally legitimate. This is to say that we in such cases have a domain of legitimate normative plurality and therefore of liberality and tolerance.[5]

In addition to these two 'discursively redeemable' validity claims, Habermas introduces the concept of a general claim of trustworthiness, of the speaker's being serious, a claim that is 'redeemed' by living together with the speaker, not by discussion alone. Habermas also talks about a claim of intelligibility as a precondition for dialogue (and for discourse – although this, I would say, is a precondition that is frequently discussed in connection with claims of truth or of rightness).

These claims entail huge problems.[6] One way of reasoning is found among contextualists (e.g. Wittgensteinians).[7] Concrete situated cases are asked for: in what sense do we always make these four validity claims? What about irony and cases of diminished or distorted awareness? What about deception and con-fusion, treason and manipulation? And in what sense are there such sharp and clear-cut distinctions between these validity claims? For instance, do we not also have 'institutional facts', which do not fit into the simple dichotomy between facts and norms?

Such questions lead to the debate on universality and contextuality. One kind of defense on behalf of universal pragmatics is related to the distinction between justification and application, the former being universal, the latter contextual.

Melioristic and Fallibilistic Gradualism?

There is more to be said about this debate on universality and contextuality, but first I would like briefly to spell out my own conception of some of these problems. I will refer to five notions, namely *meliorism*, the *primacy of the negative*, *gradualism*, the use of *examples*, and the *irreducibility of practice*.[8]

Focusing on the notion consensus, we may recall that the notion of a rational consensus cannot be seen as a necessary, nor as a sufficient, condition for validity.[9] In this sense rational consensus is not a criteriological notion of validity. It is essential that the notion of consensus (rational consensus) be related to the notion of argumentation and to the notion of the 'compelling force of the better argument'. In a certain sense I find it convincing to think of the notion of the 'best argument' as an unavoidable regulative idea, constituting an ultimate obligation for rationality. Our immediate obligation, however, is the 'best argument here and now', though always conceived as what in principle could, and often should, be critically tested once more, in order to be improved or changed. In working critically against what is *not good enough* we thus strive toward what is better. The even-better argument is therefore an obligation, transcending the best given argument, but without being known to be the final truth.[10] This rationally founded, dynamic triple obligation – from the best given, to the better, toward the best – represents a *melioristic* notion of argumentative validation.

The *primacy of the negative* is built into this meliorism at the outset: the immediate discursive obligation is the avoidance of what is worse. This primacy, I assume, can also be elaborated convincingly by looking into cases of *arguments from absurdity*: in violating some precondition for intelligibility (as in cases of category mistakes) we obtain an absurdity, whose constitutive role can be reflectively illuminated by looking closely at the context to which it belongs. Through this *via negativa* we may gain insight into preconditions of various kinds. I assume that the claim, in universal pragmatics, of a deep grammar of pragmatic competence can fruitfully be interpreted and treated in this way.[11]

The concept of *gradualism* is entailed by the concept of meliorism and the concept of the primacy of the negative: the discursive practice of improving and of avoiding what is worse implies a graduality as to the notion of argumentation. And this gradualistic meliorism represents a fallibilistic process.[12]

Examples are productive for philosophical reasoning, not only in order to illustrate pedagogically points already made, but also in order to try out our preconceptions, since examples, despite their conceptual constitution, do preserve a relative autonomy.[13] Thought-experiments related to the analysis of examples are useful not only for clarifying a point, but also in trying out conceptual preconditions; this is what is accomplished by using arguments from absurdity. Such analyses can even be undertaken in order to get a good grasp of what a discourse can possibly be.[14]

Pragmatics is not reducible to semantics. One could say that in interpreting speech acts merely in the semantic perspective, one loses the aspect of competence, praxis, and tacit knowledge. What one loses is the competence presupposed. To Wittgensteinians these presuppositions indicate the 'stubbornness' of *practice* and of *tacit insight*, to pragmaticians they represent enabling competences, and to transcendental pragmaticians they represent undeniable, reflective insights obtained in a performative mode.[15]

By incorporating more conceptual flexibility and embeddedness, these points entail, in my view, a strengthening of universal pragmatics. With these modifications, I tend to accept the main claims of universal pragmatics, including that of a universalistic notion of rationality, based on self-reflection and the pragmatic 'force' of the 'better argument'.[16]

Lifeworld Modernization Interpreted through Universal Pragmatics

The Habermasian notion of *lifeworld modernization* is deeply integrated in his notion of *universal pragmatics*. We have seen how universal pragmatics and discourse ethics are interrelated, to the extent that the triple distinctions of universal validity claims, of worlds, of attitudes, and of modes of communication are fundamental both to universal pragmatics and to discourse theory, discourse ethics included. In adapting the Kohlbergian scheme of moral development, Habermas reinterprets this scheme from his own perspective of a 'decentered world understanding', thereby reinterpreting stages and transitions and introducing discourse ethics as the highest moral position.[17]

The same pattern of an interrelating interpretation is found in the Habermasian conception of lifeworld rationalization: it is conceived of in the perspective of his notion of communicative action, which again is tightly correlated to universal pragmatics and discourse theory. A rationalized modernity implies not only an increase in purposive rationality, related to the 'system', but also increased 'discursibility' concerning worldviews, beliefs, and norms in the lifeworld. Lifeworld modernization is thus a maturation toward reciprocity and universal role taking, reflexibility, and universalizability.

At the same time as the Habermasian research project is explicitly fallible and vulnerable, it also represents a kind of *hermeneutic holism* at the level of basic conceptions, reinterpreting and integrating other projects and perspectives. This has the double effect of weakening both potential challenges and potential support.

When, for instance, stages five and six in the Kohlbergian scheme are philosophically reinterpreted, they can no longer deliver empirical support for Habermas, but neither do they represent an empirical challenge.

Weber talked in terms of ideal types. The basic notions in Habermas are explicitly *idealizations*, as is the chosen analytic unit of universal pragmatics. This means that contextualist objections taken from the realm of ordinary language are misconceived.[18] But for the same reason, the burden of theoretically justifying these very idealizations becomes that much greater.

A conceptual-hermeneutic consistency covering a large field of projects and perspectives is certainly a convincing contribution in this respect. But then it is relevant to ask for the empirical foundation of these other projects; and, as in the case of Kohlberg, this might turn out to be a tricky question.[19] To the extent that these idealizations are conceived of as competences and abilities, distinct from the level of performance, it is particularly difficult to test them.[20] But at this point an extended use of arguments from absurdity could most probably be helpful. Here it becomes most appropriate to ask for possible justifications of inherent 'adequacy claims' and 'unavoidability claims'. However, at an intermediate level of abstraction, there are, in Habermas, strikingly few case studies which might have been helpful in checking 'claims of conceptual adequacy'.[21]

Finally, given the theoretical level at which Habermas is working, given this comprehensive project embracing a socio-historical perspective that includes a self-referentially consistent notion of rationality, it is not easy to come up with a better alternative. For one thing, Habermas has elaborated his conceptual perspective through extended and thorough *Auseinandersetzungen* with major theoreticians in various fields. However, in another sense it is indeed rather easy to find weak points, and in some cases it is also possible to indicate alternatives (as in Habermas's 'system-theoretical' interpretation of both economy and politics.)[22]

(a) Ethics versus morality

At this point I will refer to a double attack on the Habermasian approach, on the one hand from transcendental pragmaticians, who blame him for diluting the rational core by moving too far toward empirical and historical reasoning, and on the other hand from social scientists, who blame him for being too transcendental and for not paying sufficient attention to the contextualization required to make the project acceptable.[23]

It might be true, as transcendental pragmaticians say, that Habermas's explicit doubts about the possibility and importance of transcendental reasoning are contradicted by his own use of arguments from self-referential consistency in criticizing other philosophers, such as French postmodernists.[24] However, Habermas is far from rejecting this kind of reasoning, even though he thinks that some philosophical doubt has to be taken into account for any verbalization, also in a performative self-reflection, and even though he thinks gradualistically about the relationship between philosophy and scientific research and therefore welcomes any support, and challenge, from relevant research programmes.

Transcendental pragmaticians, I assume, have a valid point in defending the hard core of self-reference related to discourse.[25] They are right in referring to the unavoidability of discursive rationality in cases of doubt and dissent. But even so, there is a need for arguments showing that discursive rationality is embedded in society, i.e. for arguments of the kind elaborated by Habermas; without such arguments the appeal to discursive solutions will have relatively little force outside of argumentations. To be sure, one might maintain that the status of such an appeal to discursive rationality (aiming at people outside discourse) is merely 'practical': seeing whether it works is in each case an open question. Nevertheless, it is clearly relevant to investigate in what sense discursive rationality is embedded in a modern society (which is what Habermas does). And an affirmative answer is not merely theoretically interesting; it can also help to promote rationality in a modern lifeworld. In this sense also, transcendental pragmaticians have an interest in the elaboration of a theory of communicative action, including a notion of lifeworld modernization, that shows its interconnections to discursive rationality. To the extent that this programme appears convincing, it does not threaten the idea of universal rationality and universal basic norms; rather, it lends support to our reason for having faith in the practical importance of this idea.[26]

It is fairly clear that Habermas, too, relies on self-referential arguments as part of his notion of discursive rationality, even though he concentrates on research which aims at showing the embeddedness of this kind of rationality in a modern society. We can therefore say that the transcendental pragmaticians and Habermas share a double concern for self-referential rationality and for its embeddedness in non-discursive communication. Even though they emphasize these two concerns differently, it is difficult to see that the difference is as great as it is sometimes claimed to be.[27]

We have seen that there might be some reason to assume that the transcendental pragmaticians are right in emphasizing that Habermas at times seems to disregard the need for self-reflection and to pay too much attention to actual ethics (*die Sittlichkeit*). But we have also seen that, at this point, it is relevant to recall the tendency in Habermas to reinterpret other projects from within his own philosophical perspective. To the extent that this is the case, it implies that Habermasian references to lifeworld ethics (*Sittlichkeit*) as a normative foundation should *not* be conceived of as an appeal to *historical contingency*, implying a lack of a rational foundation and, finally, to relativism. The major point is this: lifeworld development *is already philosophically interpreted* from the perspective of universal pragmatics and discourse ethics. It could therefore be asked whether the transcendental pragmaticians, in objecting in these terms, disregard the normative interpretation that has already reconstructed what otherwise could have been interpreted as historically contingent.[28]

To be sure, there is an ambiguity in Habermas's use of the term "lifeworld", an ambiguity that might be of importance at this point.

On the one hand, Habermas seems to hold on to a phenomeno-logical notion of a lifeworld, as an unthematized and (*qua* totality) unthematizable horizon for our thoughts and actions. On the other hand, he elaborates a notion of a modernized lifeworld restructured according to the principles of discourse theory and universal pragmatics. The former notion entails a historicity that can rightly be said to imply a relativism in a certain sense, also concerning fundamental normative questions. The latter notion is clearly one that entails discursive rationality and thereby the kind of normative foundation asked for by transcendental pragmaticians. As we have seen,[29] Habermas explicitly talks about modernization as a process moving away from the former notion of a lifeworld toward the latter.[30]

However, at this point Habermas elaborates the distinction between questions of justice and questions of cultural values. For one thing, he makes a distinction between the possibility of adapting a hypothetical attitude to the social world (with its questions of justice) and the impossibility for an acting individual to create a distance between himself and the practice of everyday life (i.e. his identity and values). Cultural values embodied in life forms and life histories "permeate the fabric of the communicative practice of everyday life through which the individual's life is shaped and his identity secured."[31] Cultural values are connected to ideas of the good life:[32]

"They shape the identity of groups and individuals in such a way that they form an integral part of culture and personality.

A person who questions the forms of life in which his identity has been shaped questions his very existence. The distancing produced by life crises of that kind is of another sort than the distance of a norm-testing participant in discourse from the facticity of existing institutions."[33]

Lifeworld modernization means discursive questioning of morality as *justice* – "the social world becomes increasingly moralized."[34] At the same time, this discursive questioning becomes "divorced from its background in the lifeworld," whereas questions of the *good life* are shaped "*within* the horizon of a concrete historical form of life or an individual life style."[35]

In other words, Habermas explicitly elaborates a distinction between *questions of justice*, which can be discursively treated because of the rationalization inherent in lifeworld modernization, and *value questions*, questions of identity and of the good life, which remain "answerable within the horizon of lifeworld certainties."[36] He distinguishes between morality (*Moral*) and ethics (*Sittlichkeit*). But as we can see from this quotation, this distinction does not imply that the ethics of a specific form of life (*die Sittlichkeit*) is to be understood as contingent for those living within this specific socio-cultural horizon.

All in all, we could say that the objections made by transcendental pragmaticians have to be qualified relative to these two notions of a lifeworld: (i) Questions of justice are 'moralized' by lifeworld modernization. (ii) Only questions of value remain within the horizon of a particular lifeworld, and these values may be deeply rooted in "the identity of groups and individuals in such a way that they form an integral part of culture and personality."

(b) Universal justice versus contextual values

Arguments from contextualists against the Habermasian notion of lifeworld modernization are of different kinds. (There are different kinds of contextualists.)

A philosophical type of contextualist arguments has already been mentioned in connection with the use of case studies and arguments from absurdity; I will not repeat these points at this stage.[37] However, when social scientists and historians blame Habermas for being too transcendental and universal, and not sufficiently empirical and contextual, it is important to consider whether these objections are made with an awareness of the conceptual level at which Habermas is working,[38] i.e. an awareness of the notion of discursive rationality (as inescapable), which is an integrated part of his project. Empirical and historical arguments in favor of greater contextuality could thus easily miss the target. For instance, they can miss the point as it is presented by Habermas by over-looking the fact that he is largely working in terms of idealizations (concerning competences). But there is still room for arguments against the very idea of idealizations with such a high degree of immunity to falsification. These arguments, however, can no longer be purely empirical or historical; they have to be elaborated methodologically and epistemologically.

This brings us back to the question of the *idealizations* in Habermas's project:[39] his choice, in universal pragmatics, of "propositionally differentiated and institutionally unbound, explicit, context-independent speech actions" as an "analytic unit" is such an idealization.[40] Habermas argues for it along various lines. He argues in favor of a primacy of communicative actions relative to instrumental, strategic, and even symbolic actions. He argues that this "analytic unit" is best suited to reveal the universal pragmatics of communicative action. Thus this "analytic unit" and universal pragmatics (and the theory of communicative action) are *mutually interpreted*, and the same goes for the notion of modernization in terms of rationalization and differentiation.[41] This means that objections against this idealized "analytic unit" cannot be taken immediately from our experience of varieties of language usage, such as irony, poetry, jokes, and rhetoric. And it means that there is some mutual support between universal pragmatics elaborated from this idealization and the notion of lifeworld modernization, interpreted in the perspective of universal pragmatics.

To the extent that we allow ourselves to assume that the differentiations in the notion of modernization have some footing in the modern world itself, we could also say that the idealizations of universal pragmatics have "become more adequate to reality" because reality itself has become more segmented into relatively pure institutions, such as scientific disciplines and jurisprudence, demanding linguistic unambiguity and explicit claims about truth or rightness.[42]

Nevertheless it can rightly be argued that pragmatic skills are needed, also in cases of truth claims in scientific discussions or of rightness claims in juridical discussions. Now, pragmatic competences are what universal pragmatics is supposed to be all about. The question is whether through his idealizations Habermas somehow tends to misrepresent these pragmatic competences by 'semanticizing' them.[43]

It is certainly true that he addresses these issues explicitly. Pragmatic competence is the main concern of universal pragmatics. He also explicitly addresses the problem of contextual application and of 'motivational anchoring'.[44] The question is therefore not whether he addresses these questions – he does – but whether his suggestions are considered convincing, which is a tricky question.

This is where the arguments in favor of the irreducibility of practice and tacit knowledge should be addressed, following up the problems of application and contextualization.[45] And this, I think, could still be seen as a problematic point, even if we give Habermas full mileage for the conceptual level on which he works and for all he says about application and contextualization.[46] The question is whether we find his viewpoint fair: we have seen (in the previous chapter) that the distinction between *justification* and *application* requires further clarification.[47] Such a distinction might have a job to do in some contexts, but it is inadequate in the sense that it does not do justice to the (conceptual) fact that *understanding* is necessary both for justification and for application. Understanding implies pragmatic competence, as well as some insight into what is being talked about. When we do not talk self-referentially about the conditions for talking, what is talked *about* is somehow 'out there'. The point is not only that there might be ambiguous contexts, making it difficult to know how to apply the notion of justice correctly, but that a person who has discursively acquired the highest notion of justice must also have acquired thereby some insight into what justice would look like in some appropriate context. It is counterintuitive that a person can discursively reach the highest insight into the notion of justice yet not know how to recognize it when it is applied contextually. But

Habermas does not claim that this is the case. On the contrary:
"This integration of cognitive operations and emotional disposi-
tions and attitudes in justifying and applying norms characterizes
the *mature* capacity for moral judgment."

"This concept of maturity".... "should flow from an adequate
description of the highest stage of morality itself."[48]

Again, the question is whether Habermas treats the problem in a
way that is philosophically satisfactory. Here his way of presenting
the distinction between justification and application might once
again be questioned: it might be semantically true that the notion
of justification differs from that of contextual application. But
pragmatically, when we look at the pragmatic competences and
skills required, the matter is more subtle. Recall the Wittgensteinian
argument in favor of the inseparability of a rule and the application
of the rule; at some stage practice is required, the ability (acquired
through practice) to know how to identify phenomena and how to
use a rule.[49]

We could proceed in the following way: Habermas has recently
emphasized a mutual connection between the discursive acquisition
of the notion of *justice* and the acquisition of the notion of
solidarity.[50] Justice means universalizability acquired through role
taking, beginning with role taking and identification with one's
own society, leading up to an ideal or universal role taking (on the
basis of which non-universalizable features in one's own society
can be criticized).[51] – An immediate response is the following. If
justice is acquired through such a process of role taking, if justice
and solidarity are thus intertwined, then it is hard to see how the
very notion of justice could be purified from insight in its contextual meaning.[52]

Furthermore, we recall that the highest moral stage requires real
discourse in order to obtain what is called *universalizable
interpretations of needs*. Intersubjectively, this means socialization
for reciprocity, but initially rooted in a specific cultural context
with particular persons. Universalizability of needs or interests is
not understood as a recognition of objective needs, but as a dis-

cursive agreement concerning the most appropriate interpretation
of needs (or interests). If there were naturally (or metaphysically)
given needs (and need interpretations), real discourse would not
have been required, a rational recognition of the real needs (the
correct conception of what the real needs are) would have sufficed.
However, in discussing need interpretations we are not discussing
self-referentially the norms necessarily presupposed in discourse.
We are discussing norms as 'content' (within the 'frame' of discourse constitutive norms). And we are discussing their interpretation, that is, the appropriateness of the language in terms of
which they are formulated, or rather, what would be the most
appropriate language among those 'languages' proposed by the
various interpretations. We do discuss the adequacy of the different
conceptual perspectives. These languages, or conceptual perspectives, are ultimately 'situated'; they have a contextual backing. The
aim of such a discourse is that of reaching an agreement about an
interpretation. We seek universalizable interpretations of needs. But
in so doing we have to understand what the different interpretations
actually mean, that is, we have to understand their contextual
meaning.[53] There is thus a close relationship between a practical
discourse concerning interpretations of needs and an understanding
of the contextual meaning of the various proposals for an acceptable interpretation. In this sense the notion of contextuality is
already presupposed in the notion of a real discourse aimed at
universalizable interpretations of needs.

In the Apelian tradition there are paradigmatic distinctions
between universalistic justification, contextual application, and an
ethics of responsibility. Universalistic justification is understood
transcendental-pragmatically in terms of self-referential irrefutability. This is the so-called part A_1 of discourse ethics.[54]
Contextual application is understood hermeneutically in terms of
fallible discourses of application and conceptual adequacy. This is
part A_2 of discourse ethics. An ethics of responsibility is conceived
of as potentially strategic.[55] This is part B of discourse ethics.
This tripartite distinction indicates how problems of cultural and
conceptual plurality and of irrationality and strategic action are

addressed and elaborated in the Apelian tradition. The distinctions are paradigmatic; they are founded on differences of principle. But in practice there are transitions between these paradigm cases. Thus there are problems on two levels: those related to the status of these paradigmatic cases themselves, and those related to the transition from one paradigmatic case to another (i.e. between reflective justification and hermeneutic application, and between each of these two and an ethics of responsibility). If the hermeneutic question of an adequate conceptual application implies contextuality, and therefore some kind of relativity, how could we 'mediate' between this linguistically rooted contextualism and a claim of strict universality concerning our verbal expressions on the basis of reflective justification? How should we think of the practical transitions back and forth between hermeneutic understanding and strategic responsibility?[56]

Habermas, on the other hand, elaborates the question of universalistic justification and of contextual application in terms of a distinction between formal-pragmatic idealizations and the performance of speech acts, at the same time as his formal pragmatics is interpreted through his theory of moral maturation and his theory of modernization. The notion of justification thus acquires its Hegelian flavor, and the notion of contextual application receives a special interpretation in modern societies (with their various differentiated and rationalized contexts): for the principle of justice there is a development toward universalizability, but the question of values remains relative to the plurality of cultural traditions.

The question of application in the Habermasian perspective has for instance been elaborated by Klaus Günther,[57] who argues in favor of a notion of 'application discourse'. The contextualist question of conceptual adequacy is understood here in terms not of a pre-modern *phronesis* but of discursive solutions, and, we may add, in a setting of modern differentiated and rationalized contexts, primarily related to justice. Günther strongly emphasizes impartiality as a basic procedural norm for such application discourses (*Anwendungsdiskurse*).

It is appropriate to argue in favor of an application discourse, in addition to the justification discourse, in which the questions of conceptual adequacy and contextuality are emphasized. It is also reasonable to emphasize the norm of impartiality as a constitutive norm for such application discourses. But this is less novel than it might appear. Impartiality is a constitutive norm for justification discourse (i.e. for discourses concerning the validity claims of truth and of rightness): mutual recognition among the participants and equal opportunity to take part are discourse-constitutive norms, together with the norm of mutual role taking. A norm of impartiality for application discourses, enabling all relevant conceptual perspectives to emerge, is therefore not only a reasonable idea but also one which involves well-known problems: I refer to the problems of a final consensus, in which all possible perspectives are taken into account, or, in negative terms, for which all possible hindrances are both realized and simultaneously eliminated.[58] There are two strategies one can employ in trying to solve these problems. One is related to the theory of modernization (and maturation): in modern societies there is a plurality of contexts, but these contexts are partly rationalized and specialized in a way which reduces the manifoldness of conceptual perspectives adequate for each context. This is a main point in the Habermasian approach, and also in Günther. The other strategy consists of arguing in 'negativistic' and melioristic terms. This is a main point in my approach, and Günther seems to employ this strategy as well.[59] The latter strategy entails a fallibilistic meliorism, in which conceptual inadequacies are pursued and 'sublated', but without any claim of having reached The Adequate conceptual perspective (or the all-embracing synthesis of all relevant perspectives). For one thing, the possibility of new conceptual perspectives is not denied.

A combination of these two strategies, one from the theory of modernization and the other from a fallibilistic version of hermeneutics, makes the Güntherian approach to the problem of application and contextualization congenial to my own approach.[60] By bringing together a melioristic (and 'negativistic') version of hermeneutics and a blend of formal pragmatics and theory of

modernization, this approach represents an attempt at reinterpretative 'mediation' between the Habermasian and the Apelian
tradition (but probably more Wittgensteinian in its flavor than suits
either Habermas, Apel, or Günther).

Dichotomy or Graduality?
Justice versus Need Interpretation

We return to our discussion of the Habermasian notion of justice
as universalizability and the problems of discursive consensus and
contextual application.

Even though the notion of universalizability is interpreted discursively, as a free and enlightened agreement in real discourse, this
does not imply that its moral validity is exhausted by this agreement alone: it would be a trivialization to think of theoretical
discourse in terms of the slogan 'consensus because of truth', and
practical discourse in terms of the slogan 'rightness because of
consensus'. Practical validity claims also include *conceptual
adequacy claims*, and these are not merely to be seen as a matter
of *free agreement*: in some cases it can be pointed out that there
are conceptual perspectives that are *less* adequate than others. This
point of relative appropriateness does not take us the whole way
back to a claim of 'objectively correct interpretations' in a
naturalistic or metaphysical sense. But it implies that there is *a
cognitive element* in claims of practical validity, in addition to that
of discursive consensus. This possibility of a rational consensus
concerning conceptual adequacy in practical discourses (for instance in discourses on need interpretations and interest interpretations) does at the same time imply, though, a certain *contextuality*: the chosen linguistic perspective is found to be adequate for
the type of question that is under investigation. It is found to be
adequate for a certain kind of case, for a certain context.[61]

However, the declared distinction between questions of justice
and questions of value seems to get blurred, and necessarily so, as

soon as we approach the question of universalizable interpretations of such phenomena as needs and interests.[62] We may ask, to what extent are interpretations of needs and interests influenced by value questions? And it seems fair to answer: to the extent that we discursively aim at universalizable interpretations of needs or interests, and not merely at universalizable meta-norms for fairness, it is difficult to see how we can avoid the issue of *values*, i.e. of contextual concepts of what is good or desirable. This implies that the question of contextualization is already present within the notion of justice (as this notion is understood by Habermas).[63]

Habermas, who is somewhat of a gradualist concerning the relationship between philosophy and other forms of research, tends to stick firmly to a *dichotomist* position concerning the relation between the question of *justice* and that of *values*, and his reasons for holding on to such a strict distinction might be the same as those that motivate Apel to hold on to the uniqueness and purity of philosophical reflection, namely the intuition that rational and normative universality should be defended against relativistic contextualizations.[64]

To the extent that the core of the universal-pragmatic (or formal-pragmatic) notion of justice is understood in terms of a reciprocal recognition among discussants, and in terms of an obligation in favor of the better argument, I have no fundamental objections. I also go along with further elaborations of discourse-constitutive norms, as in the perspective of self-reflection. But there are definitely problems when Habermas interprets the notion of *justice* in terms of '*generalizable interpretations of needs*' (or of interests).[65] It is, for instance, questionable whether there could be rational consensus concerning the interpretation of needs and interests, as in cases of scarcity of vital resources caused by ecological and demographic crises.[66] In such cases it is not easy to envisage any generalizable solution on the substantial level (even though we could in principle envisage a rational consensus about what are steps necessary in order to try to avoid such crises emerging in the first place, and even though we could in principle envisage discursive ways of settling the meta-ethical question of decision procedures).

The philosophical strength of the formulation 'generalizable interpretations of needs' stems from its emphasis on needs as 'interpretable': needs are not brute facts, objectively given, nor merely subjective preferences, they are linguistically 'mediated' and capable of change and of improvement. It is not the dictum of some sectoral expert, nor the private preference as registered on the market, but rationally 'laundered' preferences that represent what could and should be generalized. Needs (and interests) should be treated discursively. A real discourse implies normative validation, but also a learning process by role taking among the participants; a real discourse is thus both validating and educative. In some cases it might even be therapeutic.

However, in order rightly to know our own needs and interests, it does not suffice to be *discursively competent*. Some *Bildung* is also needed, as a personal, cultural development *through education and self-participatory experience*. Without such cultural development through tradition and personal appropriation, we would not be able to discuss the generalizability of our interpretations of needs and interests.

But if the deeper understanding of our needs requires not merely a formal discursive competence but also some historical and sociological insight and experience through personal participation, it is unavoidable that the question of justice in terms of the generalizability of the interpretation of our needs becomes involved in the diversity of forms of life. In short, to the extent that the discursive 'laundering' of our interpretations of needs demands some competence among the participants in terms of *education* and of *experience,* we are already working within a horizon of cultural contextuality. I would therefore argue in favor of *gradualism* between the question of justice and the question of values. Once justice is defined in terms of generalizable interpretations of needs, the supposed dichotomy between justice and values yields to gradualism.

This gradualism implies that the theoretical tension between justification and contextualization is considerably reduced. But does it also imply a slippery slope toward ethical relativism? I don't think so. In defending gradualism, I still maintain a universalistic core, partly in terms of self-referential argumentation conceived of as arguments from absurdity, partly in terms of a meliorism directed toward 'the negative', toward that which is relatively worse. This, it seems to me, is all we have, and all we need to have in order to avoid a self-defeating and destructive relativism.

If this position were to be called transcendental, it should be added that its strength is its 'weakness', that is, its caution. It is also a position that realizes the need for a permanent struggle, on various levels, in order to make possible the educative and cultural conditions for a discursive rationality. The goal is that of a political culture in terms of an interplay of various dimensions, a balance that is good enough, or rather, not worse than necessary.[67]

To maintain such a political culture is a diverse and endless task, implying also a concern for the preconditions for socio-cultural and ecological reproduction. The moral requirement of a modern society, it seems to me, consists ultimately in this dual obligation to secure a discursive rationality and to promote this precarious balance of the plurality of institutions and value spheres which is required for a meaningful discourse. Many have valuable contributions to make to the discussion of how this never-ending task should be undertaken, nobody has the final solution.

Practical Rationality Embedded

If a distinction were to be maintained between justice and values, one could argue in favor of restricting the notion of justice to discourse-constitutive norms (and their implications), and thus not including the more substantial questions of interpretations of needs. In this sense we could stick to a formal conception of justice, without trying to embrace the questions of the content of such interpretations, including problems of their plausible consequences

and side-effects, which make the idea of a possible (rational) consensus an unlikely one.[68]

Against such a proposal one could object that a 'formal' notion
of justice is far too restrictive: we are then left ultimately with
discourse-constitutive norms and with no more than a hope of
possible normative agreement in cases of controversy over more
substantial questions of justice. Since some specific language is
always involved in substantial questions of justice, we can never
avoid an element of contextual relativism; and we can therefore
hardly expect any widespread consensus in real questions of justice
(or injustice).

The answer could run as follows:

(1) The specific epistemic status of *discourse-constitutive norms* is
worth emphasizing. Even if it could be shown that they have only
restricted practical implications, it is still important to bring such
cases of normative unavoidability (and, in that sense, of normative
universality) into the open.[69]

(2) As indicated earlier, there are arguments in favor of the claim
that there are normative implications *from* the discourse-constitutive
norms *to* the level of normative questions within a discourse: for
this reason, some partiality and irrationalism are ruled out on the
level of substantial normative questions. This is far from trivial.[70]

(3) Even if it should turn out to be the case that we cannot expect
any widespread consensus in substantial questions of justice, in the
sense of universal discursive agreements about just answers, this
does not rule out the possibility that a *discursive treatment of
substantial questions of justice* is both *feasible and desirable*: a
discursive procedure could most probably *exclude* some positions
and perspectives as relatively *less acceptable*.[71] For instance, 'the
power of the negative' is operative whenever cases of unequal
treatment of equals or of equal treatment of unequals are
demonstrated, whenever a relative one-sidedness or imbalance in

the conceptual perspective is shown, and whenever facts are shown to be disregarded, or implications not drawn.[72] By excluding some answers as unacceptable, and thus achieving a consensus about the relative injustice of some positions, we have obtained a certain *'laundering' of possible positions.* And among those positions for or against which no consensus is obtained, we could legitimately decide by some other procedure (arrived at discursively), such as voting or compromise (or we can point to tolerance, if no decision is possible nor necessary).

(4) It is furthermore of practical importance that the various (more or less 'contingent') *conditions for discourse* be highlighted and defended according to the situation. Such conditions for discursive rationality embrace the notion of a 'normative notion of political culture' (such as appropriately differentiated institutions and socialized maturity). Education and public debate, cultural development and plural experiences are essential elements here.[73] These elements could, and should, be defended and improved.[74]

In this sense a *melioristic practice* is at work. A higher degree of justice and of rationality is obtainable, even when there is no discursive unanimity and no final answer. Piecemeal exclusion of cases of injustice, and attempts at a gradual improvement of the overall competence of the participants, and of the quality of the positions between which we finally have to decide, all this is itself an important achievement in the pursuit of justice.[75] This work is itself fallible. But it can be shown to function in many cases, and this experience is sufficient for our continuous efforts. In practice it is not a question of reaching the ideal, but of avoiding what is worse than it need be. This is all we need, theoretically and practically.[76]

Transcendental Pragmatics versus Lifeworld Modernization

I will now sum up by commenting on what I see as crucial points of controversy between Apel and Habermas on the question of the universality of reason, practical reason included.

Apel insists, as opposed to Habermas, on a paradigmatic difference between empirical and reconstructive research on the one hand and philosophical reflection on the other:[77] philosophy as 'strict reflection' on the normative preconditions for reflection provides an ultimate ethical justification in terms of self-referential undeniability. Apel thus relies on arguments from absurdity[78] where absurdity is conceived in terms of self-reflective *Nicht-hintergehbarkeit*.[79] Some fallibilism is already present in verbalizing such self-reflective insight, but not in the sense of fallibilism in empirical or reconstructive research. Here we have a rock bottom for rationality.[80] Since self-reflection in a performative mode is a speech act, and not merely a mental act, the unavoidable preconditions for self-reflection are also unavoidable preconditions for argumentation. Thus we have a distinction between 'frame' and 'content', between undeniable preconditions for argumentation and that which is discussed, the former being *a priori* and revealed by reflection, the latter being questions open for discursive interpretation and testing. In this sense we could talk in terms of constitutive procedural norms, or meta-norms, in the former case, and in terms of applied and contextual norms in the latter. If this is taken for granted, it follows that there are no crucial philosophical problems of application or contextualization: norms and values discussed within such a discursive frame are to be interpreted according to their situatedness. But there are, as indicated above, some normative restrictions on possible substantial conclusions within the frame of a practical discourse. Since respect for the better argument and reciprocal recognition among the participants belong to the discourse-constitutive norms, it is *a priori* excluded that these norms could be denied on the level of norms discussed within a serious discourse. Basic forms of irrationalism and ethnocentrism are thus ruled out.

A few critical remarks are in place here.

The strength of an argument from absurdity depends on the nature of the absurdity involved.[81] Each case of putative undeniability has to be carefully tested discursively. The same holds true of any appeal to meaninglessness. A personal experience of meaninglessness won't do: such a criterion would imply only a precritical reference to evidence. There is thus (as shown in "Arguments from Absurdity" and "Pragmatism and Pragmatics") a permanent need for *detailed analyses* in *each case* of such a claim of absurdity, also in cases of assumed self-referential *Sinnlosigkeit* (senselessness).

With this reservation, I tend to agree with Apel's insistence on the importance of such self-referential reasoning. But I would emphasize that reciprocal recognition, as part of the undeniable preconditions for discourse, entails not only rationality but also *fallibility*: we discuss because we are finite and fallible, and need other people to overcome our one-sidedness and distortion. I would also emphasize the *procedural* nature of these arguments from absurdity: even though some reflective insights seem to remain firm and settled, what we have basically is an ongoing philosophical activity, no Theory, nor any reified theses about constitutive norms. Finally, I would emphasize that there is a *gradual* transition from absurdities of various kinds to severely empirical falsity[82] (and in this sense there might be something to be said for Habermas's insistence on differences of degree rather than a dichotomy between philosophy and empirical research).

Ultimately Apel argues 'steeply from above' (*steil von oben*): first a firm footing, securing universality, and then 'reappropriation' (*Selbsteinholung*); this is the Apelian recipe.[83] He questions Habermas's fallibilistic reconstructions 'from below', leading inductively upward. – Or rather, this is how Habermas appears from Apel's perspective. But the question is whether that perspective is fair to the hermeneutic elaboration of lifeworld modernization in Habermas, for instance to his reinterpretative adoption of Kohlberg's scheme of moral development, in which Habermas retrospectively interprets moral maturation from the point of view of discourse ethics as a normative position: there is, in Habermas, a mutual hermeneutic elaboration between normative presuppositions and theoretically interpreted empirical data. In this sense, Habermas incorporates that 'mediating position', between normativism from above and inductivism from below, which I asked for in the previous chapter (in the introductory reminder). If that is true, we would have to describe Apel's objections as one-sided.

As to Apel's own position, I find it appropriate to recall that a theory of lifeworld modernization does indeed help to support the view that agents outside the sphere of reflective and discursive activities could also plausibly be said to be motivated by universal ethics and discursive rationality. This is not denied by Apel, indeed he supports it; but it might be appropriate to recall this point when mutual merits and shortcomings are discussed.

In my view, Apel's and Habermas's positions can be interpreted and harmonized as follows: Habermas's approach is no 'induction from below', but represents a reconstructive interpretation of various theories, such as that of Kohlberg, in terms of universal pragmatics. Apel's approach is basically one of performative self-reference; as an ultimate defense against philosophical skepticism, he claims to have evidence concerning normative foundations.[84] Discourse among all concerned[85] and validation by free and enlightened consensus are taken to be requirements because their denial implies performative inconsistency. Ultimately this means it is a requirement for the optimal implementation of discursive rationality and for discursive solutions when needed.

The main controversy is that over transcendental argumentation: Apel insists on the uniqueness of what I would call 'analyses of presuppositions', primarily in terms of self-reflection. He insists on a difference of level. In this I think Apel is right; there are different epistemic levels. Habermas insists that there is no "hierarchy of argumentation games" and that we cannot bring "reasons" into a hierarchy "once and for all"; there is no "meta discourse" that can "prescribe rules" for subordinated discourses.[86]

If we interpret this pragmatically, and not as a sign of a tendency to 'externalize' pragmatic insights in terms of *statements*, I think Habermas has a point.[87] As I would like to interpret him, he does not deny the uniqueness of analyses of presuppositions (implying difference of epistemic levels), nor does he deny their importance (though I find him vague in this respect), he merely rejects a *semanticist* hierarchy of levels (I hope).[88]

I thus conclude that the arguments of this controversy between Apel and Habermas could, and should, be interpreted from a cautiously pragmatic perspective: analyses of pragmatically undeniable preconditions are thought of as ongoing activities, always left self-critically open, but not fallible in the way that substantial claims are. In referring to such reflective experiences, we can achieve valuable insights.[89]

Habermas's notion of a modernization of the lifeworld, philosophically elaborated from the sociological tradition and developmental psychology, represents, all in all, a powerful attempt at grasping modernity. The challenges from transcendental pragmaticians, in defense of the notions of argumentative rationality and normative universality are real enough, and so are some of those from social scientists and philosophical contextualists of various schools, in defense of contextuality and plurality. But these challenges are basically of a kind that keeps the debate going, not such as can claim to be passing final judgment, one way or the other. If we reinterpret pragmatic reason in melioristic and praxeological terms, we can achieve a certain middle way between the two positions, a 'mediation' which integrates contextuality and plurality, but which maintains the universality of pragmatically conceived rationality.

Postlude

Modernization of the lifeworld, in one way or many? In one, in the sense that discursive rationality is inescapable; the discursive procedure for treating theoretical questions and questions of justice is one and the same, and a discursively acquired answer is as universally valid as the quality of the arguments. In this sense, rationality in a modern world is one. We might say: in a modern world the idea of a single unifying substantial rationality is a possibility well lost. Modernity is characterized by a discursive rationality, but by many institutions and conceptual perspectives, by different disciplines and cultural horizons, and by a plurality of roles and life-styles. The question whether, at times, there could be too much differentiation and disintegration is one to be treated discursively as it arises in each case.[90] And the irrationality in modern societies (apparent in trends and potentials in technology and economy, in politics and ecology, and in socio-cultural and biological reproduction) is most certainly in need of permanent and serious questioning. A disturbing question is that of how to decide discursively the competence requirements for participation in discourse, that is, the problem of the inclusion and exclusion of potential discussants.[91] Apparently we have to live with this dilemma in a modern lifeworld, just as we have to live wondering about the borderlines of intersubjective rationality, and about the question of the possibility of 'exclusive insights'.[92]

As actual or potential participants in discursive rationality we are fallible, though for the most part we can learn from one another. Our predicament is that of having to try again, through a joint effort, in order to get further, or at least to try to avoid avoidable confusion or mistakes. In this sense, modernity is an inescapable horizon. In the same sense, philosophizing is a practical, never-ending task. Being in the same boat (as is often said), we have to cope with our problems by participating in the transforming of our vessel step by step, "far out at sea" (as some philosopher said – and to which we might add: a charming ship of perishable fools.)[93]

NOTES

1. This is reminiscent of a Quinean (holistic) research project. Cf. Habermas (*HCD*, pp. 239–240; for the abbreviation, cf. preceding chapter) who accepts William E. Connolly's characterization ("Review of T. McCarthy, The Critical Theory of Jürgen Habermas," *History and Theory*, 3(1979), pp. 397–398): "The more encompassing the theory, the greater the variety of coherence tests each of the component parts must pass."

2. Cf. Allen W. Wood's discussion of Habermas's '*Verständigung*-thesis' in defense of ethical rationalism (concerning the ethical foundation of social institutions) against both traditionalist consensualists and rational-choice pluralists ("Defense of Rationalism," in: *New German Critique*, No. 35, 1985, pp. 145–164): "Habermas' transcendental argument for rationalism gains a hold on us only because it argues that we cannot engage in the normal activities of communicative speech at all without raising validity claims to truth and normative correctness and presupposing that they are redeemable through rational discourse" (*ibid.* pp. 156–157). Despite his sympathy with this Habermasian project, Wood concludes rather negatively: "The argument would work, however, only if researchers successfully complete the program of universal pragmatics, and give it the status of a science" (*ibid.* p. 163). Wood's second suggestion, that of giving universal pragmatics "the status of a science," seems to me to ask for too much (and too little!). One thing we can expect is 'additive support' of a fallibilistic and melioristic nature, according to Habermas's own claims. He attempts to bring together mutual support from a theory of communicative action (arguing for its primacy relative to strategic and purely symbolic action), from a theory of modernization (arguing for differentiations in terms of speech modes, worlds, and validity claims), and from formal pragmatics (arguing for pragmatic competences). (And we can expect an explicitly self-referential argumentation – cultivated especially by K.-O. Apel.)

   In my opinion, Habermas's '*Verständigung*-thesis' suffers at times from an overemphasis on the putative interconnection between our *understanding* a validity claim and our *taking a stand* on its validity. I find it interesting that one of the few examples discussed by Habermas in defense of this position is one taken from mathematics, a discipline in which there is a close connection between understanding an argument and taking a stand on its validity, cf. "Entgegnung", in: *Kommunikatives Handeln*, eds. A. Honneth and H. Joas, Frankfurt a.M.: Suhrkamp, especially p. 348. In empirical research (from natural science to historiography), the relation between 'gathering evidence' and the evaluation of the main thesis is more remote; understanding the latter does not imply taking any stand on its validity. Hence it is reasonable to talk in terms of *potential* 'stand taking' (i.e. of understanding what a validation *would have* implied). This, I assume, is a trivial point. What is not trivial is the fact that Habermas very rarely discusses *cases* of what he considers to be arguments. This fact adds unnecessarily to the conceptual vagueness of such terms as *Beweis* or *Grund*.

3. Cf. e.g. "Wahrheitstheorien," published in: *Wirklichkeit und Reflexion*, ed. H. Fahrenbach, Pfüllingen: Neske, 1973, pp. 211–263. Also "What is Universal Pragmatics?", in: *CES*; pp. 1–68 (German original 1976). And elaborated in: "Intermediate Reflections" in: *TCA* I, pp. 273–337 (German original 1981). Critically, e.g. Rüdiger Bubner: "Habermas's Concept of Critical Theory," in: *HCD*, pp. 42–56. Otfried Höffe: "Kantische Skepsis gegen die transzendentale Kommunikationsethik," in: *Kommunikation und Reflexion* (= *KR*), eds. W. Kuhlmann and D. Böhler, Frankfurt a.M.: Suhrkamp, pp. 518–539 (*CEC*, pp. 193–219). Karl-Heinz Ilting: "Geltung als Konsens," in: *Neue Hefte für Philosophie*, No. 10, 1976, and "Der Geltungsgrund moralischer Normen," in: *KR*, 1982, pp. 612–648 (Engl. translation in *CEC* pp. 220–254). Herbert Schnädelbach: "Bemerkungen über Rationalität und Sprache," in: *KR*, pp. 347–368 (*CEC*, pp. 270–292). John B. Thompson: "Universal Pragmatics," in: *HCD*, pp. 116–133. Albrecht Wellmer: "Praktische Philosophie und Theorie der Gesellschaft," in: *Normen und Geschichte*, ed. Willi Oelmüller, Paderborn: Schöningh, 1979, pp. 140–174 (*CEC*, pp. 293–329). Also Albrecht Wellmer in: *Ethik und Dialog*, 1986. – For abbreviations, cf. preceding chapter.

4. It is important to keep in mind that the pragmatic notion of the 'compelling force of the better argument' is the normative core of this theory of validation. The term "consensus" should be interpreted in term of this notion (and not the other way around). (A traditional consensus theory of truth, or of justice, runs into severe problems, see e.g. my remarks in "Pragmatism and Pragmatics" in this collection; see also the first sections in this chapter.)

5. This politically important point seems to me to have been somewhat overlooked by libertarian critics, from the right as well as from the left (from Herman Lübbe to Foucauldians of various blends). (In support of

the claim that discourse ethics implies tolerance, cf. e.g. Alexy in: *CEC*, p. 179.)

6. Cf. "Pragmatism and Pragmatics".

7. Cf. e.g. Albrecht Wellmer who argues in Wittgensteinian terms in favor of a mutual 'openness' of the three claims to each other, in: "On the Dialectic of Modernism and Postmodernism," in: *Praxis International*, 4(1984), p. 360 (also pp. 351–355).

8. Cf. "Contextual and Universal Pragmatics" in this collection.

9. Arguments given in "Pragmatism and Pragmatics."

10. Cf. the tension between the notions of argument and consensus, the former being 'contental' the latter 'formal'. Cf. "Pragmatism and Pragmatics", and also A. Wellmer in: *Ethik und Dialog*, Frankfurt a.M.: Suhrkamp, 1986, pp. 82–112.

11. The study of *competence* differs from the study of *performance*. For the former, I assume, arguments from absurdity are appropriate. Cf. e.g. "Madness and Reason. *Reductio ad pathologicum* as a *via negativa* for elucidating the universal-pragmatic notion of rationality?" in this collection.

    There are additional problems when such preconditions are understood as moral norms, see e.g. Karl-Heinz Ilting: "The Basis of the Validity of Moral Norms" in: *The Communicative Ethics Controversy* (= *CEC*), eds. S. Benhabib and F. Dallmayr, Cambridge, Mass.: MIT Press, pp. 220–255. See also K. E. Tranøy in the section 'Critical Aftermath' in "Pragmatism and Pragmatics".

    At this point it is important to be aware of the distinction between norms that are discourse constitutive and norms that are discursively justified, that is, between 'norms of the frame' and 'norms *qua* content'. The former are meta-norms for the justification of the latter. As to the latter, I for one would not interpret their validity exclusively in intersubjective terms, that is, I would not emphasize the notion of consensus in the expression *consensus on generalizable need (or interest) interpretations* and simultaneously disregard the question of the *conceptual adequacy* of the interpretation. I would stress the importance of a *discursive justification of the adequacy question* of the concepts involved. This means we have a question of a (hermeneutically conceived) 'realism' also in cases of normative consensus. We have *arguments*, not only agreement. See below, 'Dichotomy or Graduality?' in this chapter. Cf. Ilting's arguments in favor of the idea that a consensus has to be a consensus *about something*: "Geltung als Konsens," in: *Neue Hefte für Philosophie*, No. 10, Göttingen, 1976. Cf. also my arguments to the same point, in: "Pragmatism and Pragmatics". However, I do not follow Ilting in his rejection of the idea that constitutive norms can also be *moral* norms (e.g. "The Basis of the Validity of Moral Norms," in: *CEC*, p. 231). Constitutive norms certainly have a peculiar status. But I find it fair to say that they also are moral norms for a discourse, indicating duties and giving reasons for moral blame when violated. Cf. again the reference to K. E. Tranøy in this note. (The community of researchers is basically a moralistic one. A violation of discourse-constitutive and research-constitutive norms, demonstrated during a doctoral disputation, most certainly represents a reason for moral blame.) Moreover, discourse is not just one game among others, from which we can freely choose to abstain. In a modern society, validating discourses represent the rational 'checking game' for all severe doubts and dissents concerning truth and rightness.

12. I would also argue in favor of gradualism in the relationship between absurdity and falsity (cf. "Arguments from Absurdity"), as well as in that between action and discourse (cf. "Contextual and Universal Pragmatics," last part).

13. Cf. "Praxeological Reflections."

14. Cf. "Contextual and Universal Pragmatics", especially the last paragraph.

15. The claim that all insight can be expressed propositionally represents a semanticist fallacy. Cf. also at this point: "Contextual and Universal Pragmatics."

16. In this sense I favor a 'contextually sensitive' conception of pragmatic rationality (cf. Seyla Benhabib, *Situating the Self* (= *StS*), Cambridge: Polity Press, 1992, pp. 180–183).

17. This can be seen as an improvement on ambiguities and shortcomings in Kohlberg's conceptions, but at the same time it implies that there is less support for Habermas in the Kohlbergian scheme.

18. See above, at the end of the paragraph "Rationality and Lifeworld".

19. As pointed out earlier in "Modernization of the Lifeworld."

20. Cf. *MCCA*, p. 187.

21. A remarkable exception is the case of the morning beer, p. 123 in *TCA* II.

22. System theory has its problems and other theoretical approaches to economy and to politics are clearly possible. Cf. T. McCarthy in: *Ial*, p. 178. However, cf. Habermas's recent elaboration of the realm of politics (law and democracy), in *Faktizität und Geltung* (1992).

23. Cf. Karl-Otto Apel: "Normative Begründung der 'Kritischen Theorie' durch Rekurs auf lebensweltliche Sittlichkeit? Ein transzendental-pragmatisch orientierter Versuch, mit Habermas gegen Habermas zu denken" in: *Zwischenbetrachtungen* (= *Z*), eds. A. Honneth et al., Frankfurt a.M.: Suhrkamp, 1989, pp. 15–65. See also: *Diskurs und Verantwortung*, Frankfurt a.M.: Suhrkamp, 1988. Harald Wenzel and Uwe Hochmuth: "Die Kontingenz von Kommunikation. Zur kritischen Theorie des kommunikativen Handelns von Jürgen Habermas" in: *Kölner Zeitschrift für Soziologie und Sozialpsychologie*, 41(1989) pp. 215–240. English translations of Apel include: *Towards a Transformation of Philosophy*, London: Routledge & Kegan Paul, 1980, and *Understanding and Explanation: A Transcendental-Pragmatic Perspective*, Cambridge Mass.: MIT Press, 1984. For Habermas's response, cf. e.g. *EzD*, especially pp. 185 ff.

24. This, for instance, is the case in Habermas's criticism of French post-modernists in: *Der philosophische Diskurs der Moderne*, Frankfurt a.M.: Suhrkamp, 1985. However, Habermas also made direct appeal to trans-cendental reasoning, as e.g. in: "Moral Consciousness and Communicative Action" (in: *MCCA*, pp. 129–130). As to his reasons for being somewhat cautious, cf. e.g. "Discourse Ethics," in: *ibid.*, pp. 82–98. Also in: "What is Universal Pragmatics," in: *Communication and the Evolution of Society (CES)*, Boston: Beacon Press, 1979, pp. 21–25. And see his extended discussion of Apel's favorite arguments employing self-reference, in: "Moral Consciousness and Communicative Action," in: *MCCA*.

25. We could claim that the challenge from 'deep skepticism' is what makes a defense of rationality urgent. Hence an experience of crisis (of 'European nihilism') is essential to see the point of such a defense. (In this respect, I assume, Apel and Habermas are probably different from Rorty and quite a number of anglophone intellectuals.)

    References to *Letztbegründung*, in addition to Karl-Otto Apel, see especially Wolfgang Kuhlmann and Dietrich Böhler. In English, e.g. D. Böhler: "Transcendental Pragmatic and Critical Morality: On the Possibility and Moral Significance of a Self-Enlightenment of Reason", in: *The Communicative Ethics Controversy (CEC)*, eds. S. Benhabib and F. Dallmayr, Cambridge, Mass.: MIT Press, 1990, pp. 111–150. In German, e.g., W. Kuhlmann: *Reflexive Letztbegründung*, Freiburg/Munich: Karl Albert, 1985; D. Böhler: *Rekonstruktive Pragmatik*, Frankfurt a.M.: Suhrkamp, 1985; and a recent collection, *Zur Anwendung der Diskursethik in Politik, Recht und Wissenschaft*, eds. Karl-Otto Apel and Matthias Kettner, Frankfurt a.M.: Suhrkamp, 1992.

26. In accepting Apel's main point concerning the pragmatic inconsistency involved in denying discourse-constitutive norms while arguing, Habermas adds: "This argument does not go far enough to convince him [the skeptic] in his capacity as an *actor* as well" (*MCCA*, p. 85). "It is by no means self-evident that rules that are unavoidable *within* discourses can also claim to be valid for regulating action *outside* of discourses" (*op.cit.* pp. 85–86). At this point Apel has accepted a "decisionistic residual problematic" in the sense of a decision of applying norms that are discursively justified (in: "Types of Rationality Today," in: *Towards a Transformation of Philosophy*, London: Routledge & Kegan Paul, 1980, p. 334; see also Herbert Schnädelbach: "Remarks about Rationality and Language," in: *The Communicative Ethics Controversy*, eds. S. Benhabib and F. Dallmayr, Cambridge Mass.: MIT Press, 1990, pp. 270–292). But Apel insists that the skeptic can only be fully defeated by arguments from strict self-reflection (*strixte Reflexion* in the sense of Wolfgang Kuhlmann, cf. *Zwischenbetrachtungen*, p. 50, note 48); only through the performative certainty of the person who reflects on his own argumentation can ultimate justification be reached. And only from the reflective insight into the irrefutability of the preconditions for argumentation can further steps be taken to reappropriate our development and our ethical life (*Selbsteinholung*). Habermas's reference to actual 'alternativelessness' is insufficient for an ultimate justification, and his reconstructive project is too inductive; both are far too fallibilistic, according to Apel.

However, Habermas views his theory of communicative action, with its speech-act inherent validity claims, as a decisive argument in favor of the view that discourse-constitutive norms have a normative bearing also outside of discourse (or argumentation): "Anyone who does not participate, or is not ready to participate in argumentation stands nevertheless 'already' in contexts of *communicative action*. In doing so, he has already naively recognized the validity claims – however counterfactually raised – that are contained in speech acts and which can be redeemed only discursively. Otherwise he could have to detach himself from the communicatively established language game of everyday practice" (*Legitimation Crisis*, Boston: Beacon Press, 1975, p. 159).

Even if a skeptic could refuse to argue (but how could he then claim to be a skeptic? Apel would ask), Habermas maintains that the skeptic cannot "even indirectly, deny that he moves in a shared sociocultural form of life, that he grew up in a web of communicative action, and that he reproduces his life in that web. In a word, the sceptic may reject morality, but he cannot reject the ethical substance (*Sittlichkeit*) of the life circumstances in which he spends his waking hours, not unless he is willing to take refuge in suicide or serious mental illness" (*MCCA*, p. 100).

27. Cf. Karl-Otto Apel, Z, pp. 15–65.

28. Cf. Apel, *ibid. (Z)*.

29. Cf. the quotation at the end of the introductory remarks in the previous chapter ("Modernization of the Lifeworld"), taken from *TCA* I, pp. 70–71.

30. He also holds that a modern society consists of both. An attempt to eliminate the notion of an unthematized horizon would have been problematic. (Hermeneuticians and Wittgensteinians alike have convincingly pointed out the irreducibility of what is implicitly given in a tradition or in our practice.)

31. Cf. Habermas in *MCCA*, p. 177.

32. For another view on the interrelation between 'the good' and 'the just' (in favor of the former), cf. Charles Taylor, *Sources of the Self. The Making of the Modern Identity*, Cambridge, Mass.: Harvard University Press, 1989.

33. *MCCA*, pp. 177 and 178. Cf. also (p. 178): "The concrete ethical life of a naively habituated lifeworld is characterized by the fusion of moral and evaluative issues. Only in a rationalized lifeworld do moral issues become independent of issues of the good life. Only then do they have to be dealt with autonomously as issues of justice....".

34. Cf. *MCCA* p. 177.

35. Cf. *MCCA* p. 178.

36. The questions of European nihilism focus not only on questions of justice but also on questions of life values and cultural and *personal identity* – who we are and what life is good for, in short, the meaning of life. (Cf. G. Skirbekk, *Nihilisme?*, Oslo: Tanum, 1958. English translation, 1973.)

37. Cf. e.g. "Arguments from Absurdity" and "Contextual and Universal Pragmatics."

38. Cf. e.g. Harald Wenzel and Uwe Hochmuth: "Die Kontingenz von Kommunikation. Zur kritischen Theorie des kommunikativen Handelns von Jürgen Habermas." in: *Kölner Zeitschrift für Soziologie und Sozialpsychologie*, 41(1989), pp. 215–240.

39. Cf. T. McCarthy's book *Ideals and Illusions* (= *IaI*), Cambridge, Mass.: MIT Press 1991.

40. *CES*, pp. 34–41.

41. Cf. Habermas in: *HCD*, p. 236: "Formal-pragmatic analysis starts with idealised cases of the communicative action that is typical of everyday life *in modern societies.*" Cf. T. McCarthy in: *IaI*, pp. 134–135.

42. Against the lingering objection that this choice still implies a problematic idealization relative to the actual use of language, *the theory of lifeworld modernization* is meant to be of some help: there is mutual support between universal pragmatics and the theory of lifeworld modernization. The idealized speech situation, which is the analytical point of departure for universal pragmatics, is not to be found in a clear-cut way in the various kinds of ambiguous and situational usages. In elaborating a

universal pragmatics, we have our attention directed not only toward mature adults (presupposing a successful process of maturation, of will formation, and of role taking), and toward sane adults (leaving aside various forms of insanity and distortion), but also toward speech acts *within a modern society*, where institutional and conceptual differentiations have enabled us to act in relatively clear-cut settings, approximately 'ideal' situations, such as the speech acts of stating in science, and the speech acts of normative claims in jurisprudence. In this sense, the *idealized* speech acts of universal pragmatics become somewhat less remote from *actual* speech acts. A modernized lifeworld, i.e. a lifeworld impregnated by the modern differentiations of truth, rightness, and authenticity, is more congenial with the notion of the four universal validity claims than the rather pre-modern world of some contextualists. In this sense I do think that there is a *certain mutual support* between the *theory of modernization* of the lifeworld and *universal pragmatics*.

However, there is an interesting tension between idealization in universal pragmatics (with a 'Kantian' flavor, being preconditions that can be elucidated by means of arguments from absurdity) and idealizations in the theory of modernization (with a 'Hegelian' flavor, in the sense that these idealizations converge with an idea of real, historical changes). In the latter case the status of the idealizations is a tricky question: what happens in history becomes relevant for the support (or challenge) of these claims (– but only indirectly, since historical facts are philosophically interpreted; this is the epistemological paradox of 'Faktizität und Geltung' in this Hegelian perspective).

43. This is a main point in Albrecht Wellmer's critical discussion, in *Ethik und Dialog*, Frankfurt a.M.: Suhrkamp, 1986.

44. For example, in *MCCA*, pp. 179 ff. See also his explicit revisionary remarks in favor of situational judgment and application, and motivation, in: "Habermas: Questions and Counter-Questions," in: *Praxis International*, 1984, Vol. 4, No. 3, pp. 246–247. Cf. also Robert Alexy on the relation between justification and realizability, in: "A Theory of Practical Discourse," in: *The Communicative Ethics Controversy* (= *CEC*), eds. S. Benhabib and F. Dallmayr, Cambridge, Mass.: MIT Press, p. 175.

For Habermas, 'rational motivation' in favor of discursive rationality is real but weak. (We are both talking about a motivation in favor of [entering into] rational discourse and a motivation on behalf of [the implementation of] its results.) Universal pragmatics, interpreted together with theories of maturation and of modernization, give support to the idea of rational motivation (before, in and after discourse). Habermas's recent work, *Faktizität und Geltung. Beiträge zur Diskurstheorie des Rechts und des demokratischen Rechtsstaats* (1992), lends support to the idea of an institutional assistance (within the frames of a democratic *Rechtsstaat*) to our real but weak motivation in favor of rationality and justice.

45. I am referring here to Wittgensteinian arguments concerning the *interrelationship between meaning and forms of life*, as discussed by A. Wellmer in: "On the Dialectic of Modernism and Postmodernism," in: *Praxis International*, Vol. 4, No. 4, 1985, pp. 351–355. I am also referring to pragmatically conceived *practice*, cf. R. Bernstein in: *Beyond Objectivism and Relativism*, Philadelphia: University of Pennsylvania Press, 1983.

46. In: *HCD*, pp. 251 ff., Habermas characterizes the need for 'mediation' "the blind spot of transcendentally orientated theories" (p. 253). "Practical reason .... has to be 'situated'" (p. 252). The dilemma to be avoided is, on the one hand, (i) skepticism ("about the cognitive claim of moral judgments"), which he ascribes to Steven Lukes, and on the other, (ii) contextualism ("asserting the right of historically situated morality [*Sittlichkeit*] against an abstractly universal morality [*Moral*]"), which he ascribes to Seyla Benhabib. "I regard both as false – the historico-philosophical no less than the sceptical" (p. 253). This shows, once again, not only that Habermas is well aware of these problems, but also that he himself criticizes a moral position based on "historically situated morality (*Sittlichkeit*)," which is the kind of criticism Apel directs at Habermas (in Apel's article in: *Zwischenbetrachtungen*, eds. A. Honneth et al., Frankfurt a.M.: Suhrkamp. 1989). The subtlety of this debate between Apel and Habermas is further illustrated by the fact that Habermas finds it appropriate to refer to Apel's position in order to "explain the *status* that the principle of universalisation assumes in the discourse ethics" (*HCD*, p. 256).

47. Cf. "Modernization of the Lifeworld." Habermas continues referring to the distinction between '*Anwendungsdiskurs*' and '*Begründungsdiskurs*', cf. e.g. his response to Sheila Briggs and Seyla Benhabib in: *Texte und Kontexte*, Frankfurt a.M.: Suhrkamp, 1991, pp. 148–151. See also the elaboration of this distinction in K. Günther, *Der Sinn für Angemessenheit. Anwendungsdiskurse in Moral und Recht* (= *SfA*), Frankfurt a.M.:

Suhrkamp, 1988.

48. *MCCA*, p. 182.

49. Pragmatics focuses on speech-act competences, not on expressions in a semantic perspective. Universal pragmatics focuses on 'depth' competences, in Habermas related to the ability to master general validity claims. This ability is a question of 'knowing one's way around', not only an ability to identify situations (or contexts), but an ability to master communicative and argumentative situations. These pragmatic (communicatively and argumentatively presupposed) competences represent 'tacit knowledge'. They can be shown and talked about retrospectively and reflectively, but cannot be expressed in straightforward propositions as if they were mere facts. This philosophical awareness therefore influences our way of writing (and reading).

50. Recently, Habermas *EzD*, e.g. pp. 149–152, 174–175.

51. "Justice and Solidarity: On the Discussion Concerning 'Stage 6'," in: *Hermeneutics and Critical Theory in Ethics and Politics*, ed. Michael Kelly, Cambridge, Mass.: MIT Press, 1990, pp. 32–52. – Habermas points convincingly to an interrelation between discourse and communality: discourse implies mutual recognition among the discussants, including role taking as part of the discursive requirement for universalization. This mutual recognition, required for a discursive 'redemption' of the normative validity claim of justice, implies a communal solidarity, implies a social identity based on mutual role taking among the members of the given community. But since discursive rationality entails an ability to reflect upon and criticize any given context, it also entails an ability to transcend and question any given form of solidarity within a community. Hence we could say that application is always contextual and that justification has contextual ties, but in the process of critique (or justification), discursive rationality entails an ability to operate trans-contextually. "Arguments extend per se beyond particular lifeworlds, for in the pragmatic presuppositions of argumentation, the normative content of the presuppositions of communicative action is extended – in universalized, abstract form and without limitations – to an ideal communication community (as Apel, following C. S. Peirce, calls it) that includes all subjects capable of speech and action" (*ibid.* p. 48).

52. Such an intertwining of justice and (universal) solidarity implies a fairly strong thesis concerning the possibility of conceptual, moral and identificational harmony, to be obtained (at the highest stage) through the process of maturation (and modernization). And then we are back to Habermas's comprehensive attempt to elaborate a theory of communicative action and of socio-cultural modernization.

As to the question of the interrelationship between imperatives supported by power and imperatives supported by normative reasons and extra-discursive contextuality, cf. Erling Skjei: "A Comment on Performative, Subject, and Proposition in Habermas' Theory of Communication", in: *Inquiry*, 28(1985), pp. 87–105.

53. Cf. the discussion of the interrelation between 'moral subject' and 'moral discussant' in the chapter "Ethical Gradualism and Discourse Ethics".

54. Cf. Dietrich Böhler, "Menschenwürde und Menschentötung. Über Diskursethik und utilitaristische Ethik," in: *Zeitschrift für Evangelische Ethik*, 35(1991), No. 3, pp. 166–186. Karl-Otto Apel, *Diskurs und Verantwortung. Das Problem des Überganges zur postkonventionellen Moral*, Frankfurt a.M.: Suhrkamp, 1988, pp. 103–153.

55. Cf. Habermas's criticism in *EzD*, pp. 185 ff., especially pp. 196–197.

56. For Apel's answer to these questions, cf. the references to Apel and Böhler in note 54.

57. Cf. *SfA* referred to earlier. Also e.g. Seyla Benhabib, *StS*.

58. Cf. "Contextual and Universal Pragmatics."

59. Cf. in *SfA* pp. 94–98. Also "Pragmatism and Pragmatics".

60. Cf. "Contextual and Universal Pragmatics" and "Modernization of the Lifeworld."

61. Again, cf. T. McCarthy *Ial*, pp. 181–199, and J. Habermas *EzD*, pp. 200–204.

62. As we know, the word 'need' is deeply ambiguous and its use often confusing or even ideological: on the one hand, we have a set of concepts concerning physiological (physical) conditions for survival (as in 'needs for food', similar to physical conditions indicated by expressions such as 'cars need oil'). These 'needs' can in principle be defined by experts in the appropriate areas. This use of the term 'need' can be extended (gradually) into the social realm, though with increasing doubt as to the significance (and strict necessity) of these 'needs'. On the other hand, extending the use of the term even further, we soon find ourselves in the field of desires and values, without any close connection to the notion of vital necessities. In order to decide on the desirability of these putative 'needs', we need (!) an enlightened discourse, among sane, experienced, and cultivated persons. (However, an appeal to 'desirability experts' ['happiness experts'] would probably function rather ideologically, repressing human autonomy and responsibility.)

63. Habermas argues in favor of the view that questions of justice, *qua* interpretation of needs or interests, can be seen, in principle, as universalizable: "Wie umfangreich der Bereich strikt verallgemeinerbarer Interessen ist, bleibt eine empirische Frage." (*EzD*, pp. 202–203, in response to T. McCarthy's objections in *IaI*). And he adds (*op.cit.* p. 203): "Nur wenn man grundsätzlich zeigen könnte, daß moralische Diskurse trotz des wachsenden Konsenses beispielsweise über Menschenrechte und Demokratie *leerlaufen* müssen, weil sich gemeinsame Interessen im Lichte inkommensurabler Sprachen *überhaupt nicht mehr* identifizieren lassen, wäre der Versuch einer deontologischen Entkopplung der Gerechtigkeits- fragen von den je kontextabhängigen Fragen des guten Lebens geschei- tert." This, I think, is to defend one's own position by demanding strong arguments from the opponents (that of showing an impossibility) and by demanding weak arguments on behalf of oneself (leaving the question open for 'empirical' tests). There are at least some middle grounds concerning plausibility and implausibility (which is exactly the terrain of Habermasian arguments from modernization). And there is a need for semantical clarifications: the terms 'need' and 'interest' are tremendously ambiguous (and in Habermas few attempts are made to clarify them); the term of an 'affected person' (mentioned in the formulation of the principle of universalisation) is also very ambiguous indeed, both in terms of actual and potential competences for inclusion – how should we define the various competences required for 'moral discussants' and how should we define the 'moral subjects' worthy of advocatory representation in

practical discourses? (Catchwords here are the borderline questions between human and non-human animals, and the question of future generations. Cf. "Ethical Gradualism and Discourse Ethics".) And the terms 'consequences and side effects' raise epistemological and sociological problems in their own right. Cf., e.g., Kristin Shrader-Frechette, *Risk and Rationality*, Berkeley, University of California Press, 1991. (Also Skirbekk, "Ecological Crisis and Technological Expertise", in G. Skirbekk, *Eco-Philosophical Manuscripts* (= *EPhM*), Bergen: Ariadne, 1992.)

Habermas occasionally criticizes Rawls for blurring the difference between meta-ethical discussions (which is a philosopher's job) and concrete ethical discussions (open for everyone). However, since Habermas says little about what kinds of 'need' and 'interest' and what notions of 'affected person' and which 'consequences and side-effects' he has in mind, it is difficult to discuss his proposal for a universalization principle (e.g. *MCCA*, pp. 65, 93 and 120). By spelling out a few cases (as Rawls does) he might have revealed some of his underlying ideas and hence furthered our understanding of what he is up to. For instance, to what extent are questions concerning the distribution of scarce resources involved, in addition to questions of recognition and questions of liberal rights? Questions of distribution are certainly crucial both in normative discussions on justice and in political discussions on the role of market economy and the welfare state, not to mention ecology issues. But Habermas does not discuss these questions from the perspective of this principle. (One such question is the population problem in China. Who should, in this case, be seen as 'moral discussants', and who as 'moral subjects' whose 'needs' ['interests'] are to be discussed? How should we approach the various 'consequences and side-effects'?)

When all this conceptual vagueness is put together, without the necessary clarification through examples, it is difficult to know what one is talking about and what would count as a counterargument. All depending on how the various terms are defined we would probably find that the principle is more or less plausible (or implausible). For quite a few definitions it seems fairly implausible to me. (Cf., e.g., Skirbekk, "Eco-Crisis and the Welfare State", *EPhM*.) But on the other hand, I think there are elements in this principle which could have been given a fruitful critical use, for instance in an ecological perspective, asking for sustainable justice. (Cf. *ibid.*, and also "Political Culture" in *EPhM*, and the section 'Practical Rationality Embedded' in this chapter.)

64. However, having indicated some reason for not neglecting the notion of contextualization, not even within the notion of discursive validation, I would like to emphasize the following point: the notion of justification should not become blurred by empirical notions. Genesis and validity should be kept apart; the logic of validation differs from that of discovery and of application. This is a classical line of defense for rationality against relativism. (Pragmatic skills and tacit knowledge do not in themselves threaten a universal pragmatic notion of validity, nor does the interrelation between the understanding of discursively justified norms and their contextual application. My answer is that of a melioristic pragmatics, cf. also previous chapters, esp. "Pragmatism and Pragmatics".)

65. Cf. note 14 in "Ethical Gradualism and Discourse Ethics".

66. Cf., e.g., S. Lukes, "Of Gods and Demons: Habermas and Practical Reason", in: *HCD*, pp. 134–148.

67. Cf. "The World Reconsidered" in *Thesis Eleven*, 30(1991), pp. 17–32. See also "Political Culture" in *EPhM*.

68. Cf., e.g., Carol C. Gould, "On the Conception of the Common Interest: Between Procedure and Substance", in *Hermeneutics and Critical Theory in Ethics and Politics*, ed. Michael Kelly, Cambridge, Mass.: MIT Press, 1990, pp. 253–273.

69. Any attempt at verbalizing these norms can in principle be disputed, but still it is fair to say that they embrace a basic reciprocal recognition among discussants and a willingness to follow 'better arguments'. In this sense equality and universalizability are involved.

70. It means that some ethnocentrism and irrationalism are ruled out.

71. This, again, is my 'negativistic' and melioristic version of 'application discourse'.

72. Cf. "Ecological Crisis and Technological Expertise" and "Science and Ethics" in Skirbekk, *EPhM*. In these essays on rational 'overcoming' of onesided expertise, the main point is to show how this melioristic 'force of the negative' operates in favor of improved solutions.

73. Cf. the normative notion of political culture in "The World Reconsidered", in: *Thesis Eleven*, (30)1991, pp. 17–32. This is my answer to the question of the transition from justification and application to an ethics of strategic responsibility (cf. the relation between part A and B in Apel's notion of discourse ethics).

74. Cf. Habermas in: *Moralität und Sittlichkeit* (= *MS*), ed. W. Kuhlmann, Frankfurt a.M.: Suhrkamp, 1986, p. 30. However, this practical work is not a task for philosophers in particular, but for everybody; cf. Habermas *ibid.* pp. 32–33. On the notion of political culture, cf. "Political Culture", Skirbekk, *EPhM*.

75. As to the application of the notion of gradualist meliorism, cf. "Ecological Crisis and Technological Expertise" (in: *EPhM*). On the attempt at a more flexible notion of discursive justice, cf. also T. McCarthy in: *Ial*, pp. 198–199.

76. In addition, we should welcome any attempt that argumentatively elucidates the core of rationality embedded in communicative speech acts and in the process of maturation and of modernization (as in Habermas).

77. Cf. *Zwischenbetrachtungen* (= *Z*), e.g. p. 19. Concerning Habermas's response to Apel's general criticism, cf. "Erläuterungen zur Diskursethik", in: *Erläuterungen zur Diskursethik* (= *EzD*), Frankfurt a.M.: Suhrkamp, pp. 185–199.

78. Cf. *Z*, e.g. p. 20 (note 7) on "sinnkritische Argumente" and what one "sinnvollerweise erwarten kann" (also e.g. p. 46: "gar nicht verstanden werden kann", "macht ... gar keinen Sinn"). And explicitly on p. 49: "eine(r) transzendentalreflexive(n) Letztbegründung durch *reductio ad absurdum*." (Cf. also K. E. Tranøy's analyses different kinds of basic cognitive norms, in the section 'Critical Aftermath' in "Pragmatism and Pragmatics".)

79. Cf. Apel in *Z*, e.g. p. 20, note 7, and p. 49.

80. Cf. also W. Kuhlmann: *Reflexive Letztbegründung*.

81. Cf. "Arguments from Absurdity."

82. *Ibid.*

83. If for a moment we disregard Popperian decisionism concerning the foundation of rationality, we could point out that Apel's approach has structural similarities with Popper's normativism 'from above'. Likewise, if we disregard Kuhnian relativism, we could point out that Habermas's approach has structural similarities with Kuhnian reconstructivism 'from below'.

84. Cf. e.g. Wolfgang Kuhlmann: "Ist die Idee einer letztbegründeten normativen Ethik überhaupt sinnvoll?," in: *Moralität und Sittlichkeit* (= *MS*), ed. W. Kuhlmann, Frankfurt a.M.: Suhrkamp, 1986, pp. 194–216.

85. As we have seen, the insistence on the presence of everybody concerned leads to the idea of an *advocatory* representation for those who are unable to participate. (Cf. e.g. Habermas: "Diskursethik – Notizen zu einem Begründungsprogramm," in: *Moralbewusstsein und kommunikatives Handeln*, Frankfurt a.M.: Suhrkamp, 1983, p. 104, and Apel: "Sprachakttheorie und transzendentale Sprachpragmatik zur Frage ethischer Normen," in: *Sprachpragmatik und Philosophie*, Frankfurt a.M.: Suhrkamp, 1976, p. 126.) This would apply to minors, but also to future generations, and finally to all 'moral subjects', also non-humans. (Cf. "Ethical Gradualism and Discourse Ethics," and also Micha Brumlik: "Über die Ansprüche Ungeborener und Unmündiger. Wie advokatorisch ist die diskursive Ethik?," in: *MS*, 1986, pp. 265–300.) The implication of the idea of an advocatory representation is, in my opinion, that 'formal questions' cannot be fully separated from 'content questions': the 'formal' question as to who should participate and who should be represented advocatorily by somebody else, has somehow to be settled *within* a discourse, as a 'content question'. Even though there is a paradigmatic distinction between discursive 'form' and 'content', the need for advocatory representation indicates the necessity of some overlap.

86. Cf. Apel in: "Normative Begründung der 'Kritischen Theorie' durch Rekurs auf lebensweltliche Sittlichkeit? Ein transzendental-pragmatisch orientierter Versuch, mit Habermas gegen Habermas zu denken", in: *Zwischenbetrachtungen*, pp. 15–65 (e.g. fn. 7, pp. 19–20). Cf. Habermas's statement: "Es gibt keine Metadiskurse in dem Sinne, daß ein höherer Diskurs einem untergeordneten Diskurs die Regeln vorschreiben könnte. Argumentationsspiele bilden keine Hierarchie." From "Entgegnung", in:

Kommunikatives Handeln, eds. A. Honneth and H. Joas, Frankfurt a.M.: Suhrkamp, 1986, pp. 327–405, quoted from p. 350. This is one of the texts specially commented upon by Apel in his article in: *Z* (cf. above). On the same point (as well as other points in Apel's criticism), cf. Habermas in: "Erläuterungen zur Diskursethik", in *EzD*, pp. 185 ff. Cf. also Habermas's comment on philosophy as characterized by *Mehrsprachigkeit* (*TuK*, pp. 41 and 48), which implies, as far as I can see, a characterization of philosophy as capable of reflective flexibility between various perspectives – more in the sense of 'trans' than 'meta'. It does not imply a 'meta-level' of a 'universal language game', but a reflexivity by which philosophy is 'liberated' from the 'immanence' of one or a few given perspectives. (In that sense we could speak of a 'higher level'.)

87. In *formulating* performative inconsistencies we run the risk of ending up with simple *semantic contradictions*, cf. this point in Albrecht Wellmer, in: *Ethik und Dialog*, Frankfurt a.M.: Suhrkamp, 1986, e.g. pp. 103–104 (note 1). In talking about pragmatic preconditions we run the risk of ending up with theoretical claims that rightly belong to the questions that should be discussed *within* a discourse. To me Habermas's 'principle of universalization' represents such a case.

88. In criticizing R. Wuthnow, he says: "Er [Wuthnow] hält die verschiedenen analytischen Ebenen nicht auseinander und bedenkt nicht den methodischen Unterschied zwischen formalpragmatisch durchgeführter Sprach-, Argumentations- und Handlungstheorie einerseits, soziologischer Handlungs- und Systemtheorie anderseits;...." (in: *Texte und Kontexte*, Frankfurt a.M.: Suhrkamp, 1991, p. 150). Eben!

89. Cf. the term 'philosophical experience' in: "Contextual and Universal Pragmatics."

90. Cf. the problem of feasible and desirable interrelationships between market economy and various types of politics.

91. How should the requirements for discursive competence be decided (the question of inclusion and exclusion)? And how should moral subjects (possibly, moral agents), who are not also moral discussants, be represented (the question of advocatory representation in practical discourses)? In both cases we have a transition between form and content

(between a discourse-constitutive frame and possible substantial answers within a practical discourse).

92. Cf. *MCCA*, pp. 177–178, on life crises.

93. Cf. *The Commercial Ark. A Book on Ecology and Ethics*, A. Nylund, A. Selvik, G. Skirbekk, A. Steigen, A. Tjønneland, Oslo: Scandinavian University Press, 1992. For the quotation, cf. Otto Neurath, "Foundations of the Social Sciences," in: *Foundations of the Unity of Science. Toward an International Encyclopedia of Unified Science*, eds. Rudolf Carnap, Charles Morris and Otto Neurath, Chicago: Chicago University Press, Vol. II, 1970, p. 47.

References

Articles published earlier have been revised. Some have been changed extensively.

"Praxeological Reflections" was originally written in Norwegian for the *Festskrift for Hans Skjervheim*, Oslo, 1976. In English in the anthology *Praxeology*, Oslo, 1983.

"Arguments from Absurdity" is a revised version of part II of *Truth and Preconditions*, Bergen, 1972. (German translation in *Wahrheitstheorien*, Frankfurt, 1977.)

"Pragmatism and Pragmatics" was originally published (under the title "Pragmatism in Apel and Habermas") in *Contemporary Philosophy*, Vol. 4, ed. G. Fløistad, The Hague, 1983, and in a revised version in *Essays in Pragmatic Philosophy I*, eds. I. Gullvåg and H. Høibraaten, Oslo, 1985.

"Madness and Reason" was published in *Årbok 1988 - modernitet, differensiering og rationalisering*, ed. H. Grimen, SVT, Bergen, 1988.

"Contextual and Universal Pragmatics" was published in *Thesis Eleven*, No. 28, 1991.

"The Pragmatic Notion of Nature" was published in *Manuscripts on Rationality*, SVT, Bergen, 1984. (German translation in *Die pragmatische Wende*, Frankfurt, 1986.)

"Ethical Gradualism and Discourse Ethics" to be published in *Festschrift for Karl-Otto Apel*, Frankfurt, 1993.

"Modernization of the Lifeworld" and "Rationality and Contextuality", unpublished.